Letters from Limbo

dpInk: DonnaInk Publications, L.L.C.

dpInk
Donnaink Publications, L.L.C.

U.S.A.

Letters from Limbo

by

PHIL FORCE

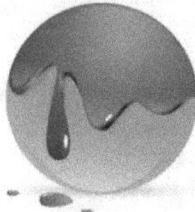

Donnaink Publications, L.L.C.

Letters from Limbo, Phil Force
dpInk: Donnaink Publications, L.L.C.
Editors; ZenCon an Art of Zen Consultancy Editor and Layout Designer.. This book is intended to provide general information on a particular subject and is not an exhaustive treatment of such subjects.

This is a work of nonfiction from the author's perspective and memory of facts and events. Much of the vernacular in this title is minced with slang and varied forms of English, editorial review provided creative liberty and the publisher takes exception for remaining misnomers, errors or omissions. Names have not been changed. Without limiting the foregoing, the author and publisher do not warrant the content will be error free or will meet any particular criteria. Neither the publisher nor author advocate drug use.

For information about permissions to reproduce selections from the book write to Permissions, dpInk: **Donnaink Publications, L.L.C.,** 129 Daisy Hill Road, Carthage, North Carolina 28327 or email: permissions@donnaink.com or call 01-888.564.7741.

For information about special discounts for bulk purchases, please contact dpInk: **Donnaink Publications, L.L.C.** Special Sales, 129 Daisy Hill Road, Carthage, North Carolina 28327, or email: special_markets@donnaink.com or call 01.888-564.7741.

dpInk: Donnaink Publications, L.L.C.
129 Daisy Hill Road   (888) 564-7741 (office)
Carthage, NC 28327   (800) 686-5603 (fax)
www.donnaink.com

The Library of Congress has catalogued this title as follows:
    Force, Phil, 2015-

Letters from Limbo | Phil Force. 1st edition.
                ISBN: 978-1-939425-51-5 (alk. paper)
                        p. cm. 237
[1. Force, Phil, 2015 - Memoir. 2. International - Memoir. 3. Cancer - Memoir. 4. Medical - Memoir. 5. Health - Memoir. 6. Philosophy - United States. 7. Relationships – Memoir. 8. Family - Memoir. 9. Recovery - Memoir. 10. Self-Improvement - Memoir.]

Printed in the United States of America.

2013936121

12 11 10 9 8 7 6 5 4 3 2 1

Contents

Third Frontier

Prelude

It's bothersome to me when a person speaks of his or her version of reality as if it were profound and the only correct perspective. Many personal ideals have similar themes but no two are identical. I believe this action is dismissive of other perspectives without even acknowledging them. I don't want to offend anyone. Offense only leads to anger and sadness; I believe there is enough of that in our world without my contribution. The views expressed here are just that and are in no way meant to be taken as absolute truth but like anyone, I believe my idea of reality is the most accurate in comparison to others that have been offered to me.

The following is an explanation of what seems to be my most significant perspective and a study of the factors that constantly alter it. I apologize if anyone believes my recollections to be inaccurate but in recognizing my perspective is different from yours, you've just proven my point. Haven't you?

lim·bo
1. Roman Catholic Theology - a region on the border of hell or heaven, serving as the abode after death of unbaptized infants (limbo of infants) and of the righteous who died before the com-ing of Christ (limbo of the fathers or limbo of the patriarchs).

2. A place or state of oblivion to which persons or things are regarded as being relegated when cast aside, forgotten, past, or out of date: My youthful hopes are in the limbo of lost dreams.

3. An intermediate, transitional, or midway state or place.

4. A place or state of imprisonment or confinement.[1]

---

[1]   Limbo.

Letters from Limbo

Chapter One.

The Tumor

At twenty, I was told a tumor was growing in the third ventricle of my brain. Before the diagnosis, I lived with my grandparents in Lake Jackson, Texas. At the time, the pressure to be in school was apparent but I wasn't ready to commit to a life's purpose, a predesigned plan. My grandmother suggested phlebotomy because it was a short class. I think she thought I would be good at it. Really, in her eyes I could have done anything. I suppose she was right in her prediction about my abilities in Phlebotomy. Of course, I wouldn't finish the scheduled course. I would be forced to put off my studies until the next year.

The first symptoms I remember occurred when I was visiting my girlfriend at the time in Austin. This girlfriend, whom we'll call "Nine," had taken over the lease on my apartment and was making use of my furniture, as my living situation at the time didn't allow room for much other than my clothing and myself. That night a great pain formed in my head but I really didn't give it much thought. It was a headache. My girlfriend's friend suggested I take a pain reliever for it and, without really thinking, I said, "They don't make pain killers for my headaches." During the night the pain grew much worse. All night, I lay awake quivering in pain.

A few years later, a second set of symptoms arose. My parents recently divorced and I helped my father move to Chandler, Arizona. I did little more than vomit for several days in a row. I actually recall vomiting in the hotel room's bathtub when my stomach issues had my backside glued to the toilet. We assumed the dry heat of Arizona was responsible for my experience for two reasons: Firstly, I hadn't experienced any symptoms that would seem to be related until the dramatic climate change. Secondly, I began to feel better once I left Arizona.

I returned from my trip to Arizona to Boerne, Texas to be with my mom. We were having lunch at a Mexican restaurant when the right side of my body went numb. I informed my mother with a half-smile. I cannot say for certain whether the half-smile was a result of mixed emotions or the actual numbness in my face. We grabbed a few tortillas to go and hurried to her family physician's office. As I made my way across the parking lot the last remaining tortilla slipped out of my right hand—I had lost the ability to grasp it properly.

I was anxious but excited. The rollercoaster that had been life was pretty timid at this point. I had become bored with my life but I now anticipated the next big dive. I didn't know whether it would result in a sharp turn or a loop but the clinking of the chain lift was apparent as I made my way up the wheel chair ramp to the physician's office.

After I explained my symptoms, the doctor sent me for an MRI. Two days later, we returned to hear the results. In a voice filled with sympathy, the doctor said, "It doesn't look good. It looks like you have a brain tumor." The coaster reached its peak with the doctor's delivery of these words.

I raised my voice with an enthusiastic, "Yes!" The reaction may sound strange but the understanding of this problem was bittersweet. I was happy we had a diagnosis but I think the enthusiastic reply was more about apathy for a situation I couldn't control more than anything else. I had joked about the possibility of a brain tumor. This "Yes!" was a realization of that joke. The joke was funny before because it was ridiculous. The doctor's delivery of those words, "It looks like you have a brain tumor" was the punch line. The joke was on me. It seemed as though it would be all downhill from here. Would I die? I'd surely experience pain in my near future. Either way, what could I do but embrace what lay before me?

They referred me to a neurologist in San Antonio who was said to be "the best." It's funny how something potentially life changing can alter our priorities and even our perspectives. I had not prayed regularly since adolescence but now I did. I was raised in a Christian family but adolescence brought on a rebellion that dismissed any desire for faith rather quickly. A desire for faith became abundantly clear when I was forced to confront my own mortality.

On operation day, my family showed up to give me support. It was late in the day and my grandmother was worried my surgeon would be tired after his other surgeries and not able to give his best performance.

I was brought to a room with one other patient. By now the pain was persistent. My world was formed by my brain and the pain I experienced came from my brain. My world was pain. Each sound in my world was a physical dart of uncomfortable sensation rolling around in my head. I hit the "nurse call" button and requested morphine. The lady visiting the other patient in the room said with a somewhat joking attitude, "Make that two."

The nurse prepared a shot, and asked me to turn onto my side. She asked if I was in school. I said "yes" with anticipation. She then explained that she was trying to get me to talk so I would be somewhat distracted when she pushed the needle in. She asked about my major. I replied in a long stream of words, "Actually, I am going to school to be a phlebotomist, so this shouldn't be that . . ." she stuck the needle into my backside and I finished my sentence, "baaad."

Shortly after the nurse left, my grandmother came in to report that my doctor would perform the surgery the following day.

My girlfriend and two of my female friends kept me company that night. I loved the attention. I was the star of the show and we laughed quite a bit. A male nurse came in to see if I needed anything. He seemed surprised to see the smile on my face and the three beautiful girls in my room. When he returned a second time he asked if we had found anything good to watch on TV. "We found the booby channel," I said, referring to the channel that was supposed to teach new mothers how to breastfeed.

The next day was a blur. A member of the hospital staff injected me with something that made me really disoriented. I remember the sounds of the construction workers at work outside. Somehow I felt like I could see them. My physical perspective was higher than it typically was and I remember witnessing the vision of the construction workers through a window frame. Before I knew it I was in some room with several people in scrubs and gowns. My doctor came by to say hi.

The next thing I knew I was in a big white room. I was wearing a loincloth and sitting in some kind of chair that suspended me a few feet off the ground in a very foreign way: my legs were stretched open as if I was straddling the empty space beneath me. I felt as though my legs were being held apart by gynecologist's stirrups. I felt an extension from my genitals running down to the floor and vibrating ever so slightly. This extension was a part of me but had no physical form that I can describe now. The room felt sterile, futuristic and foreign, as I would imagine an alien ship to feel.

I woke again, sometime later. This time I was outside in a tent, sitting with my legs extended before me. I knew I was behind enemy lines and that my mission was to remove a hose from the tent I occupied. I felt the hose in my hands but couldn't determine where it was coming from. As much as I pulled I could not get the hose free.

Two rival nurses came to where I lay and asked what happened. I said I didn't know. I would not give any information.

In an instant, I was back in my hospital room. A young female nurse stood by my bed while a male nurse hurried off.

I felt somewhat socially awkward but I was still high as a kite. "Hi," I said, "what's your name?"

She responded but the name fell on deaf ears. Then I said, as if relating my name, "I'm a bloody mess."

She smiled. Her attitude toward me was like one would have toward a drunken friend, understanding yet mildly patronizing.

When I regained consciousness a third time, I was in a bed outside the tent. Machines were hooked up to what I imagined to be the physical incarnation of myself. A nurse was talking to me. I wasn't paying attention but I remember nodding as if I understood. With a smile, I thought, Yes, I understand. Thank you.

When she left, I knew what she had asked me to do. This was the motivation of a blindly following child. I didn't understand her reasoning but I knew the action to be taken. I yanked the tape off my arm. Something came with it.

When I awoke again, I was lying in my hospital bed. I began piecing together my memories of the experience. I realized the hose from the tent was, in fact, my catheter. The tape I pulled off my arm had been used to keep my IV line in place.

Later, my neurosurgeon came to check on me and suture the wound at the back of my head. He explained that a local anesthetic would probably be more painful to administer than the sutures themselves and proceeded to apply what I remember as three stitches. I made quiet noises of pain. He asked if he was hurting me and offered what sounded like a sincere apology. I was amazed by his concern for me. He had told my mother he really liked me and was actually a little nervous about operating on me.

When I was aware enough to really comprehend, my mother told me he hadn't removed the entire tumor. During the operation he tested a small part of it and established that it was a germinoma (a type of tumor that apparently responds particularly well to radiation).

When I felt well enough, I would start my radiation therapy.

A few days into my hospital stay, the nurse came by to inquire about the date of my last bowel movement. From my reply, she decided it would be best to give me an enema. She explained that I was to delay releasing the foamy beast from my bowels until the last possible second. I turned onto my side and she injected the contents of the enema. I remained with my back end exposed and did my best to hold it. I hadn't used my legs in a few days and I didn't know how long it would take me to make it to the toilet. With a slight franticness, I made it to the bathroom, just a few feet from my bed, under my own power.

After a while in the hospital, my grandparents came into my room and said "We're going home today." I assumed that "we" included me, so I had them call for the nurse. I had to teach my legs how to walk again if we were to get home that day. The nurse brought in a pair of socks with rubber grippers on the bottom, and a wheelchair. She put the socks on my feet and then helped me stand to grasp the handles on the back of the wheelchair. The hallway was wide and split by an island where nurses worked when not directly attending to their patients. I made slow but steady laps around the hallway with the nurse and my grandparents close by. At some point during my third lap, I was almost completely walking by myself. One of my grandparents went to check me out of the hospital. The nurse then helped me make my way around to the front of the chair to sit and wheeled me out of the hospital.

I spent some time at my mother's house after that. Each Tuesday and Thursday she drove me to CTRC (Cancer Therapy Research Center). At that point, I hadn't even realized a germinoma was cancerous. The two people working the giant radiation machine were very friendly. Each day I brought a different CD and they played it for me while the very loud machine trolled back and forth, pumping radiation into my brain. One of the technicians took a liking to my music almost immediately. One day I forgot to bring any and he mentioned that he had the Beatles *Blue Album* in his car. We started that session with "Strawberry Fields."

When my radiation was finished the female technician presented me with a certificate that read, "This is to certify that Philip Force has completed a three month course in radiation therapy."

I had survived. It was almost a disappointment. Before the tumor I was bored with life and depressed. Now I had to claw my way back to that meaningless life I lived before. I was still somewhat excited though. Perhaps the life I was returning to would be very different from the one I left. I had been given a second chance and, aside from that, I finally had purpose. My brother was distraught about my father's recent move out of state. I felt my presence made a difference, even though I spent most of the time in bed.

I remember one specific night when I could hear him from my bedroom. He was lying in bed crying. I knew he missed his dad and felt abandoned. This sadness was a factor of the world that I had woken to.

I climbed onto his bed and hugged him. He made a loud, angry sound and pushed me away. I slid off his bed and stood. This wasn't the response I expected but I was still learning about my new world, the very different world that I had woken to after my journey through the various dimensions I inhabited throughout the tumor experience.

Chapter Two

Nine

When I was well enough, I went back to live with my grandparents to finish school. Shortly after that, Nine and I split up. The breakup was inevitable. I loved her deeply but had not seemed to be able to mold the love into a functioning relationship.

Nine and I had dated off and on for five years. It was common at the time for me to explain to anyone who was interested that this relationship had lasted four years longer than it should have. I was constantly picking her apart, trying to change her, constantly pointing out what I saw as flaws. She often said or did things that seemed cliché and mindless to me. There is a quote attributed to Thomas Merton that would seem fitting, "The beginning of love is to let those we love be themselves, and not to twist them to fit our own image. Otherwise we love only the reflection of ourselves we find in them."[2]

While I was dealing with these problems, my mother told me something that really rang true for me. She said that things we dislike the most in other people are often things we dislike about ourselves. I think this holds especially true when it comes to the people we love the most. Maybe my picking her apart was a reflection of the shame I had for my own imperfections. I pulled this girl apart by her imperfections because I was constantly hearing that voice of scrutiny over my own flaws. Maybe I wanted her to be perfect because I could not. Then again, maybe it was not about her being perfect at all. Maybe I tried to tear her down so I could feel better about my own imperfection.

She was never enough for me. At the time these "flaws" seemed like problems that would destroy our relationship. Maybe I let them destroy it.

---

2   Thomas Merton quotes, 1999-2009.

When this request for improvement first began it was not intended to be so much for my benefit but more for hers. I saw these problems in her and tried to help her better herself by fixing them. I suppose it became more about me when she failed to fix what I saw as problems. It then became about my inability to remedy what I saw as flawed in her.

It has been said, a person must love him or herself before he or she can love someone else. My personal history has led me to believe this is true. I believe one must love him or herself before he or she can allow others to love him or her. I suppose any good seen in me was likely taken as lip service and insincere. I don't know I ever really loved myself before my experience with cancer. I did feel pride for my accomplishments but all it took was one perceived conviction in disagreement of the greatness of my accomplishments for me to become instantly humbled. Not all contradicting views had this effect on me but I often perceived negative opinions of me with no proof of their existence.

I held her so high in my mind. Maybe I never really loved her but was just infatuated with the idea of her. I dated a friend of hers briefly, one of the many times we broke up. The friend eventually ended things with me. She said this was because she couldn't look at me without seeing her friend (my ex-girlfriend). The way she explained it was that it wasn't so much a guilt thing on her part but that I carried the love and the hurt of my ex-girlfriend with me constantly.

I cheated on Nine a few times when we dated. The enjoyment of such an act was fleeting at best. The act inspired a shameful feeling of self-destruction. Afterward, I was numb, remorseful and completely disconnected all at the same time. It was the idea I had screwed up again and now had to go confess and hope for forgiveness. I think I cheated on her for one reason: I was happy and felt undeserving of such happiness. Something so good could never last for me. I was most familiar with emotional pain so I caused myself pain in order to gain a sense of familiarity.

It's been years since I've had a desire to be with her but near the beginning of my current relationship I still occasionally dreamed about her. I felt guilty every time I woke up to the memory of one of these dreams. In some dreams, I was lying next to her, asleep. In others, I was cheating on my present girlfriend with her. I didn't experience the act of sex or the superficial satisfaction I associated with having sex, only the before and after. When I dreamed I was cheating with her I felt a kind of defeated nonchalance reminiscent of when I cheated on her.

I once wrote, "I'll never be enough for you to be enough for me. Do you remember the electricity of the dawn-forgotten beach? Not a lot has changed, as anyone can see. I'm still gift wrapping my soul for ones I will never reach." My problems with her were reflected problems with myself.

She once told me, I put her on a pedestal. As strange as it seemed I knew it to be true. It had been a habit of mine for a long time. Maybe it wasn't so much my admiration for her and the others before her but my distaste for myself and the rest of the world. While we were dating, I wrote a poem entitled "Magnolia." I was writing about her and my inability to make things right between us. I wrote, "I can change," because I desperately wanted to be a person who would not cheat on her.

I have since discovered I cannot change who I am. I don't believe anyone can. I can only evolve and become a better me by changing my actions. I cannot change the past, it has a lot to do with who I am today. I can only add to what is me, and try to improve the ratio of things I like to things I don't like. We cannot change who we are, because our personal histories form our identities. We can only change our actions to better ourselves. When one is young, love is experimental. It is a learning experience in which one is bound to make mistakes.

Chapter Three

Back at "Home"

I stayed in my grandparent's second house, which was around 11 miles away from their primary residence. It was a beautiful place, on the San Bernard River. My grandmother had a knack for decorating in creative ways. The most unique feature of this house was the palm tree leaf ceiling. Dried palm leaves covered the otherwise bare wood ceiling of half of the den. In spite of the beauty, I felt alone and depressed.

My grandmother once asked why I seemed sad most of the time. I didn't wear my sadness on my sleeve but rather on my shoulders. I tried not to let it affect my relationship with them. I told her I knew there was comfort in familiarity and maybe I was just used to being sad. "So, what you're saying is, you're happy being sad?" I disagreed but really couldn't explain it any better.

During the day, I spent time with my grandparents and did chores in exchange for money. At night, I worked on my music. I spent hours placing drum, guitar, vocal, and ambient tracks on my computer. My dog Rocky lived with me and I talked to him as though he understood. I think he did understand, at least my emotion, which was normally very defeated and lonely.

Looking back now, I think he was, appropriately enough, my best friend. Though I remember joking at the time, in a somewhat self-pitying manner, that my grandparents were my only peers.

They saw me as a child. Perhaps they were right but being a person who desired the respect he hoped he deserved, and knowing his only daily contact with the rest of the human race didn't consider him an equal, was difficult. Still, they did more than I ever would have asked of them. They housed me. They fed me. They even clothed me because, according to them, my attire made me look like a child or a "teeny bopper," as it was put. I didn't always agree with them but it wasn't my place to. I am grateful for what they did for me.

My immediate family came to visit once. Most of my extended family lived, and continue to live, in that area and my mother wanted to make a trip to see everyone. My brother Collin, my sister Catherine, and my sister's boyfriend ended up staying a night with me at the river house. The next day, I was visiting with my grandparents at their house—as I did most every day—when they asked about the sleeping arrangements the night before. I told them my sister and her boyfriend had slept in the same bed. They were very upset with her.

My grandmother asked as if she already knew the answer, "You would never have a girl spend the night with you at the river house, would you?"

I gave my head the slightest of shakes. She asked again in a playful, yet insistent manner. I quickly spoke the word "no" to appease her. They made it clear I could not have a girl stay with me in their house until I was thirty, which just happened to be the age of my second cousin who was coming that weekend with her "boy toy."

Shortly after this conversation, Nine called from Austin. It had been several months and we'd had very little communication between us. She had arranged to have a male friend drive her to meet me halfway. I wasn't sure if I wanted to see her; she had been seeing someone new and using different mind-altering substances but I was bored and very lonely, so I drove to meet her in New Braunfels. I didn't look at her the entire drive and we barely spoke. I was disgusted with her. When we got back to the house, I was tired and ready to shower and get to bed. I asked her to come with me as I made my way to the bathroom.

Despite my state of mind, I wanted to share in her company. I was angry for the pain she had caused and afraid of the potential for future pain but somewhat excited to experience the company of this new incarnation of the person I once loved so desperately.

We entered the bathroom and I closed the door. I began to undress. We had seen each other naked many times, of course but this time was different. I felt exposed. I was still barely able to look at her but I managed to pathetically tug at her shirt as if to say, "Take it off." She took off her shirt and I finished undressing. I turned on the water and stepped into the shower. She asked if I wanted her to get in and I said it would be all right. We were silent for a few minutes and then I blurted, "Did you fuck him on my bed?"

The word "fuck" created such a disturbing wave in me. I had gone months without using it and then in a bout of anger I said it but I felt too empowered by my anger, and worried about her response to care.

She said, "No, that's our place."

I wrapped my arms around her and started to sob. "Did you fuck him at all?" I asked through my gasping breaths.

"No."

I cried some more and then finished my shower. We proceeded to the bedroom.

The next day we went to the local shopping mall. She mentioned in conversation that she'd had some kind of temporary STD in recent history. I almost thought she was joking.

"How did that happen?" I asked with a kind of worried smile.

She reminded me that she had been seeing someone else. "I thought you said you didn't fuck him?" I said with a whirl winded mix of emotion. After speaking with her for a minute, it became clear she hadn't understood my teary inquisition in the shower the night before. I went back into defensive mode for a while. Again, I couldn't look at her and had nothing to say. I knew she hadn't meant to mislead me but it took time to come to terms with the fact that I had acted, the night before, on false information.

That betrayed feeling shortly faded and we made our way back to the river house. Halfway down the road, we passed my grandparents' car. We pulled into the driveway and I got out to unlock the gate.

My grandparents pulled up behind us. My grandmother got out of the car and came around to the driver's side. She leaned down to look at me through the open window and said something along the lines of, "You're in big trouble mister."

She told Nine, who was still technically my ex-girlfriend, to get into her car. Then she told me to meet them at their house. I told my grandmother I could drive us both but she refused.

Things had cooled off by the time I got there. We four sat at their coffee table and talked. I wanted to be completely honest with them. Without much delay I blurted, "So, we had sex last night."

I felt Nine's disbelief and shock in my statement. My grandfather reminded me that my sister was not welcome to come stay at their second house anymore because she had had a boy stay with her. He seemed to be implying I might not be welcome to stay there anymore either.

I began to cry. "I didn't mean to mislead you," I said, feeling what I imagined Nine felt an hour or so before when she realized she had accidentally misled me.

We spoke more. My grandmother asked if we were intending to start seeing each other seriously again. I looked at Nine as she looked back at me and said to my grandmother that I didn't really know. She said with a knowing tone that we "should probably figure that out." After all of the tears, my grandma looked to me and said, "Love is blind, isn't it?" I felt a release of anxiety with the understanding in her voice.

We stayed at their house that night, in the same room but in separate twin size beds.

After that we started talking regularly again. Things seemed like they might finally work for us.

My mother understood I wasn't happy in my situation and, when I had completed my course in phlebotomy, she suggested I come live with her in Boerne. I was hesitant. She didn't really want my dog in her new house. I couldn't blame her but eventually it seemed to be too self-destructive to stay where I was. My grandparents loved me but they didn't respect me as an adult. I began to see myself as more and more inadequate.

My mother was very insistent about my coming to stay with her. She assured me Rocky would be fine living in her backyard. So I moved to Boerne but Rocky wasn't happy. We got him a cage so he could sleep in my room without shedding all over my mother's new carpet but he desperately wanted to be near me. Some nights he spent hours crying, and eventually barking, for my attention. I hope God shows more care for us than we do for the creatures we govern. I didn't blame my mother for wanting him to stay off her carpet. I just wished there had been a better alternative.

My love life began to fall apart again. Sometimes Nine didn't return my calls for weeks. Eventually, I ended the relationship. I believed she was still using mind-altering substances and, while I had no problem with the idea of it, it did seem to contribute to the problems between us. Shortly after I ended the relationship her mother called to ask if I knew where Nine was. She had been missing for weeks. I said I hadn't heard from her but that she was likely somewhere getting high. I took a very knowing tone as if to say, "What are we going to do with this girl?"

Her mother agreed she was likely getting high. Nine would later confirm my suspicion she was using a mind-altering substance during her retreat.

Sometime later she contacted me. She was alive. She and I tried again but it lasted about a week. After I had left messages for a few days in a row, she finally called. I still recall the conversation. She was practically pleading with me, stating I couldn't end the relationship now . . . she was just starting to get things together. There is an old parable that goes "If a dog is burned by scalding water he will fear cold water too." I had been burned many times before. I wasn't taking the chance that the water might be hot.

A few months after our final break up, I fell in love with someone new. It would seem like I moved way too fast but I had been over the idea of my last love even while still trying to make it work. The new girlfriend, whom we'll call "Thirteen," actually helped me through the heartbreak I experienced over Nine. One night shortly after the tumor surgery, we spent time in my bedroom at my mom's house watching TV and listening to music. A song came on that reminded me of Nine. I sighed and changed the track. "I'm not going to make you deal with that," I said.

Chapter Four

My Little Sister and Her Husband

One night my little sister Catherine called our mother claiming her live-in boyfriend was on some kind of hallucinogen and being abusive. I drove to her apartment to provide some protection for her. My mother called when I was on the way and asked me to call with the address when I got there. I knew how to get there by the use of landmarks but hadn't yet attained an actual street address.

I found my sister in the parking lot with two men. Neither of whom were her boyfriend. I asked if she was okay and then introduced myself to the guys. I asked for her address because I was uncertain and wanted to clarify before relaying the information to my mother. My sister wouldn't tell me because she didn't want our mother to call the cops on her loaded boyfriend.

We stood there talking for a while. Then the boyfriend showed up. The two men and I stood intently between him and Catherine.

"Can I help you with something?" one of the guys asked in a cocky voice.

The boyfriend responded in a similar but more irritated tone, "I'd like to talk to my girlfriend." He took a step toward her.

Her friend inserted his body into her boyfriend's path. "You can talk from there."

They talked for a second while my sister's friend made certain to keep the distance between them. The voices escalated quickly. Soon, he left in anger. A few minutes later conversation was interrupted by metallic banging sounds in the distance. I looked to find him ramming his fists into the nearby dumpster. He turned and started in our direction. The two guys and I again moved between him and my sister. They made threats and then he looked at me. We had been friendly at one time. I think he was feeling bad about being treated like a threat. "So," he asked, "you want to kick my ass now, too?"

"No, I don't want to kick your ass."

He said, "See?" and proceeded to grasp my shoulder.

I didn't want to be his friend at that moment. I responded very quickly, "Don't touch me, though." It seemed to hurt his feelings.

He and the other males continued to threaten each other and then one of my sister's friends threw his nearly full beer can at his face. He left and then her friend made a "Tommy Boy" reference, "not so much here or here" as he pointed up and down his face "but right here." He then pointed along the center of his face.

We went into one of Catherine's friend's apartments upstairs. A few minutes later one of her friends spotted him across the parking lot, in the wooded area, talking loudly to himself. We didn't see him after that.

A few months later, she called to talk to our mother. I answered and said our mother wasn't home. She said casually, as if just to update me on the situation, "So, I'm pregnant."

Was this really happening? I asked her very calmly who the father was.

"Who do you think?" Of course, the child was the seed of the abusive boyfriend.

A few days later, the two of them came over for lunch with the family. I shook his hand, looked him in the eye, and asked how he was doing. I hated the idea of my sister having his child but I had to make the best of the situation.

They married and then shortly after she miscarried. It's sad how society's rules evoke actions that are not necessarily the best path for anyone involved.

She recently revealed to me he filed for divorce about a year later. She only agreed to the divorce after considering the physical abuse he had inflicted on her. Was this really the world I had left the year before? It was too surreal, like an exaggeration of the world I once knew.

Chapter Five.

Dad

I slept a lot. The sleeping was, at this point, more from feeling bad physically and less from being depressed but I still battled with depression regularly. I sometimes thought up interesting ways to kill myself but it was more for entertainment purposes and less serious considerations. For the most part, I was happy. For the first time in years, I was optimistic about my love life. I had been trying to make love happen since middle school. This time it fell in my lap.

My father and I had been building a relationship since I helped him move to Arizona. I'm sure my living with his mother helped a great deal. Of course, I suppose the fact I was threatened with a very serious health condition didn't hurt. He had been paying for a lot on my behalf. He even gave me a thousand dollars spending money each month on a credit card I had used when I worked for him several years before. Then, for no apparent reason, the phone calls slowly got fewer and one day he just stopped returning my calls. I did get the chance to speak with him on occasion when he called to talk to my brother but these seemed to be conversations of convenience.

One afternoon I was sleeping when my brother woke me to tell me our father was on the phone. I said I would call after I woke up and got something to eat. I assumed this was an inconsiderate act on my brother's part and not an act of my father's will. My mother told me later that my father seemed very angry, and that he expressed a plan to cut me off from all monetary support.

When I called, he answered his phone with his full name, as if he didn't know me. This came as a surprise as I expected him to recognize the call was coming from my phone. I have experienced similar answers to my calls to him since. I have even made habit of a greeting similar to this myself in recent history but this interaction seemed motivated by anger. I suspect he knew I was calling.

"Hey. It's Phil," I said with an optimistic, inquisitive tone.

"So here's the deal. I've already canceled your credit card," he said. "You've got about a week on your cell phone and probably two on your car insurance."

I didn't know what to say. I told him I hadn't meant to offend him.

"I know you're not used to it and it's probably because of the way you were raised but when I say jump, you say how high. So, good luck."

The only words I could muster were "Okay. Bye."

He hung up.

I stopped trying to use my credit card but apparently he never stopped paying for my phone or insurance. I stopped receiving my proof of insurance but managed to get a current copy each time it expired. And, I received a text message from the phone company each month after he paid for my phone. I sent him several letters apologizing but I never received a response. I wasn't sure I blamed him. We hadn't had the best relationship.

The story of one of my most significant experiences with my father begins when I was fifteen. Late one night, I located his car keys on the kitchen counter and took his car to go pick up some friends. When returning home, I turned off the car, killed the headlights and pulled into the exact spot of the driveway from where I had left. But I couldn't get the key out of the ignition. I let my foot off the brake and the car started moving toward the garage. I frantically, repetitively, pressed my foot against the brake knowing that each inch the car rolled forward was another inch it would be out of place. But the brakes did not respond as I expected them to. The car finally came to rest against the garage door with a loud bang. At that point, I knew that my parents would conclude, by the position of the car, that something was amiss.

I started the car and pulled back about ten feet to what I guessed was its original position. I, now a little rattled, held my foot firmly against the brake and shakily tried again to remove the key from the ignition.

A figure entered my peripherals. It was my mother coming from the front door of our house. "What are you doing up?" I asked. I was caught but wouldn't address the fact until I had to. "God told me to come out here," she replied. She would later admit Rocky had barked when I hit the garage. "What are you doing?"

"I can't get the key out."

Then I realized the car needed to be in park for the key to be removed. I clumsily moved the gearshift into park and pulled the key out of the ignition.

The next evening my mother and I were driving back from the retail store, Target. It was getting dark and she had the headlights on. When we neared our house she asked, "What is that?"

As we got closer I realized my father was sitting on the ground in front of the mailbox. Mom rolled down my window to speak to him. I sat between them, my mother in the driver's seat next to me and my father on the ground outside the car. "What are you doing?"

"Nothing," was all he said.

"You're scaring me."

He said something small to reassure her. We left him there and drove up the driveway.

I got out of the car carrying a shopping bag containing the new No Doubt CD "Return of Saturn" my mother had bought for me. I think she knew I was remorseful and I had no plans to take my father's car in the future. I still remember what I had on, a short-sleeved shirt and a blue necktie that had belonged to my grandfather before he passed away when I was three.

"Hey you!" called my dad.

I looked up to see my father was much closer, walking toward me. He told my mother to go inside and grabbed me by the arm. His firm grip guided me toward the side of the house.

He stopped walking, faced me toward him and began shouting. "Who do you think you are?"

I didn't know what to say. I was in a defensive state of mind. He proceeded to throw a few punches to my face and body. What was happening? My mother came around the corner as if to investigate.

"Go inside," he told her.

I was in a daze.

Once my mother left, he went back to striking me on the face and body. "Fight back!" he demanded. I barely felt his strikes as this apparent dream continued. I fell to the ground a few times, each time being pulled back up by my grandfather's necktie to meet one of my father's fists.

After a few moments of this, he stopped and asked in an angrier tone, "Who do you think you are? Do you know what would have happened if you had hit someone?"

I was brought out of my state of submissive ragdoll and began to process the words my father spoke. At least there was no longer any doubt as to what this was about.

I knew I should have been in trouble but had little idea how severe it would be, as I had not experienced any consequence until this point and suspected my actions were more a rite of passage. "That would mean no college for Catherine, no college for Collin." I understand what he meant by this statement now but didn't really think about it at the time. He obviously knew more about the world than I did and I had little doubt he knew what he was talking about. He then told me to go inside.

With little emotion, I went to my room and slid between the covers on my bed. I was supposed to cry. I focused on the words, "Who do you think you are?"

Who did I think I was? I could have killed someone or worse ruined my sibling's chances of a future. I started to tear up and then it began to sink in. Lying on my side, I cried uncontrollably for a few minutes and then my dad came in the room. I rolled onto my back to face him. The objective now was to not anger him. I realized the spot I had branded with a lighter on my shoulder was exposed and pulled the blanket up so he wouldn't see it.

He seemed empowered by my tears. "I want some answers!"

I assumed he was going to inquire the purpose of my trip the night before. I can't be certain I would have told him the truth, that two female friends had begged me to pick them up and that I aimed to please. This would have only worked as evidence to support his accusation that my act of insolence was motivated by a chance to, as he put it, get my dick wet.

He asked what I wanted for my future.

I said I didn't know.

"You'd better figure it out or we can go out there and I'll kick your ass again."

Was that what had happened?

I told him what I thought he wanted to hear. I said I wanted to go to college and maybe start a family someday.

He said something along the lines of, "Good. Now do it." He left the room.

Sometime later, Mom came in. She explained his father used to beat him. The way she said, "beat" I knew she was referring to what he had done to me. I was still somewhat disoriented. I don't think she ever forgave him for that night. And, I don't believe she has forgiven herself for standing idly by.

Years later, he would tell me his actions that night were his way of trying to tell me not to grow up so fast.

A few years after that night, on the side lawn of my parent's house, I found myself working for my father and living in an apartment he paid for. My parents were seeing a psychologist for problems with my sister. I was depressed and alone. I made my own hours, so it was easy to decide I needed a few extra hours of sleep each morning.

After a while, the few hours of sleep turned into all day ordeals. When my dad confronted me about this, he had me follow him and my mother into his home office, which had previously been my bedroom. I said I knew I wasn't doing my job the way I was supposed to and that I would do better. My dad said he had asked my sister's psychologist about my situation. Her response was that I saw him as the "asshole" who beat me up when I was fifteen.

He then spoke, with some sadness in his voice, "So I'll just ask you. Will you ever be able to forgive me?"

I explained that the issue at hand wasn't a result of our less than perfect history. I said my sister felt unloved and that he didn't listen to my mother. It was easier for me to play psychologist than address any real issues between us. I told him, in my mother's presence, that I saw flaws in his marriage.

When I was about nineteen, my mom asked what I thought about the idea of her divorcing my father. Would it be okay if she divorced such an "abusive" man? I was excited for her. I said it would be fine. She couldn't forgive him for that infamous night when I was fifteen, I showed her that I saw flaws in her marriage and I gave her my blessing in her decision to separate from him. It would be easy to see how these three events might have contributed to my parent's divorce. I don't think he was right to do what he did but I couldn't blame him if he blamed me for some of the problems that attributed to his divorce.

Another illustration of our imperfect history together, features a much younger version of myself. When I was in the third grade a friend and I would often make the walk through the neighborhood roads between my house and his in search of amusement. One day, this friend and I were walking to his house, when his dog, who accompanied us on this trip, wondered onto a neighbor's lawn. The owner of the house was out in his yard. In a very angry manner he kicked her and she ran back to her master. My friend protested but the man wouldn't listen.

Later that day, we walked back to my house. I had already forgotten about the incident but apparently my friend couldn't get it off his mind. Once we reached my upstairs bedroom he asked to borrow a piece of paper. I had received some kind of artsy stationery from a relative as a gift. I was excited and handed him a piece.

He gathered a writing utensil from my desk and wrote very slowly, as someone that age does,

"Fuck you, you son of a bitch."

We laughed about it as he folded the paper and wrote, "From your mother" on the outside. He put it in the man's mailbox as we passed by later that day.

A few days later we were walking to my friend's house when this man was again outside.

We tried to walk past without looking at him.

"Hey," he called.

We looked at him as if to say, "Who, us?"

"Come here a second," he said.

My friend went first and I followed. The first step to not getting caught, is to not act guilty. The man held up my unique sheet of paper. "Did you write this?"

My friend said we hadn't and I let him speak for me. I looked on, silently rooting for my friend's ability to tell a believable lie.

"Do you know who did?"

"Yeah," my friend said, "I think they live over there." He pointed to some houses on a distant hill.

When the man looked my friend took off running, breaking the cardinal rule, "Don't act guilty." We were caught. I kept my eyes focused on my fleeing friend and said in a quiet, defeated tone, "He's getting away."

My neighbor grabbed me by the arm and started walking, much in the way my father would years later as a preface to our one-sided brawl on the side lawn. My friend stopped in the road just in front of this neighbor's house and the man grabbed his arm with his other hand. "Which one of you lives closer?"

My friend informed the man that I did. He forcibly guided us to the front door of my mother's house and knocked. My mother answered. He explained the situation and showed her the note we had left in his mailbox.

My mother had my friend and me come into the living room and sit. My friend sat in my mother's chair. It was a light brown, Lazy Boy style rocking chair. I sat in my father's chair. The huge creature that normally occupied this chair would be home to deal with me soon.

When my friend's mother got there to pick him up, I was sent to my room. I was never more jealous of a friend for having divorced parents.

I spent a few hours in my bedroom. Later, my dad came in holding the paper we had left in my neighbor's mailbox. He spoke calmly and I mirrored his emotion.

"Why did you use that word?" he asked.

I took a stance common among third-graders. I didn't know. I was obviously guilty but couldn't explain my actions. The actions taken weren't even the product of my will but I took joy in the act.

He then asked if I knew what the word meant. I said I didn't.

"Do you know what a vagina is?" I said I did. Without understanding the sexual functionality of a vagina, the word was very clinical.

"It means to stick a penis in a vagina."

He asked what I thought my punishment should be. I took it very seriously and set out a stream of cliché punishments: "I should get three spankings and I should be grounded for two weeks. And, I should be sent to bed without dinner."

He grabbed me and spun me around, holding my left arm to keep me from moving away. He slapped my backside hard enough to lift me off the carpet. Instinctively, I threw my open right hand behind me. He yanked my hand out of the way and slapped me again. I threw my hand back; he removed it and slapped me a third time. He then said in a stern voice that I was grounded for something like two weeks and was to have no dinner that night.

It was exactly what I had asked for. I really felt I deserved more. There was strong significance in this word. I didn't know why it was significant but I felt like I wasn't supposed to know. It was interesting to me though, that the F word resulted in me being handled in such a similar manner by both my father and this stranger, a firm hold of my scrawny bicep. Does this self-inflicted punishment of my past contribute to the fact I, as an adult, have often held masochistic tendencies? It typically takes repetition of a pattern to make it a habit. Despite its significance, I can't imagine this one incident would have completely molded a pattern in me as an adult. Although, it might have laid the foundation for the self-punishment in which I willfully engaged as I was growing up. Am I trying to punish myself for not being perfect? I often feel a sense of shame without being able to identify its source. I have done wrong in my life but if I'm to feel guilt, shouldn't I at least know what I'm feeling guilty about?

School was difficult for me. When I was an adolescent, my father discussed with me some facts about my personal history that were apparently more significant than I'd previously understood. Back then, any time he wanted to talk he would tell me to go get the football so we could pass it back and forth. The first few times I thought he was just trying to spend time with me but I soon noticed the pattern of his motivation. Every time we were to "throw the ball" I was in trouble for something.

One particular time, he was frustrated because I was doing poorly in school. He seemed earnest and asked what the problem was. I had the typical teenage attitude of "I don't know. It's my problem. Don't worry about it."

He told me one of my elementary school teachers had expressed the idea that I wasn't being challenged. He said I was then moved to an advanced class. "That didn't work either, so what's the problem?"

Coming from him, the words felt very critical, like he was revoking the idea of intelligence he had placed on me. I often felt like I wasn't the son he wanted. My self-esteem was often formed by my failures in school and Dad's apparent opinion of me just cemented the perspective I had developed of myself. Looking back on the conversation, I see his actions were out of concern and love, even if they came off in a critical way.

We moved a few times when I was growing up. It seemed like Dad always had a new job in a new town. Looking at it now, I don't suppose we moved more than a few times but still, I think this could have contributed to the fact that my social skills are still not where I feel they should be. I always felt like the new kid, outside looking in on these cliques of friends that had formed the year before. I remained disconnected, suspecting that at the end of the year we would move again and I would be the new kid somewhere else. It was such a shock when we stayed in

Austin. I had to learn how to be friendly and cordial. We would move again before I finished high school, this time to Boerne, Texas. I think the reason he struggled so hard for me was because he didn't want me to end up like him, moving from job to job trying to make something work.

Chapter Six

The False World

As much as I've been through over the past few years, I am surprisingly optimistic. The best advice I've gotten was from someone who wasn't necessarily giving advice. A friend of mine is a recovering addict. She once told me she has to take it one day at a time to stay sober. In my mind that meant she could pat herself on the back for each day but as soon as she started commending herself for the time she'd spent sober, she risked feeling like she'd accomplished something and could quit fighting. Some days it's a fight for me to get out of bed and think positively but if I focus on this day and try to make the best of it, I end up feeling better than I would if I gave in to the lingering, comparatively minute pain, or depression. As insignificant as they seem, they are inconsistencies in life and that's not insignificant at all.

Life after the tumor has been, at times, so surreal. Everything feels like a copy of what my life was before. I expected some huge change to occur while I was dealing with the tumor. I half expected to die. Maybe this world is an artist's lucid dream. The subconscious mind is a powerful thing and it makes sense that my life now would so closely resemble my life before, if this were indeed a fantastic illusion. When I dream I sometimes have what seem like synthetic memories. In the dream state I could swear my memories occurred in my past but I wouldn't have to swear because they're memories. They're like any other part of my perspective, authentic in the moment.

It's possible my conscious memories are formulated. Even if this isn't a dream world, it's possible my memories are not authentic. I know my memory of my own personal history is not always accurate. The only factor that makes theory fact is second party perspective, and no two beliefs are ever completely alike. So, what makes history fact? My ideas of events in my personal history are based on my perspective. They're based on my thinking when I was experiencing each event and the way I've come to see each event now.

Throughout the steps taken to rid me of my ailment, my brain tissue was exposed to uncommon stimuli. During the partial removal of the tumor, my brain was accessed through a hole in the back of my head. My brain tissue was exposed. After the surgery, I spent small periods of time each week for weeks having my head shot with what I assume was ionizing radiation, the specific type of radiation used in radio-therapy for the treatment of cancer.[3] A small cancerous mass was removed from the third ventricle of my brain. Who could say my current outlook is correct?

Then there are people who do things that, to me, seem completely irrational and they don't question their actions. Strangely enough, I believe Kay from "Men in Black" said it best, "A person is smart. People are dumb, panicky dangerous animals and you know it."[4] What would you think if you witnessed a species of animal with fairly irrational thinking habits build giant, fragile machines that moved at incredible speeds and then climb inside and travel at those speeds? The automobile is a common part of daily human life.

According to the most recent statistics from FARS (Fatality Analysis Reporting System), the total number of highway fatalities in 2008 was 34,017, and still something like 200,000,000 United States citizens have valid driver's licenses; 196,165,666 according to state-master.com.[5] I'm one of them. The freeway is a cacophony of free-will. Every movement these huge mechanical beasts make is the product of a human's judgment. This would not seem like a very rational system.

Are these thoughts rational? Are they even based on fact or is this just a game I play to keep my brain busy? I have started to notice inconsistencies in the world around me. They are small things like passing three cars broken down and parked on the side of the highway on my daily drive to work when I rarely see a single car in this position on any day. Sometimes I remember my dreams as reality. It can be hard to tell the difference.

For a while after the tumor, I would see unidentifiable images in my line of vision for just part of a second at a time. As far back as I can remember I have, on occasion, seen these apparent manifestations in my peripheral vision. I suspect everyone does to an extent but these were quite prevalent. Maybe the glasses I've worn since my experience with the tumor were responsible for these visions. Maybe, as a member of a generation that was often raised by the television, I've been programmed to

---

3   Types of Radiation Used to Treat Cancer, 2009.
4   Memorable Quotes For, 1990-2009.
5   Transportation Statistics, 2003-2009.

believe anything behind a sheet of glass is the product of a fictitious world. Maybe the idea of this television world comes from the thought that nothing is real. Often my life seems like a bad TV drama. Advertisements seem like satire. Morning talk shows seem like statements from sources opposed to the current state of the typical human perspective. And why not? Television is simply art reflecting life. The world before the tumor often seemed like life reflecting art; so, why not the world after?

If everything is a bad copy of how I remember it, then maybe the imagination that created this supposed false world is not as strong as my analytical brain. The other day I was transferring some of my poetry to my computer. I noticed the significance in the line "They cancer my brain" in one poem. The very next poem was written to what I imagined was a second consciousness in my head. I believe now that I was likely writing to the tumor that could have just recently formed in my brain.

If I'm dreaming, my subconscious could be playing tricks on me. If I'm dreaming, I could be the consciousness I felt those few years ago. In my mind, the poetry was written before the tumor. I remember writing it but maybe nothing is truly real. I remember questioning the genuineness of my physical perspective, even before the tumor. I had conversations with several people about it. One person in particular, whom we can call "Pablo Honey," helped me establish there is no proof of anything other than energy. I am experiencing something; therefore something exists.

If nothing is distorted it is still nothing. It doesn't matter how much something is distorted by the light years it has traveled to get to me. Much like my brain tumor, if I can sense something then something exists. If I am dreaming, these thoughts had to come from somewhere. Maybe I'm in a coma and someone has left the television on in my room. Before all this, I heard television had helped people in similar situations. I recall a story of a girl experiencing episodes of the sitcom Seinfeld from her coma bed. I can almost hear the TV now: "FARS says the total . . ."

I was in a car accident a few years ago. I have always religiously worn my seatbelt but that particular day I felt something was different. Somehow I think I knew of the accident to be and my masochistic ways inspired me to tempt fate by not wearing it. They said we should have died. Aside from a few broken bones we weren't any worse for the wear. How did I sense this disruption to my life unless time is not a line but an infinite?

This was not a secluded incident. I have had many experiences that would be considered intuition. Many people all over the world have. I believe we all, at times, possess the ability to see the future in different ways. Still, most of us would not seem to understand what we're seeing when we see it. This phenomenon could not be possible unless on Earth, or maybe only in my mind, time has no beginning or end.

The timeline in the dream world would seem infinite. I have heard some people dream about both past and future events. I often mistake memories of dreams for memories of my personal history. Déjà vu is defined as "Psychology, the illusion of having previously experienced something actually being encountered for the first time."[6] If time is infinite in our subconscious minds then the phenomenon of déjà vu is no more than our subconscious recognizing something that's happening because it in a sense has already experienced it. The same idea applies to premonition. If time is infinite then premonition is simply a subconscious knowledge of occurrences on the infinite timeline being brought into the conscious line of thought.

Perhaps I'm experiencing the false world we often see the dream world to be. This would be an easy explanation for these otherwise unexplainable phenomena; but who of us can claim absolute knowledge of the authenticity of this world? If real is what we perceive to be real, then most dreams are real to us in the moment. We excuse dreams as figments of the brain because history dictates future and our personal histories often lead us to believe these experiences are falsified. In reality, whether they are false or not, they are simply alternate realities. If our physical world is based on perspective, then who can say which experiences are fabricated by our brains? It's been theorized that there is an unlimited number of alternate realities. If these dreams are realities to us, they could very well be visions into other possible dimensions. What dimension did I wake to after the tumor experience?

Maybe the fact that most of us can't see forward in our conscious state is the result of the fact that we can't understand infinity. If we could see, unrestrictedly, both forward and backward then we would have the potential to see infinitely and our human minds would not be able to understand it. Time, from the human perspective, is a line fragment. There is a beginning and an end. In this dimension, time is a line. It has no visible beginning or end but limited to this dimension, it can only move forward or backward. If we consider time in the other possible dimensions then time is truly infinite. It stretches in every direction to no foreseeable end. Perhaps "time" is the wrong term. The term time is only a fixture in my perspective.

Without a profound name for it, does time exist? How can we know if our flawed perspectives are the only measurement we have of it?

Einstein theorized that time is relative to the momentum of the person holding the perspective of time with his theory of time dilation.[7] The phrase, "Time flies when you're having fun" is a common one. Although it would seem to have been meant to illustrate a difference in perspective

---

[6] 2009.
[7] Time Traveler, 2005.

when it comes to enjoyment and displeasure in an activity, this old saying clearly illustrates the idea that time is relative.

Perhaps my theories of a false reality are just products of habitual patterns. Often, I distance myself from the reality that is my physical pain. I suppose this is a form of meditation. I sink in behind my outer shell of a body. My perspective of the outside world is very distant, as if that of a dream. The pain ceases to be so intense because it ceases to reach the part of my world into which I retreat. My world could genuinely feel false as a result of regularly using this method of distancing my pain by somewhat falsifying my world. Still, if history dictates future, this would not seem to be the world I left when I went under for my tumor operation. This present does not seem to be the future of my past. Then again, perhaps this world feels unreal because I have distanced myself from my past.

If this world is authentic in the standard sense of the word then it is likely the tumor altered the way my brain forms my perspective. I recently spent some time staring into the clear blue sky above the parking lot near the business office where I have recently purchased my glasses. After a short period of looking into the vast blue space, it started to form shapes within itself. It looked as though I was rapidly being sucked backward through a giant pit of blue spheres. I have trouble forming a rational explanation for this. I know from past experience that when I stare at a fixed bright object long enough, like a television or a light bulb, I tend to see its phantom outline when I look into darkness; but these images appeared after looking into a somewhat bright fixture with no outlined definition other than the horizon in my peripherals. After looking for a short time I saw shapes that were not recently presented to my eyes. Were they hallucinations? Were these balls a product of my malfunctioning vision, perhaps patterns inside my eyes that distorted my view of the sky; or were they true to the physical incarnation of what I was looking at?

Perhaps this sky was not the sky with which I was familiar. Perhaps the sky has always looked like this and I never saw it before because I never cared to see it. I have yet to see these shapes in the sky again. I believe all things happen for a reason. I suppose this vision could have been the product of a greater purpose or meant to help me see past this physical world. Then again it could have simply been a product of the world I've lived in since awaking from my experience with the brain tumor. Perhaps these phenomena are not the products of a false world but are a part of the world I have lived in since birth.

Chapter Seven

Allen and the Little Girl
Who Loved Me

Recently I visited with a longtime friend who we'll call "Jo." I mentioned I was working on recording my music. She has always been a fan of it. She claims love for a song I did with an old musical project of mine and, on this visit, she asked if I would record a version of it for her. I was not the original author of the melody but decided it would be all right to record a version for her use. I think Jo appreciates the song because she witnessed the happenings that inspired it.

I was seventeen and living at home in Boerne. I had gotten my G.E.D. mainly because the small town seemed to nurture teenage sex and drug use. Despite my dabbling in both, I no longer wanted anything to do with that lifestyle. The small town politics I dealt with daily were certainly a further deterrent to staying in school. Allen, my best friend of something like nine years, asked me to move into an apartment with him in Austin. There was much incentive: my girlfriend and most of my friends lived in Austin. I lived in Boerne but, emotionally, I'd never left Austin. I had made the hour and a half drive several times in the middle of the night just to see my friends.

Allen called and told me he had signed a lease on an efficiency apartment before we had really talked about when I would be coming to town. I moved in as soon as I could, which took only a few minutes as my belongings included little more than a nightstand, a mattress, and a backpack. His belongings were already in the apartment when I got there. They included a mattress, some clothes, and a shotgun.

We drank a lot, which was not a good idea, considering we both had parents who had had problems with alcohol. One day he told me about a dream he'd had. It involved a girl whose rejection he had been grieving over. In the dream, we threw a party in our new apartment and this girl came. He went into the closet for his father's shotgun, for which he had one shell. I followed him. I put the shell in my shirt pocket and left. I walked outside and along the walkway. He quickly caught up with me, pushed me against the wall and took the shell from my pocket.

Then he went into our one closet and, as he put it, blew his brains out. This concerned me more than it seemed to concern him.

A few nights later I had a friend over and Allen drank until he was really intoxicated. He laid on his bed yelling incomprehensible half-sentences. Then he said without much change in his tone, "Where is my shotgun?"

I casually, with every effort not to clue him in to my planned action, stepped into the small alcove where the bathroom sink and closet were. I removed the shell from the gun and put it in my shirt pocket. I had already passed through the door and my visitor was standing in the doorway when I realized Allen had gotten up off his bed.

"Where is my bullet?" he slurred.

"I don't know," I said with a slight laugh. His slurred speech and determination were humorous.

"I know you have it."

I admitted having it and said I would give it back to him later. He followed me outside, yelling all the way. When I got near my car I started to run. My visitor friend did the same. I still thought it was funny but I was becoming annoyed.

As we closed our car doors he reached the rear bumper. He tried to lift the back end of my car so I couldn't leave. Because my car was front wheel drive, I was able to slowly back up until he had to drop the rear end. He lifted on the bumper again. I backed up a little more until he dropped it again. Eventually I made it far enough that I could peel out of the parking lot.

When I got back that night the apartment was trashed. It was then I realized the seriousness of this situation. Shortly after that, I found other living arrangements. He was very angry with me for leaving. I went back a day or so later to get the last of my things. I brought a male friend, who we'll call Woody, because I wasn't sure what to expect from Allen.

He asked me for my share of the rent. I said I didn't feel I should have had to pay my portion of the rent considering I only stayed for something like two weeks, he trashed some of my things, and that I had to leave to possibly save my life. He seemed hurt by the last of these reasons. He said I should know he would never hurt me. He said he needed the money, that I owed it to him, and that if I hadn't occupied my half of the efficiency, he could have found another roommate. My mother had given me the amount I needed for rent. I told him I didn't feel good about it and handed him the money.

Woody and I left the apartment. A few seconds later, Allen opened the door and threw the money into the air. There was a light breeze; it would have blown away if Woody hadn't gone to gather it. I believed that, because of this, Allen blamed me for his credit problems. I suspected that eventually he would try to kill himself and I didn't want to be around when it happened. His actions were selfish. If he wanted to end his life, I wasn't going to try to stop him again.

About a year later his little sister called to say he had shot himself in the head. When I hung up with her I laughed about it. Good riddance. I was angry with him but I was his brother a lot longer than he was mine. He had a rough childhood and as much as I took them for granted, my family was his second family. Someone once told me that he really admired me. As much as

I try not to hate anything, I hate that I didn't try harder to save him from himself.

Are my memories so tragic because they are not actually memories, or am I subconsciously making efforts to remember the bad times and block out the memories of the good times? This could be the comfort in sadness I tried to explain to my grandmother those few years ago. Then again, I suppose the bad times mark points of significant change. Change has made me who I am today, so these moments had the greatest impact on my perspective because they seem so regrettable.

I dreamed about Allen a few months ago. In my dream I woke up in tears. I was crying into a cloth of some kind. I reached over to a glass on my nightstand and wrung the tears into it. When I woke I realized the significance of this. After his death I wrote a song that was aesthetically inspired by the Deftones song "Minerva."

And now we repent all of the tears that we have spent on you.

You'd have given up before we filled the cup. You wanted to.

That day I told a coworker about the dream. Not long afterward, a woman came into my place of business. Her name was Minerva.

I had been careless with my friendship with Allen. We were "best friends" in our third grade class at Oak Hill Elementary. He never talked down to me. He was always there for me, although I think it did a lot for him to be able to do that. He became a part of my family and loved me very much. I think he probably admired my life more than I know. He didn't get along with his parents at any point I can remember. From what I've been told, I believe them to have been both physically and emotionally abusive. I recall once, going with Allen to pick up his younger siblings at a battered women's shelter. We waited outside the gate as his siblings made their way out. I don't remember seeing his mother there.

She was always so worried we were getting into trouble. It was a reasonable concern but the forms of the trouble she accused us of seemed a little extreme and even contradicting. This time was the mid-nineties and we had taken a liking to the "Banger" group in school. After leaving his mom's house, we often painted our fingernails black then removed the nail polish on our way back. For a while he kept a bottle of nail polish remover in the creek near his house. We often walked through this creek to get to the Gatti Town parking lot. I can still smell the nail polish remover and feel the damp sensation on my fingers that was so apparent after removing the nail polish twice in one day. Once or twice his mother caught us wearing the polish. I remember making efforts to keep my hands in my pockets so she wouldn't see it. She became concerned her son and his best friend were homosexuals.

She once walked in on Allen rapping along with an Eminem song on the radio. It just so happened the line that she heard was "I can't figure out which Spice Girl I wanna impregnate." This opened new doors of suspicion. She also got it in her head we were in, or going to join, a gang. I joked with Allen we should start a homosexual gang in which the initiation would be to impregnate a girl.

I don't remember much about his father aside from his large collection of pornography from the seventies and red-hot temper and my suspicions he was abusive to Allen. If my father did so much damage in one evening, how much had Allen's parents done over his lifetime? Although, and I don't suspect this was his intention, I suppose it inflicted a fair amount of pain to them when he killed himself. I've heard it said when a person kills himself, his mother dies with him. The image of his parents' red, teary faces at his funeral is still heartbreaking to me.

Allen lived with my family for a short while. His mom had decided that he could not live with her any longer. It was something she had done many times before. They shouted and tussled pretty regularly. Often he ended up staying at a friend's house or sleeping in the neighborhood park for a few nights. We spent a lot of time in that park. It was in walking distance from his house. I took his sister's virginity in that park. We once stayed the night in a wooded area of the park after one of the many times his mother had kicked him out. He took a bottle of alcohol from his father's collection and we drank and fell asleep. The next morning I awoke to police officers questioning us about our purpose in the park. Allen told me later he had chucked the bottle into the trees before anyone knew we had been drinking. Apparently, there was a curfew on all city parks.

When Allen was living with us, my father set conditions. He was to quit smoking pot and quit drinking alcohol. He lived in an office separate from the house, so he came and went as he wanted. This office would later become my teenage bachelor pad. Allen told me he had quit smoking pot, with a few exceptions, and he hadn't been drinking at all. But he wanted to have one last party for his upcoming birthday. This didn't work out well for him. Allen told me the story from his perspective later.

One evening, he was in his room talking to a friend on our portable phone about the upcoming keg party when my dad began to bang on his door. "I was listening on the other phone!" he said. "You're outta here!"

It would seem my dad cut bait and ran when things got hard with Allen. Perhaps he was just trying to show him some "tough love." I can't blame my father for his actions, as I cut ties with Allen when things got difficult as well. I don't know if I was wrong for doing but I do feel guilt about it.

It makes sense, considering the probability of the credit problems my actions caused him, now I suspect my credit is being destroyed because I cannot afford to pay my medical bills. I don't know if its karma or fate or my subconscious punishing me but it is poetic justice. I walked away from Allen when things got difficult. I wish I could have stayed. I wish I had attempted to help him through his problems. At the time, I viewed his actions as inconsiderate and something to distance myself from to protect myself. I now believe, if we don't help others confront their self-destructive ways, we are enabling them. I'm not suggesting we confront people about actions we see as flawed out of selfishness or self-righteousness but empower them to face habits that even they should know are destructive.

I dreamed about Allen again recently. At first, I was only in the company of a mutual friend. He had a swingout cylinder revolver in his right hand. The cylinder was in the open position and he started to lose ammunition. Then Allen was there. He suggested our friend load the empty chamber with his pocketknife. After a clumsy and futile attempt at this, he swung the cylinder into place and aimed the barrel of the gun through his lips toward the back of his mouth. I, with some regret in my tone, asked him not to. He proceeded to pull the trigger.

Then Allen said, in a rather monotonous tone, "That looks like a good idea." He took the revolver with his right hand and aimed it at his right temple. I lovingly and gently tried to redirect the barrel away from his head. He extended his arm toward me and fired a shot into my torso. I watched the wound as it slowly released a spring of blood. I thought of the cell phone in my right front pocket and my prospective ability to call for medical help. Within a second or two the gun was pointed back at his temple and releasing a bullet into his head.

I suppose this dream was supposed to help me realize that I likely couldn't have helped him with any amount of love but I still regret not giving more than I did. I guess it really comes down to the value of one's own life and how it compares with the value of a loved one's. I didn't ask for the drama he added to my life, nor did I do anything, to my knowledge, to provoke it but I suppose his baggage was mine because he was such a large part of my life.

I believe we are put into situations for specific reasons. I don't know if I acted in the way I was supposed to but I believe I grew from the experience. The song I wrote years before about my experience with him was very angry. I felt justified in the lines "*Has he fallen yet? Is he falling yet?*" I was angry with Allen for playing with the idea of killing himself. I now have nothing but love for him.

Chapter Eight

Allen and the Little Girl
Who Loved Me pt. 2

Allen was closest with his younger sister. My sister was about her age and when we were younger I wanted nothing to do with her. Allen acted the same way toward his sister when I was around but somewhere through all of the distaste for each other, a bond was formed.

I was fifteen and had just recently discovered the physical translation of that word that my father so eloquently explained when I was in the third grade—fuck. I thought I was in love.

Looking at it now, it was probably a love for the idea of love I'd heard about in pop songs. I had discovered for myself the thing much of the world revolved around. Allen's sister was a year or so younger which, in my mind, made Allen and me the experts in everything.

I had heard about the promiscuity of teenagers and, considering I was now one of them, I wanted to share this new discovery with my best friend's sister. It was actually not premeditated but more of a testing of boundaries for me. She showed little interest. When I took the condom out of my wallet and applied it she told me with a certain certainty I had just wasted a condom. She said it wasn't going to happen but never told me not to or made any effort to stop me. I can try to justify it to myself but now, knowing her admitted struggle with telling a person "No," this almost feels like rape.

I shouldn't have slept with my friend's sister but in my mind this was one of those forgivable sins. I didn't realize how severely it would affect everyone involved. I started cheating on my girlfriend with Allen's sister regularly. It's strange how acts of intimacy are forcibly attempted after a physical relationship is born. We often try to fool ourselves into believing we have an emotional connection when all we have is a genital connection. This could be why most of my past relationships began with an act of sex. I felt intimately close to her but I was completely blind to the fact she was in love with me. I was trying out my new promiscuous ability and couldn't see past myself.

I would go to his parent's house to spend time with him and end up in his sister's bedroom. After the first time with his sister, I asked Allen how he felt about my physical relationship with her. It wasn't until years later he told me how much it killed him. Looking at it from the external point of view I have now, I realize I was taking advantage of, and even taking away, an important ally. Perhaps I wasn't removing her from him but putting distance between them.

The day of Allen's funeral, I was inspired to cut all ties with her. She was sitting beside me on my couch in my apartment in Austin. We hadn't seen each other in years and she was telling me how she was uncontrollably attracted to guys that were not good to her. I leaned over and kissed her lips. She didn't return the kiss. "What do you think is happening here?" she asked.

I told her I was sorry. I hugged her and said that despite what she thought, she didn't need "assholes like me."

I was careless with her when we were younger and careless with her brother years later. For a brief moment, I thought I wanted to start a relationship with her. We had already slept together and in my mind it was less risk. Also, I've always related myself to the number 11. I knew in my head, if I ever reached that many sexual partners, I would have already been with the one I was supposed to be with for the rest of my life. I had recently seen the end of my 11th physical relationship and was wondering if this girl were the one. Looking at it now, I see how selfish the kiss might have been. She had just lost her brother, and I was exploring the possibility of an intimate relationship. It's almost laughable I made this attempt seconds after her admission of attraction for the wrong kind of guy but I was in a state of desperation.

She contacted me years later. She seemed well. I was filled with intense emotion just by the sight of her picture on Myspace. I had tried to do what I thought would be best for her years before by distancing myself from her. I can't say I never wondered how she was but I wouldn't expose her to my carelessness any longer. Then here she was, years later, telling me she wanted to be my friend. Not just my Myspace "friend" (a link that connected my profile page on the Internet social network of "Myspace" to her profile page) but my friend.

I spoke to her on the phone shortly after that initial contact. I finally got a chance to apologize for the way I used her. How ridiculous is it an apology would have to serve as reparations for the way I treated her? It was a very emotional conversation. We spoke about the past we lived both together and separately. She shined new light on the time we spent together and said she'd forgiven me a long time ago. It was so emotionally powerful just to talk to her. She confirmed my suspicions of her abusive childhood and revealed the fact her siblings had experienced abuse as well. She said something about the lack of abusive figures in her life except for "of course" her parents. How sad was it that she could say this with such nonchalance? How incredible was it she could say it with no pain in her voice? She doesn't have ill will toward them. It's only now I realize I was a part of a much larger cycle in her painful upbringing. I am truly inspired by her.

Chapter Nine

"Christian," the Adjective I
(Homosexuality is Gay)

As cliché as the statement may have become, I consider myself to be spiritual, as opposed to religious. Ideas of "Religion" would seem to carry great weight. They are black and white and seem to leave little room for interpretation. Religion can be defined as "a set of beliefs concerning the cause, nature, and purpose of the universe especially when considered as the creation of a superhuman agency or agencies, usually involving devotional or ritual observances, and often containing a moral code governing the conduct of human affairs."[8]

Is it the "governing" moral code God has set for us that has us watch our steps so closely? We are often hesitant to forgive others. Do we feel, because the Christian bible says we were made in God's image, that he would not or should not forgive us? My experience of Christianity has led me to believe that many different incarnations of Christianity want us to feel guilty for being flawed. After all, if an infallible being created me in his image should I not be perfect too?

When I was growing up my grandmother liked to tell me I was perfect. When I was three, my grandfather, Philip Charles Force, passed away. (I believe I was named after him because he was sick with cancer when I was born.) I was very sick as a baby and I've been told it was good for my grandmother to be able to care for me. I think she saw me as perfect. This might be one of the reasons I have trouble forgiving myself for the slightest mistake. I know now that no one is perfect but believed for a long time I was supposed to be.

---

[8] "Religion," 2009.

One definition of human is "Subject to or indicative of the weaknesses, imperfections, and fragility associated with humans: a mistake that shows he's only human; human frailty."[9]

We are flawed because we are human. Hence the phrase "It's only human." I will not feel guilty for behaving in accordance with the way I was created but I was raised in a Christian home. I was made to go to church each Sunday.

Could this be why I sometimes feel guilty for being imperfect? I believe the modern "Christian" heart is in the right place but a lot of the Ideas get wrapped up into Christianity seem immoral. We often believe ourselves worthy of forgiveness. Many of us believe this while simultaneously condemning others for their actions. Perhaps it is not we that should not be forgiven but they.

Some people seem to be full of hate for other members of the human race; and maybe, again, because we were "created in his image" we feel God should hate in the way we do.

The Bible does say God hates. It even says God hates certain people.

Psalm 11:5 says, "The LORD tests the righteous but his soul hates the wicked and the one who loves violence."[10]

So God hates but I have witnessed even Fred Phelps, the person responsible for "godhatesfags.com" and pastor of Westboro Baptist Church, say God's hate is different than ours. I believe God's hate is out of love for his children. He hates that which hurts us. A human's hate is blind but God's hate is divine. I believe God does not hate "fags" any more than he hates people who don't treat their body as a temple.

1 Corinthians 6:19 says, "Or do you not know that your body is a temple of the Holy Spirit within you, whom you have from God? You are not your own,"[11]

Even if the members of the Westboro Baptist Church were all health nuts, I don't see them picketing outside, even one of the 140,655 convenience stores in the United States[12] that likely sell all kinds of junk food, not to mention cigarettes.

What about the obvious sins? The Ten Commandments seem like a good place to start. Why not draw light to the children who are disrespectful to their parents, or draw attention to those who lie?

The story of Sodom and Gomorrah seems to paint God's view of homosexuality as disapproving. In Leviticus 18:22 it is written, "You shall not lie with a male as with a woman; it is an abomination."[3]

---

9 "Human."
10 English standard version, 2001.
11 "U.S. c-store count," 2006.
12 "Translations of Malakoi and Arsenokoitai through History (I Cor 6:9)," 1998.

There would seem to be many references to the sin of sodomy and acts we relate to homosexuality in The Old Testament but the word "homosexual," of course, was not the original text form of this idea. In fact, according to Jeramy Townsley, the word has been translated nearly 40 times. If you have Internet access, visit http://www.jeramyt.org/gay/gaytrans.html.

In John 8:7, Jesus, when confronted with the adulterous past of a teacher, is quoted as having said, "Let him who is without sin among you be the first to throw a stone at her."

1 John 1:8 seems to say we all have sin. "If we say we have no sin, we deceive ourselves, and the truth is not in us."

1 John 1:9 says we are "clean" through our confessions of sin[3] but this does not seem to mean we are without sin, only forgiven.

Therefore, I conclude that the lesson from John 8:7 is that we should not pass judgment on others. My favorite passage at the moment is Romans 14:10: "Why do you pass judgment on your brother? Or you, why do you despise your brother? For we will all stand before the judgment seat of God."

If homosexuality were a sin, I suspect it would be forgivable. The English Standard Version of Luke 24:47 says, "And that repentance and forgiveness of sins should be proclaimed in his name to all nations, beginning from Jerusalem."[13] but the King James Version uses the word 'remission' in place of "forgiveness."

This seems to state that a sin must cease in order for it to be forgiven. So, if the homosexual is not truly remorseful for his actions and does not cease to continue them, is he not forgiven for his imperfection? Was the internal struggle against sin supposed to be an unbalanced one? Would it really be harder for one person to avoid sin than it is for another?

Despite popular theory, homosexuality does not seem to be a question of morality. I don't believe the feelings associated with it to even be a choice. Studies have found physical differences in homosexual and heterosexual biology.

In 1977, the American Journal of Psychiatry printed an article of the title "Plasma Testosterone in Homosexual and Heterosexual Women," written by NK Gartrell; DL Loriaux and TN Chase. In this article, they reveal the results of a study of testosterone levels within 40 age matched women. Twenty-one of these women were homosexual and the remaining 19 were heterosexual. The study showed the testosterone levels in the homosexual women to be at an average of 38% higher than the levels in heterosexual women, and while the homosexual women's testosterone levels stayed about the same despite the age of the test subject, the heterosexual's testosterone levels changed significantly with age.

---

[13]   Blakeslee & Blakeslee, 2007.

According to Dr. Pascale Michelon of *sharpbrains.com*, the left inferior parietal cortex is larger in bilinguals just as quantity of grey matter changes in a musician's level of expertise. Our brains change physical form through our experiences. Its individual parts wither or grow depending on how they are used. One could theorize that the female participants from Gartrell, Loriaux and Chase's case study develop testosterone because of their chosen sexual preference but this change is of the brain tissue and nowhere near the ovaries and the adrenal gland, which produce testosterone in women.[14]

Leviticus 5:6 speaks of a lamb being sacrificed as a sin offering. It's not uncommon to read of animals being sacrificed to God in the Old Testament and John 1:29 says, "The next day he saw Jesus coming toward him, and said, 'Behold, the Lamb of God, who takes away the sin of the world!'"

John 3:16 is probably the most commonly known scripture in the Bible. If you were raised in a Christian home, you can likely recite it before proceeding to read it here. "For God so loved the world, that he gave his only Son, that whoever believes in him should not perish but have eternal life."

If you believe the Christian Bible is fairly accurate and in the power of Jesus Christ then you likely believe that everyone has sin but more importantly that God forgave our sin with the death of his son.

Forget for a second about the hypocrisy of specific judgments or the holes in the logic behind such hate. It is not a person's place to judge other people by God's law but God's place.

Romans 2:1, "Therefore you have no excuse, O man, every one of you who judges. For in passing judgment on another you condemn yourself, because you, the judge, practice the very same things."

I believe the commandments of Leviticus were meant to rule the Israelites represented in the story. Some of the laws set forth in Leviticus do not seem to hold relativity to the societies we live in. The bible does say God does not change but we have. Some consequences of things in that time do not seem to apply any more. Procedures when it comes to a menstruating woman (Leviticus 15:19-30) or when dealing with Leprosy (Leviticus 13) would seem fairly irrelevant in our age.

Leviticus 19:19 says not to wear a garment made of two kinds of material.[3] The King James version says "of linen and woolen."

It has been suggested that this was intended to mean women's clothing but I suppose that's my point. Our interpretations of the Hebrew-Aramaic and Greek scriptures are subject to speculation because they were first subject to interpretation.

---

[14]   "Diagnose-Me.com, High Female Testosterone Level."

The laws of Leviticus, despite the likely benefits they had in the time they were decreed to Moses, do not make sense from a protection stance. God's laws are meant to protect his children. I know my analytical mind is not the defining perspective. I do believe, from a logical standpoint, that a loving, all-knowing creator would set guidelines for us in an attempt to help us avoid being hurt by things we don't understand. I could never know all God knows; seeing his perspective is a likely impossibility but my analytical mind defines my perspective.

I cannot see the good in denying one's most inner feelings if the actions birthed by these feelings don't hurt anyone. I guess it comes down to one's willingness to believe his or her fellow human being's claims. Perhaps its naivety but I believe a person when he or she claims to have an inherent attraction to someone of the same sex. So, what if it's not a choice to have these feelings but a physical inclination? Should a person deny him or herself the satisfaction of his or her innermost, profound urges if the urges are for things that would not cause pain to another? I have heard of men with homosexual tendencies living heterosexual lives. Can they truly be happy? I can't imagine shutting away these feelings and feeling content. If they cannot be happy, would God want them to deny themselves this happiness?

Pastor Ted Haggard struggled much with his homosexual desires but he acted on them.[15] I guess it comes down to your definition of choice. I'm sure most are familiar with the phrase, "no choice", as in "I had no choice," but that statement would seem to never be completely true. We always have a choice, whether it is to act, despite the logical outcome, or simply to resist when something is forced upon us. I suppose this latter example is what Pastor Ted Haggard must have experienced. I suppose if someone were to physically beat me until I gave him my wallet, I would have to choose to end the beating. Would God have wanted Pastor Ted Haggard to experience the pain and condemnation that came with his desires and the acting out of said desires? Even if the tendency toward homosexuality is a physical difference in the brain, we still have a choice whether to act on it or not. But what value is a choice between unhappiness and happiness?

The Bible says everything that is good comes from God. James 1:17 says, "Every good gift and every perfect gift is from above, coming down from the Father of lights with whom there is no variation or shadow due to change."

I guess this scripture's applicability depends on your definition of "good." 1 Corinthians 13:4-7 says, "Love is patient and kind; love does not envy or boast; it is not arrogant or rude. It does not insist on its own way; it is not irritable or resentful; it does not rejoice at wrongdoing but

---

15   "Haggard to King: I'm guilty enough of so many things," 2009.

rejoices with the truth. Love bears all things, believes all things, hopes all things, endures all things."

I know from personal experience that heterosexual relationships don't always manage to reflect this description. If a love between two people of the same sex is symptomatic of everything said in 1 Corinthians 13:4-7 then is it not good? If we agree it is good, and we agree with James 1:17, then we must conclude the love is a gift from God.

The word Christian is defined as "of, pertaining to, or derived from Jesus Christ or his teachings."[16] However, words' meanings are not the same as their definitions. In this world, a person's perspective is judged by his or her actions. When we put labels like "Christian" on perspectives then a person's actions can be misused as a way of defining faith.

The problem with the "Christian" label is so many things have been carried out "in the name of God" for the "Christian way." The word Christian has so much baggage that I try to be as careful as I can with it. Likewise, even though I believe in the teachings of Jesus Christ, I rarely refer to myself as a "Christian."

1 John 1:8-9 says, "If we say we have no sin, we deceive ourselves, and the truth is not in us. If we confess our sins, he is faithful and just to forgive us our sins and to cleanse us from all unrighteousness."

It says that we must ask for forgiveness to be forgiven. This seems to suggest we must truly be remorseful and attempt not to carry out sinful acts of the past again but it also says none of us is without sin. This is every person who has not asked for forgiveness and every person who has.

I think we as humans, have so many problems with ourselves we often try to pull other people down to our level but if we remember anything from elementary school it should be making someone else feel bad doesn't make us feel better. We even have laws against homosexual acts[17] and laws prevent homosexuals from having the same rights the rest of us have, such as the legally recognized union of marriage. What happened to "separation of church and state"? Even if homosexuality were a sin, it would be a question of morality, of "church" and not of law or "state."

I believe we are all God's children. If we weren't, then he wouldn't have taken the time to set rules for all of us. The rules would say "only for God's chosen." John 3:16 says, God gave his son to "the world." God loves "the world."

This idea must hurt some people but if God gave his son's life for some of us, he gave it for every last adultering, stealing, and if it indeed is a sin, gay sex-having one of us, so we could be clean in his eyes.

---

16   "Christian."
17   Johnson, 2009.

Colossians 2:13 says, "And you, who were dead in your trespasses and the uncircumcision of your flesh, God made alive together with him, having forgiven us all our trespasses."

Chapter Ten

Perspective Evitcepsrep

All I have is my own beliefs. I cannot prove to myself, without a reasonable doubt anything but my beliefs exist. This includes everything and everyone in my world. Any information my brain carries was first translated into something my brain could understand. The human eye uses rods and cones to form mental images we know as physical perception. These rods and cones have photoreceptors that convert the energy of sight many times. What starts as light energy is converted to signals, which are sent to the brain via the optic nerve.[18] The sense of touch originates in the nerve endings in the dermis layer of the skin. The information is then carried up the spinal cord to the brain.[19]

The sense of smell comes from things called odor particles. The odor particles fit into nerve cells specific to each smell in the olfactory bulb. Then the information is sent along the olfactory nerve to the brain.[20] The sense of sound is created when sound wave vibrations hit the eardrum. The eardrum sends vibrations through the hammer, the anvil, and the stirrup (the three smallest bones in the human body). The vibrations then take hold of the cilia in the cochlea. The cilia translates the vibrations into information, which is sent to the brain via the Auditory nerve.[21] When food begins the digestive process in the mouth, receptor cells in the taste buds send the received information to the brain through sensory nerves.[22] Each of our perceived senses are a result of systems linked to our brains.

---

18   "The Retina."
19   "Your Sense of Touch."
20   "Your Sense of Smell."
21   "Your Sense of Hearing, How You Hear."
22   "Your Sense of Taste."

Each of these senses is a part of the system that gives us our individual perspective but when these senses intertwine, our perception of the external world is not always accurate. The McGurk effect displays the way our brains link two lines of information being received and forms a conclusion about the outside world. If you have Internet access you can find a video online but be wary of any kind of video delay or stutter as this separation of video sensory and audio sensory will alter your perception. The video visually displays a person speaking one syllable while the audio plays the sound of the person speaking another simultaneously. A large majority of people clearly hear a third syllable's sound not displayed in the video at all. The brain takes into consideration the shape and motion of the mouth one's eyes witness and the sounds one's ears hear and comes to a conclusion.[23] The McGurk effect clearly shows a link between the sense of hearing and the sense of sight in producing one's perception of speech.

I recall a day from my youth that was spent in its near entirety playing a first person computer game. When I finally gave in to the urgent sensation that in the past had meant a need to relieve my bladder, I was a zombie. I got up from my mother's computer and made my way down the hallway with my arms lying limp at my sides. When I got to the bathroom door, I moved my right thumb as if I were still at the computer, tapping a malfunctioning space bar on the keyboard. After a few attempts, I realized the futility in my attempt to open the bathroom door by twitching my thumb at my side but this command had become hardwired in my brain. The jerking motion of my thumb had, in recent history, opened doors.

I have no guarantee my brain's translation of the information it receives about the external world will be in conjunction with the way the world is perceived by everyone else. In fact, I'm fairly sure my brain often mistranslates this received information. Even if every aspect of my conceptual understanding before the tumor was exactly correct, since the tumor my brain has had the tendency to form a physical perspective of the external world, which differs greatly from the physical perspective I often held before the tumor. Where I used to see one image, I now often see two.

I can only assume others share my basic experience of a first person perspective. If this is so, then everyone's idea of the world is never absolutely correct because everyone's interpretation of the world is different. Everyone's interpretation of the world is different because everyone's first person perspective could not possibly share an exact experience with another first person perspective. The most obvious cause of this is each person's physical incarnation's position on the grid of the

---

23   http://www.media.uio.no/personer/arntm/McGurk_english.html.

physical world. When we only get parts of a puzzle (a happening) we tend to use our problem solving abilities to piece together the puzzle.

You hear a gunshot in the next room. When you rush to see what the disturbance was, you find a man holding a gun over the bleeding, unconscious woman on the floor. In these few seconds of your brain absorbing information from the outside world, you have likely already drawn a conclusion and possibly acted out the scene in your head. You know this was a married couple who'd been having relationship troubles. You believe you heard the woman in conversation with her secret lover earlier that day.

You can only conclude this was murder. What you didn't experience was the long, tearful conversation that had just occurred in this room before the woman pointed the gun to her head and took her own life. You also didn't witness the man reach down for the gun with the motivation of taking his own life. What is the difference in physical perspective and point of view? Physical observation is unassuming. Point of view, or perspective, is what we get when we combine physical observation with problem solving.

Have you ever seen something indefinable out of the corner of your eye only to find nothing like what you saw existed where you saw it? Have you ever said, "I could have sworn . . ." or misheard someone? Have you ever been too quick to judge something or someone? Our perspectives are constantly changing. Historical happenings have been perceived very differently. There are some of us who "know" Lee Harvey Oswald acted alone in the assassination of John F. Kennedy. Then, there are those of us who "know" there was a second gunman on the grassy knoll. Ideas like this are often excused as conspiracy theories, staging of the moon landing, aliens. These theories that seem so easily dismissed are examples of difference in perspective. They are the products of different analytical abilities.

In the fifteenth century most of humankind "knew" the Earth was flat. What we assume we know about our world is constantly changing. We now "know" it is spherical. Perspective can alter what we "know." Some people "know" we humans evolved from primates. Others "know" we were created the way we are today. The world of science is constantly changing its collective mind about what is and isn't.

Eggs were good for us and then only egg whites were good for us, because the yolks caused a raise in bad cholesterol. Last I checked, we had decided egg yolks were no longer such a serious threat.

The list goes on. Recently we decided Pluto was no longer a planet. Last I heard, it was classified as a micro-planet. I suppose the word planet is an invention of humankind and therefore, we can redefine it as we wish but nothing has changed other than our perspective. For some time, I worked as a phlebotomist. As I recall, after taking a person's blood from their cubital fossa (front of the elbow), it was common practice for the blood taker to suggest the patient bend his or her elbow to hold a piece of gauze or cotton over the wound. Now it is believed, such an act tends to result in a bruise caused by the vein bleeding under the skin.

What of the idea of a daily eight glasses of water? It has been suggested recently by the scientific community, imbibing that much water could, if anything, have adverse effects. Could such examples be excused as scientific advancement? Are we really so much more advanced than our former selves that we can now, without the slightest bit of doubt "know" things about our bodies and even our world?

A while back, I visited a childhood friend and his wife at his apartment. It was weird to think of this person as married because I had only known him as the teenage boy who attended the small underfunded Christian school of my seventh grade year of education. They seemed to be doing well and I expressed to his wife I was happy to see this. She said "it" is about being happy with what you have.

When I spoke the same sentence to my friend, he made the statement one is never happy with what he has. The statements were nearly identical. They focused on what they had and yet they seemed to be polar opposites in their message. These were two people sharing the same basic encounters of life in the physical world and yet they held majorly contrast-ing experiences of the lives they shared. I suppose these two perspectives have a lot to do with personal needs. This seems to make a strong state-ment about how perspectives vary.

What of personal history? In my experience, I have discovered the mind's eye can, and does, play back events differently from how they were first interpreted. Perspective is rarely identical. It's affected by an individual's physical perspective, personal history, and belief systems. We are affected differently by recent events and by not so recent events. Recent events affect our temporary mood while not so recent events create the roots of our perspectives.

I recently experienced a perspective I had not held in years. I suspect some would dismiss it as nostalgia but it was so much more than that. I was listening to an album I'd spent a large part of my early teenage years listening to when the world physically changed. There was no change in the physical attributes of the world, only the way I experienced them. It was the beauty of the innocent, and even ignorant, teenage angst I had experienced years before. It was seeing the freeway for its physical incarnation and not what its physical body allowed me.

It was blindness and perceived strength because of the blindness. My physical perspective reverted, and completely changed, because of the induced emotional feelings of a song. This instability of perspective is what makes such difference in each person's general view of the world possible.

These differences in each general perspective are what allow us to disagree with each other. When we debate we should present our opinions as opinions and not as absolute truths.

We should state we believe or we disagree. Our perspectives alter our opinions and therefore no opinion is absolutely correct for anyone but the person who birthed it.

I can say, "We should" change our actions without feeling I am being judgmental because "We should" is a philosophical suggestion while "You should" can be judgmental.

When we form opinions about flaws in other people's chosen actions, we are likely assuming we understand their perspective and/or understand the consequences of their actions better than they do. I can never truly know what is right for anyone other than myself because my perspective is the only one familiar to me. At the same time, I can recognize patterns as harmful in others and offer my opinion, and the line of thought that supports my opinion.

If our external world is based on perception, is it vanity that makes us so angry when other people don't see the world the same way? For that matter, what is insane? Insanity really is just a perspective few can relate to. It is possible that schizophrenics "can" hear voices instead of "do" hear voices. Maybe they can sense something we "sane" people cannot.

Many believe a spiritual world links to ours; that there are energies in this world we are often blind to. What is it that makes us so quick to condemn someone when they can sense this world we have to have faith in? What makes us so sure we are right?

Perspectives change with culture. According to "The Body Has a Mind of Its Own," a study was done by Richard Nisbett and Kaiping Peng where both Asian and American students were instructed to describe an animated water scene. The American students tended to describe the big fish featured in the picture, while the Japanese students described the background and the scene as a whole and paid less attention to the fish.[24] This is a clear example of personal history affecting perspective.

If I saw the color blue when I saw something the rest of the world would perceive as red, I would still call it red. The world would have raised me to believe what I see as blue is called "red." If I saw the color blue when I looked at a fire truck, I would give the shade the name "red" because other members of my world would have raised me to believe the color of the fire truck is red. The names we give colors are completely reliant upon our personal history. It could be argued, different colors evoke different feelings and our experience of the color would not feel genuine if we experienced an uncommon emotional reaction to the shade.

---

[24]   Blakeslee, & Blakeslee, 2007.

Red is supposed to make a person excited. Blue is supposed to be soothing but if you think about it, red is the color of many exciting things and blue is the color of many soothing things.

Red is the color we relate to fire and poison. Blue is the color we relate to the ocean and the sky on a clear day. Maybe we relate these colors to their accompanying feelings because of their counter parts in our physical world. I suppose I would find blue exciting if it were the color of poison.

In our world, color is often used to label things, even if the labeling system is not consciously human-made. Where do you think we get the color "sky blue"?

Our perception of color, or anything for that matter, is much like a computer program; our brain translates the signal of this vision into something it can understand as the color blue.

This process seems very similar to a computer translating binary code into an image. So our brains are vast collections of systems like computer programs. I suppose a thing like color-blindness could only be a system in the brain not behaving in the way it was designed. I think, often, we are blinded to the world by what we expect to find. How many times has someone overlooked something out of place because they didn't expect to find it there?

Theoretically, if our computer brains are all made by the same manufacturer, then we should all read the information we receive the same way but our brains have many more altering factors than a basic desktop.

The most prevalent of these factors is freewill. We alter our perspectives greatly by how the perceived affects us. My father has claimed the ability to alter "the truth" in his mind so he is never wrong. We cannot all be my father but I believe we all do this, at least at a subconscious level. If we don't want to believe something we can choose not to. Therefore freewill and absolute anything cannot exist together. There is always perspective, which is all we as humans have.

If our world is based on perspective and we have the ability to change the way we see the world around us, then what we *expect* to find can alter what we *do* find in our world. Many times in my life, I've realized I probably did something incorrectly. I've had this undeniable feeling I made a mistake somewhere in the process of this action but I had already reaped the rewards I could not have experienced without taking the correct actions. Maybe this was just my typical paranoia, my fear of imperfection in myself, or maybe because at the time I thought I had done things correctly, I reaped the reward I expected.

When a commute is taken every day, it becomes a program in a person's mind. No longer are you reading street signs or counting mileage. The daily drive to work is nothing but landmarks. Turn left when you get to the interstate. Turn right next to the gas station that carries your brand of whatever. If we know beyond a reasonable doubt that we were to take a left at the gas station instead of a right, would we still make it to work? It would be a simple malfunction in the mapping system in our brain. If we can willfully change our own perception of the world around us within our heads then we should be able to change the world around us based on what we expect to find. The problem is that we have no way to prove or disprove this theory. It is only logical from our perspectives that our expectations of our world are accurate.

If perspective can change based on what we expect to find, then how do we know we're not blinded by our expectations? There are those who would ask, "What about the fact two people can perceive the same thing without previous conversation about it but second party perspective cannot prove anything because we cannot prove a second party's perspective even exists?" Our brains may tell us we heard the second party make a statement or witnessed a second party do something but we can never know for certain that anything other than our own thought has happened at all. What about the fact that two people can see the same thing and perceive it completely differently?

In my personal past, history has dictated the future and the only tool I have to interpret my world is my personal history. I have learned if I don't eat, I end up hungry, and if I don't work, I end up without money. It doesn't matter if the world is how I perceive it. I do certain things to feel the way I want. But there is something to be said about mind over matter. Positive thinking can bring positive results. In a world based on malleable perspective, there would seem to be little that cannot be altered by a willful change in perspective.

There is a strong link between our mental and emotional perspectives and the physical world. When I was recovering from the brain tumor I learned that cancer survivors who thought positively had a less likely chance of developing cancer again. Scientists have proof depression hurts the physical body. I know from experience, depression manifests itself physically. According to Rob Stein, Washington Post Staff Writer, the human body ages much more rapidly when it's under emotional stress.[25] Fortunately, emotion can be controlled by the conscious mind. If a person truly does not want to be angry or hurt about something, he or she can use his or her ability to change his or her perspective.

To willfully change one's inner emotional response can be difficult. In order for a person to change his or her emotional state, he or she must first change his or her perspective. And changing one's perspective can feel like lying to oneself. Deciding we want to feel, or not to feel a certain way, isn't ignoring one's feelings, it's the first step to changing the way we perceive the situation so we may have new feelings about it. We'll go deeper into this later.

---

[25]   2004,

We are afraid of lying to ourselves, yet we lie to ourselves constantly without realizing it. When we are in love, we are often blind to someone's flaws. I personally have held false ideas of my loved ones' greatness in my mind. My personal history is littered with this defective mental pattern. I know I've often been guilty of being in love with the idea of the person but unable to make a true connection. The feelings I had were real because the only perspective I needed for them to be real was my own but the views I had of these people were the result of my desire, not logic.

I have found that a loving parent can often be blinded to his child's flaws. I know my girlfriend seems to have a great opinion of her dog—her child—despite the fact she sees the disobedience he displays on a regular basis. She can see the individual acts but does not form the perspective that he is disobedient.

I think we all would like the ability to see the world in definite terms but the problem with that is there is no definite world, only perspective. If I can change the world around me through my perspective, I wonder how much effect I have on things that are seemingly out of my reach.

I mentioned earlier in this chapter that my physical perspective of the world would often seem to differ from others'. I often have double vision. Most of the time my analytical mind can dismiss the idea of a second cloned object but the part of my brain translates the physical world into an image I can understand, has had this one major malfunction since I started to notice symptoms of the coming tumor experience several years ago. What if I didn't know everything was supposed to project itself as a single image in my brain? If all I have is my own perspective, and perspective is often wrong, how can I be certain I was ever right about the physical world to begin with? It's true that I physically sense one object when I touch it but I visually experience two hands extending toward the object. This is still a product of the senses. So which sense is right? If I unwillingly duplicate my perception of things in the physical world, how can I be sure I don't unknowingly change them?

Chapter Eleven

Christian, the Adjective II
isms, ams and anities, Oh My!

In the broad scale of possibilities, there are little differences in the largest religions in the world and yet we kill each other over the subtleties. Christianity and Judaism base their beliefs on three major factors. The first two are the belief there is a Supreme Being and in the coming of the Messiah. The third is, there is an after-life.[26]

Islam can be broken into six basic beliefs: the sole existence of one God, the existence of angels, faith in scriptures, faith in prophets, a judgment day and predestination, or the idea that God is eternal and knows what choices we will make in spite of the fact we have free-will.[27] None of these six basic beliefs rival anything in the Christian bible but more importantly, two of the six beliefs are the belief in one God and the belief in the Day of Judgment and resurrection (life after death), two beliefs Christianity would seem to be built upon.

According to Salman Hakim of mnsu.edu, Muslims have faith that, on this day of resurrection and judgment, every person who has passed, will rise from the grave and be judged according to their actions.[2] This sounds an awful lot like the happenings described in John 5:28-29 of the Christian Bible: "Do not marvel at this, for an hour is coming when all who are in the tombs will hear his voice and come out, those who have done good to the resurrection of life, and those who have done evil to the resurrection of judgment."[28]

The Qur'an says in Surah 112 "Say: He is Allah, the One and Only; Allah, the Eternal, Absolute; He begetteth not, nor is He begotten; and

---

26   "From Judaism to . . ."
27   Hakim, 2009.
28   English standard version, 2001.

there is none like unto Him."[29] Common Christian belief is of mono-theism. Many analytical minds see this and decide the views of Christianity and Islam are contradictory. After all, how could "Allah" be the only true god if "Yahweh" is the only true god?

Why would God allow so many different views if there was only one that was correct? Why would God allow so many different beliefs and religions if they were not all views of him?

We can argue everyone has freewill and the ability to ignore the truth about the one true god but would God really condemn the majority and deliver the minority?

What about those who never hear of him or his love? Are they not shown the same love those who are familiar with his teachings are? Even if they have heard of the Christian God's love, I would imagine to give up the beliefs a person has held his or her entire life for a different set of beliefs would take a lot of time and thinking. It seems to be common belief in the United States that all who don't subscribe to Christianity will not see God's grace. The Christian bible teaches of a merciful god, a god who, in my opinion, would not allow a nation of children to be raised with one set of beliefs and to live by those beliefs only to be wrong and damned to hell or nonexistence for all of eternity.

In 1997, Russell Ash reported the United States as being an 85% Christian nation.[30] If you believe in the teachings of Jesus Christ and were born in the United States then you did not have to search very far to find your beliefs.

Each religion has its differences but each holy doctrine was written by a human. There are many words used to refer to God in the Hebrew scripture: El, Elohim, El Shaddai, Adonai, Yehova, El Elyon, El-Olam. El-Berith and Zur, to name a few. El translates to "God (mighty, strong, and prominent)" while Adonai is represented by "Lord" in English Bibles.[31] What if the Christian idea of Yahweh or Jehovah or God is the same as the Muslim idea of Allah? Allah is simply the Arabic word for "God."[32]

I have heard witness to the "injustice" in the Qur'an but I have yet to see it myself. The idea most commonly presented to me is the idea the Qur'an commands followers to "Kill Infidels." This has commonly been presented as a theme behind the actions of extremist groups but in my research, I have found that most of the Muslim faith believe these inter-pretations to be unfounded.

---

[29]   Al Ikhlâs.
[30]   Top 10 Largest, 2000.
[31]   Dolphin, 2008.
[32]   Allah, 1997-2007.

Hinduism is based on the belief in a supreme being known as Brahman and in reincarnation.[33] Reincarnation paints a slightly different picture of death from those commonly painted in other beliefs listed but it still follows the basic idea of life after death. A theme of Hinduism is the idea that our purpose on Earth is to realize that we are a part of God.[34] One could translate the verse Ecclesiastes 12:7 from the Christian bible to mean that we are a part of God. It says, "and the dust returns to the earth as it was, and the spirit returns to God who gave it."

As author Kersey Graves recorded, Hindu's Krishna has many things in common with Christianity's Jesus. Their stories are almost identical. They were both called the Son of God, born to this world as the sons of carpenters. They were both visited at birth by wise men who were guided by a star. When the parents of the children fled after being warned by angels that their babies were to be put to death, they stayed in very similarly named towns. Jesus' parents stayed in Muturea, while Krishna's parents stayed in Mathura. They both performed miracles and ascended to heaven when they were resurrected.[35] So, is this just an incredible coincidence? Perhaps. It is common belief that Krishna was born 3228 B.C.E., while it is speculated that Jesus was born somewhere between 4 and 7 B.C.E.[10] It seems more likely the story of Krishna was the original story of Jesus, or the story of Jesus was simply created by someone with little imagination or respect for a person's original work. Why could it not be both? John 14:6 says, "Jesus said to him, 'I am the way, and the truth, and the life. No one comes to the Father except through me.'"[3] So, must we call him "Jesus" to know God?

Many Buddhists regard Buddhism as more of a way of life than a religion but it would seem to fit the template of religion fairly well. In Buddhism the Buddhanature, or Tathagatagarbha, is believed to be a hidden, eternal and immortal part of every animate creature.[36] This sounds an awful lot like the soul that is common in Christian beliefs. Buddhists believe in Karma and rebirth in another life according to one's karma.[37] All together these religions were present among 72.1% of the world's population in 2002.[38] According to Adherents.com at the time of this writing, these religions are present in 74.22% of the world's population.[39] We all have the same basic beliefs. There is at least one Supreme Being

---

[33]   Dominguez, 2006.
[34]   Hinduism - 4000 to 2500 BCE, 2008.
[35]   Robinson, 2001-2007.
[36]   Page, 2010.
[37]   Sayadaw, 2008.
[38]   Atlas of Faiths, 2002.
[39]   2007.

and there is an afterlife. Many of us believe we can affect our afterlives by our actions on this earth. Christian and Islamic beliefs are very similar. We share many of the same historic figures including Abraham and even Jesus. In fact, Sura 19 of the Qur'an tells the story of the virgin mother Maryam giving birth to a "pure son."[40] This sounds a lot like the Christmas story that most Christians grow up hearing. There are so many similarities and we divide ourselves by our differences.

Even Satanism is not so different. It often is followed by many misconceptions. The word Satanism often conjures visions of people in robes making sacrifices to the dark lord. I have come to understand the common modern incarnation of Satanism as having more to do with instant gratification and pleasure within this world and less about caring for or even believing in anything beyond it. We are all in pursuit of happiness. We just seem to have different ideas about what will make us happy. Satan's fall from grace is represented in Isaiah 14:12-15 in the Christian bible[3] and throughout the bible he is not portrayed as a forgiving or understanding being in the least. When you think about it, it seems silly to think someone would worship a being he or she believes will cause him or her endless pain in the afterlife.

Egyptian Mythology, if it is safe to call it mythology, tells the story of a god, Osiris, who was first born to this world as a human to the original king of Egypt. After Osiris established himself as a truly great king, his brother Set (Seth) murdered him for his throne.[41] Osiris became the king of the afterlife and Set became the god of Desert, Storms and Chaos, among other things, and was eventually viewed as a god of evil.[42]

Modern day Satanism is argued to have been birthed from ideas related to Egyptian mythology's set. Set and Christianity's "Satan" do seem to have many similarities. Satan is often viewed as the nemesis of or rival to God. If Egypt's representation of Set was an earlier incarnation of Christianity's Satan, then "Osiris" would be a close match to Christianity's Jesus. This does not mean we are simply refabricating old fictitious stories. I believe modern day religion may very well be evolutions of older religions but this does not mean they are fabricated altogether.

To me, these similarities seem like cultural differences to one singular idea.

Look at Greek mythology. Zeus was believed to be the ruler of gods.[43] In Christianity Jesus is often a part of the holy trinity. In the Latin

---

[40]   2002.
[41]   McDevitt, 1997-2007.
[42]   Seawright, 1999-2003.
[43]   "Information about," 2002.

language of Spanish Jesus is pronounced hāsoōs. These two religions were divided by at least 800 years, yet the name of the Greek king of gods is very similar to the name of one third of the head of Christianity. Greek mythology was polytheistic.[44] Christianity and Islam have angels. Are these really differences in beliefs or simply differences in translations of one belief? Hebrew's "Elohim" has plural connotations.[6]

The term Elohim seems to give room for polytheistic interpretation. If the term god can mean, a powerful ruler, who's to say that this idea of polytheism is not referring to archangels or the co rulers of the Jehovah's Witness belief, the 144,000 described in Revelation 7 and 14? How can we divide ourselves over such miniscule differences?

Perhaps we let religious wars rage between ourselves because we believe, if another religion is correct in its views, then that would make us wrong. Their declaration of the one true god would mean we are simply talking to ourselves when we pray. Again, look at John 14:6, "Jesus said to him, 'I am the way, and the truth, and the life. No one comes to the Father except through me.'" This seems to state that if you do not believe Jesus was the Messiah, you cannot possibly know God but when analyzing anything beyond this world, one has to keep in mind its abstract nature. How can we, beings bound by physical laws, comprehend something that is not? Jesus was a physical incarnation in the Book of John. I suppose he is, now, something different to each who believes there is truth behind his teachings.

I am not convinced that, simply because two religions have differences, one of them has to be wrong. A god who is forgiving and understanding would listen to a prayer no matter what name he was given by the person praying. After all, language is a creation of human-kind. The technicalities of a religion are inconsequential. What matters most is the belief in, and the relationship with, God, no matter what you call him, her, or it. It seems the major differences in our religions are simply the factors on which we choose to focus. The human mind cannot possibly understand things of the spiritual world and, the fact that something seems to be contradictory in the physical world doesn't necessarily make it so in the spiritual world. We fight over our differences when we should be uniting for the purpose of our similarities. Romans 2:10 says, "But glory and honor and peace for everyone who does well, the Jew first and also the Greek."[3]

We often relate our own beliefs to the teachings of our religion even though the religion itself may or may not have any relation to them. This seems to be how a thing like the willed death of another can be carried out "in the name of God." It would seem to make little sense that people of such similar beliefs can fight and kill each other over their differences and

---

44   "Polytheism - Ancient World," 2009.

people who have fairly contrary beliefs, like Christians and Atheists, can live in a seemingly harmonious state. Perhaps we can manage this because we appreciate difference as long as it doesn't threaten our beliefs. To each side, the contrary is an extreme that should not be taken seriously.

It has been said it's human nature to wonder where we come from. Some would say this was the root of our "creation" of the idea of God. They would say we subconsciously wanted a creator so we could better define ourselves and have meaning in our lives. If religions feature so many similar beliefs then I suppose these beliefs are the products of instinct and not the products of influence. If all of these different systems of belief came from the same basic instinct of inquiry then they would likely have, at least, the fundamentals in common. The differences could be excused as products of the environment that nurtured these beliefs.

There would seem to be a lack of proof to support any religious perspective. I think the lack of proof for the existence of a creator was God's intention. The story of Matthew 14:22-33 seems to illustrate the need for faith. Peter is standing on the surface of the sea and begins to sink only when his faith fails. Only when he believes in his ability to walk on water does his ability exist.[3] Much in this way, God does not truly work in our lives until we believe he can. Without proof we need faith.

I believe the faith we choose is largely influenced by the environment in which we are raised. The largest religion in the United States is Christianity. According to factbook.net, a large portion of Africa is Muslim, while the Middle East is predominately Muslim.[45] The fact that these statistics do not constantly fluctuate any significant amount leads me to believe that we, for the most part, believe what our parents believed. Most who adhere to Judaism inherit their religious perspectives from their parents. This has become so common that the term "Jewish" tends to refer to both a religion and a nationality. We believe what our parents believed because their belief system is the belief system to which we've had the most exposure.

Our entire general idea of the world is based on personal history. Our intake influences our beliefs and even our actions. Our ears hear sounds. Our brains interpret the sounds as theories of religious influence. Our eyes see forms in the physical world move. Our brains translate these movements to actions, and then our analytical brains attempt to define the motivation behind these actions. We then determine if these beliefs or actions fit into our personal ideas of the world. We decide if we want to make these beliefs or actions our own. Each individual occurrence in our personal histories has had a hand in shaping our current perspectives.

Our religions are not as different as we sometimes like to think. It seems it would take a strong vanity to know our way is the only correct

---

[45]   *Muslim Population by Country.*

one without exploring the possibilities of any other way. Perhaps it's each person's personal experiences with things of the supernatural. If we look at each religion as a brand, we can say we each like our own brand. It has little to do with the superiority of the brand but more to do with familiarity with the brand. If the product does what it is supposed to do, we keep buying it. We buy our parents' brand of fabric softener, shop at the same stores as they did and subscribe to the same religious beliefs.

We cannot understand many things about God. Instead of condemning people for their beliefs we should constantly be trying to evolve our own. How petty do we have to be to be divided by such subtle differences? As unfortunate as it is, we would seem to find differences to establish purpose in our lives. After all, what is a life without a mission? Are we really killing each other out of boredom? I believe most would agree there are things worth dying for. Are there things worth killing for? If not, then the need to die for said things would be much less. The problem with this is that we take human life over things that do not really seem worth killing over.

The physical world would seem to be run by humankind. After all, Genesis 1:26 says we were given domain over the entire earth, "Then God said, 'Let us make man in our image, after our likeness. And, let them have dominion over the fish of the sea and over the birds of the heavens and over the livestock and over all the earth and over every creeping thing that creeps on the earth.'" This world would seem to be the domain of humankind and our freewill. Our conscious decisions constantly affect the world around us. Perhaps if I hadn't ignored the overwhelming headaches those few years ago, I would not be dealing with the vision problems I am today. I was young and had delusions of invincibility but I might have had a strong impact on the world I live in today. It's like Newton's *Third Law of Motion* states, "For every action there is an equal and opposite reaction."[46] Or maybe you prefer The Clash: "If I go there will be trouble. An' if I stay it will be double." Well, I stayed and now my perspective of the physical world is double. Either way, of all living creatures on Earth, humankind would seem to have the strongest effect on humankind.

I guess it's somewhat counterintuitive to quote from the source of a large part of modern religion in an attempt to expose what seem to be flaws in logic behind certain parts of it. But perhaps religion wasn't the objective in the composition of the Christian Bible. What if faith was the goal? I understand how we, as a species, would, without the intention of a creator, create religion from a basic source of faith. We like things preassembled. Why would we do our own soul searching when we could simply take the word of someone who seems more experienced in things of the spiritual world? The problem with that is no one has any proof his

---

[46] *Newton's Three Laws.*

or her beliefs are correct. If we take other's views as divine truths then we are giving their speculation the power of absolute faith.

Exodus 34:11-14 says, "Observe what I command you this day. Behold, I will drive out before you the Amorites, the Canaanites, the Hittites, the Perizzites, the Hivites, and the Jebusites. Take care, lest you make a covenant with the inhabitants of the land to which you go, lest it become a snare in your midst. You shall tear down their altars and break their pillars and cut down their Asherim (for you shall worship no other god, for the LORD, whose name is Jealous, is a jealous God)," I have heard this passage interpreted to mean the Jewish people were being commanded to claim trespass of the Amorites, the Canaanites, the Hittites, the Perizzites, the Hivites, and the Jebusites and deliver justice by tearing down their altars. This passage would seem to, not only state that all others are wrong but also give power to those who believe in the Christian God to insult other's beliefs.

Romans 2:10 says: "but glory and honor and peace for everyone who does good, the Jew first and also the Greek."

How could something like the actions said to be encouraged in Exodus 34:11-14 possibly keep glory, honor and peace among humankind? My interpretation of Exodus 34:11-14 is a little different. I believe the commandment was to not be swayed by the cultures of the lands they were traveling through but to stay loyal to what they believed. I believe the tearing down of these altars and pillars was metaphorical and internal.

Would God want us to fight over the differences in our religious choices? I don't believe so. As much as we like to view our creator as vengeful, the Old Testament paints this picture well—it's humans, not God, who would seem to condemn humans for their actions. The problem is our closed-minded approach to faith. The problem is unswayable beliefs. The problem is our replacement of spirituality and thought with religion. Religion is a group of beliefs and rituals birthed by humans. I'm not questioning the legitimacy of faith in a higher power but I see flaws in the systematic beliefs that we have molded around the faith.

Perhaps the problem with these systems is the fact they are systems. Systems work in a certain way, because they were designed to do so. Water evaporates and rains back to the earth because precipitation is a system. The amount of precipitation in certain areas of the earth will vary but small amounts of water on the earth's surface will inevitably evaporate and eventually fall back to earth. Laws govern this system but systems created by humans are flawed because humankind's laws are not divine.

I suppose we turn beliefs into belief systems so we can validate our perspectives by sharing them. I am reminded of comedian, Mitch Hedburg's joke about the club sandwich. "I like my sandwiches with three pieces of bread. So do I. Let's form a club then . . . how do you feel about frilly toothpicks? I'm for 'em! Well, this club is formed . . ."[47] Perhaps each religion is simply a club, a group of people with common perspectives. The greatest will tends to birth the truth in isolated situations and ultimately the majority's idea of profound truth. These clubs are likely just the products of the most determined perspectives at given times. These willful people likely insisted on the profoundness of their perspectives to convince others to share their perspectives in an effort to feel validated in their ideas. The writers of the Christian Bible were not dictated to by God. They are said to have been inspired by God. Each story is subject to flaw because the writers were human and imperfect.

I believe any faith of a spiritual nature is a good thing. I have noticed many close to me tend to have their opinions of a person greatly altered by the person's spiritual beliefs. Some beliefs seem rooted in ideas so different from their own that the beliefs seem to hold a certain absurdity. Most don't seem to see that different faiths give us hope. They give us reason to be good to each other. But I do see the difference in faith and religion. Faith brings hope and is open for interpretation. Religion is based in beliefs and tends to condemn any beliefs that seem contrary.

Karl Marx said, "Religion is the opium of the people" or "opiate of the masses" depending on your translation.[48] Some say this statement was to mean religion was created to keep society in a subservient, obedient state. After all, the Christian Bible teaches us to obey the laws of humankind.

Romans 13:1 says, "Let every person be subject to the governing authorities.

For there is no authority except from God, and those that exist have been instituted by God."

This idea reminds me of the drug known as "Soma" in Aldous Huxley's, "Brave New World" (1932). "All the advantages of Christianity and alcohol; none of their defects" but the Christian Bible would seem to encourage us to resist any ruling hand that goes against God's law. Acts 5:16-42 seems to give the power of example to the apostles that broke laws created by worldly authority to teach God's law. The story even says God enabled them to do so. I suppose this scripture would be as Huxley put it, one of religion's "defects."

Then again, by this interpretation of Marx's statement, religion should currently be keeping a state of peace in those who subscribed to these religious beliefs. Look at how well that worked during the Crusades. Faith is good but belief structures in man are bound to contradict based on perspective, and because our perspectives are so definite to us, we take strong offense to opposing beliefs.

---

[47] Mitch Hedberg quotes, 2009.
[48] Martin, 1996-2009.

Perhaps this interpretation of Marx's statement is not completely accurate. Perhaps religion is humankind's attempt at peace. If we look at the savage from "Brave New World," we might learn something about religion. He comes from a world distant from any popular belief of modern society. He sees flaws in the logic of society and is treated as an outsider, or perhaps something more profound than an outsider, a source for entertainment, a spectacle of peculiar difference. But Huxley made it clear his subjects of modern society were of childlike minds. One aspect of my childhood experience was the rules set forth by my parents and the repercussions that followed when I disobeyed. In Genesis of the Christian Bible we are first depicted as ignorant. God tries to keep us ignorant by decreeing that we are not to eat of the tree of the knowledge of good and evil.[3] By this depiction we could assume the idea of God is an idea meant to keep us uninquisitive and sub-servient.

After all, we only suffered the repercussions of sin after the tree was eaten from; but according to the story, the tree was put there by an all-powerful god. We were told not to because of the effect that sin would have but we were given a choice, simply so we could choose. It was direction my parents tried to give me, not laws for their benefit. I believe these doctrines of faith are intended to guide us, not rule us. Faith can be a very good thing if we are responsible in the ways we use it. Perhaps we allow religion to blind us to certain subtleties to our world. If we, to an extent, experience what we expect to experience, then every belief we hold morphs the world around us.

Aldous Huxley said, "All gods are homemade, and it is we who pull their strings, and so, give them the power to pull ours."[49] One could speculate that faith in a divine plan is a way of dealing with one's own shortcomings. I can see how one might see faith as a way to deal with an uncontrollable external world. If there is a divine plan then we all are intended to fail at times.

Karl Marx is quoted as having said, "Religion is the impotence of the human mind to deal with occurrences it cannot understand."[50] If there is a divine plan then someone with our interest in mind controls the external world. Perhaps the decision to have faith is the act of altering one's perspective to be happy. If we know that having faith in a greater purpose or higher power gives us hope, then why wouldn't we allow ourselves such a luxury? Would a world without religion be similar to the world John Lennon painted in his song "Imagine"—"nothing to kill or die for"?

I suppose we would likely have less motivation to kill. After all, many of the world's wars have been based on religious beliefs. Then again, I suppose we would have less motivation not to kill.

---

[49] Aldous Huxley quotes.
[50] Karl Marx quotes.

Without that mentally painted shame finger in the sky we might be less inclined to follow any moral laws. Still, the conscience is not simply a fear of repercussions in an afterlife. I have known atheists to have strong consciences but religion gives us hope. Without hope we are less likely to follow the rules. Without hope we have nothing to lose. Religion would seem to hold the potential for a more peaceful society but this doesn't mean religious beliefs are unfounded. Religion may well be an attempt at defining our worlds and ourselves but this does not mean our definitions, despite the variety, are inaccurate.

Reflection in Limbo and Magnolia (The Perfect Child)

I often relive my day's social interactions in my head. I think it's the perfectionist in me trying to find ways to improve my communication skills; although I have to admit that, when the conversation went well from my perspective, it often feels more like a celebration of my social victory. I often replay my mistakes in my head. I envision the socially proper or correct action being taken on my part but the dark reality of my mistake always ends up playing in my mind's eye. I suppose I would rather live with my imperfection than lie to myself. I nearly always expect negative consequences when I've made a mistake or when I didn't do things according to my standard of perfection. Maybe this goes back to the need to be the perfect person I was told I was when I was younger.

I've only recently come to realize how skewed my view of myself was when I was a child. I used to slap myself in the face when I wasn't performing to my greatest ability. I would hit myself just hard enough that I would be able to feel it a few seconds afterward. I didn't want to damage myself physically, just punish myself for my imperfection. Even then I knew there was something not right about what I was doing. I saw my state as one of those you hear about, the people with problems, the people not fit for society. That just made it worse.

My father once asked me why I picked my scabs from my wounds. "It can't feel good," he said. He was right but I couldn't give him an answer. I believe, now, that this was done in my quest for perfection. I know other parents have had this problem with their children but I believe my motivation might have been different. I suppose the average child's purpose for this would be curiosity or the joy some of us get from something some might see as gross. My purpose was perfection. I actually willfully endured this sometimes-painful process on the path to perfection. These scabs didn't belong on my knees. For some reason a bleeding wound felt cleaner. I suppose the idea still seems cleaner for some reason.

As mentioned in the chapter entitled "Dad", I experienced much trouble in school. Late in my elementary school experience I would cry every night during my homework. I remember at least one specific time I intentionally let my tears hit the homework paper. I hoped somehow my teacher would recognize them as tears and at least ask about them. Maybe I just wanted pity or, more likely, attention. I was very lonely. I know now I'm not perfect. I will make mistakes in the future. I also know I will be regretful for my mistakes despite the fact that they are inevitable. I fail often. Perhaps this relation of shame for failure goes back to this idea that I can't live up to my father's idea of whom I should be.

When I was a little older I began to experience a recurring dream about the office building behind our Austin home that would later become Allen's bedroom and then mine. A long cement path stretched from the driveway, along the side of the house where my father and I had scuffled, down to a small enclosure meant for keeping animals. Between the front driveway and the "bunny hut", as we called it, the path connected the back porch with this office building. In my dream state, it was dark and I felt a strong sense of urgency. I hurried from the back door of my house across the porch to the sidewalk. Despite the urgency, I still followed social protocol by not crossing the grass but taking the longer path to the sidewalk. I hurried around to the back of the building and stood atop a mentally abstract object. Two household trashcans were kept there, so it's likely this was some incarnation of a trashcan. It felt unstable at first, as a trashcan would. Facing a window on the back of this building, I slid the left pane open and looked in with deep intent. I felt a rush of energy on my face. The only word I can find to describe it more specifically is wind but it wasn't wind. It was physical but not specific to any physical sensation I've felt outside this dream. I had this dream several times afterward, years apart. Sometimes, I'd all but forgotten about it when it came back to me.

I remember one specific instance the dream happened with an incredible quickness. I only recall the last part: I was standing on this abstract, physical object; the window was already open. Despite the fact that I somewhat anticipated the rush, it was actually more jolting because of its speed. After each incarnation of this dream I found myself waking rapidly to an experience of a larger amount of adrenaline than I've felt in any other setting, and the sensation of blood filling my face. I believe this dream was about fear of the unknown, my seemingly uncertain future. I was told I had great potential but somehow I was failing miserably. I was failing in what I was born to succeed in, using my brain.

I recall an English class in middle school in which we were told to write a poem about our past, present and future using the different levels of a house as metaphors. The first two, the basement and the ground floor, my past and my present, were full of typical teenage angst.

Upon reviewing this poem a short time after writing it, parts of the third metaphorical incarnation seemed liked grammatical stumbling. This stumbling was, for some reason, bothersome to me for years to come:

"The upstairs in my house is the attic.

There is no way to get to this place.

Dark and ignored, it cannot be explored, for its deepness I cannot face."

This was originally intended to represent uncertainty in my future, a lack of mental commitment to any one path. But even my teacher recognized there was a deeper message present. I feared my future because I had grown to expect failure in my past.

Lack of experience causes mistakes. Since the tumor experience, I have tended to autopilot through most tasks. This is likely a result of the distance caused by the pain of trying to visually focus on the physical world. Failure to live in this world would result in a lack of experience. Perhaps I make more mistakes than I would expect to because I don't really live in the physical world. I distance myself from the world and, because of this distance, tend to fail more often.

Maybe I relive my conversations because I am looking for flaws in myself. Perhaps I am, as I suggested to my grandmother, acting in pursuit of familiarity. I have had self-esteem problems since I can remember. Maybe this focus on my flaws is motivated by an attempt to keep a familiar perspective of myself. I once told Nine she was perfect. Perhaps this claim was simply the product of my desire to see perfection in her. She quickly denied the compliment. Years later, I found myself on the receiving end of the same compliment when my significant other spoke those same words to me. I denied the compliment but I was somewhat happy about being able to deny it. I tried to teach Nine so much but I suppose, in this case, she was the incarnate of the example.

My world is based on my perspective. I'm still learning about my perspective, so I'm still learning about my world. If our brains grow according to how we use them, then every minute of every day affects our skill and perspectives. I believe now, that life moves in a fluent motion. There will be good and bad in everything no matter how hard perfection is chased.

I am constantly looking for meaning in my world. I often recognize seemingly random happenings to be more than they appear. Sometimes I give in to the idea that God is trying to send me in a certain direction, literally or figuratively, and I go with it. Sometimes it's as simple as taking a different way home. I often flip the blinker in my car on beat with the music playing through my car stereo to see if the world around me falls in sync with it. Occasionally it does seem to sync up. Often the world around me will fall into beat with the music my ears are hearing on its own but this phenomenon could very well be the product of an over-active imagination.

Perhaps I review my daily conversations because I am trying to find significance, or even "coincidence", in my interaction with other humans. When I wrote the poem called "Magnolia" the topic was somewhat different from the idea of it. The topic was my history of infidelity in my relationship. The idea was that in spite of what I wanted at the time, history could repeat itself. When I was writing it, I stumbled onto something that would not seem to be fully understandable by the conscious brain. I'd written the phone number to Magnolia Café on the piece of paper on which I was now composing my poem. I wrote,

"I saw myself fall.
I said I saw myself fall.
I said, I said, I saw myself fall.
I said I saw myself say, I said, I saw myself fall."

And there it was when I got to the peak of the chorus, "Magnolia." I was writing about something I couldn't completely understand and what would seem like fate or a higher power, or even my subconscious, put that word in its place in the song. I now refer to things that we, as humans, can partially understand but know we cannot completely comprehend as "magnolias", icebergs of comprehension, much larger than the visible portions.

I have also given "magnolia" two more specific definitions: "The apparentness of the purpose of tools of fate" or "something inside of a copy or a different representation of itself." This first definition is why, earlier in this chapter, in the statement about reviewing my daily conversation, the word "coincidence" is in quotes. I believe that sometimes, if not always, coincidences are actually magnolias. They were predestined to happen. The best way I can describe this second, more tangible idea of "magnolia" is the illusion of seeing without a horizon that we experience when we look into a mirror with a mirror behind us. It would seem as though we could see forever.

I came to these definitions by my encounter of the word when I was composing the "Magnolia" poem. The first definition comes from the idea that the word magnolia was meant to be there when I climaxed my chorus. So, was this a work of a higher power, or a creation of parts of my brain I could not begin to understand? My outside world constantly mirrors what's going on in my mind. My mind is a part of the world. It's possible the world is simple enough that noticing similarities and patterns is inevitable. After all, everything is subject to, and a part of, the systems the physical world and spiritual world alike were built upon. I cannot be certain whether I saw it coming in my subconscious or a higher power actually predestined it to be there but I can't imagine how either would change the definition. After all, what is the difference between a product of the subconscious and fate? If God created everything and nothing falls outside of God's understanding then they could very well be the same thing.

The second definition is probably the more obvious one. The line goes: "I said, I saw myself say, I said, I saw myself fall.'' This second definition is derived from the idea of me watching myself see myself fall. I was inside myself. If something is inside itself, as I was in the poem, then the chain could be endless. Infinity is the most prominent example of something we can only partially understand, hence the idea of looking into two mirrors at once as an illustration of "magnolia."

I sometimes wonder if everything about me, everything that is me, everything that's in my head was preplanned. There are several levels on which this could exist. Maybe it's the will of the world I live in to be, in a sense, a mirage. Maybe everything I experience is, for the lack of a better word, a program. Everything happens the way it does because it was written in code. This still leaves the need for a programmer, a designer, a god.

I've recently noticed more definition in the physical world around me. This definition is familiar but I had long forgotten about it. Perhaps I'm finally getting used to my limited vision and coming back into the "real" world. Or maybe the "real" world is not real at all and my altered vision is not so much a handicap but a gift.

The doctor who's been trying to help me with my eyes once told me my eye problems are most common in people who've had severe brain trauma, like a brain tumor. I know the trauma changed my physical perspective of the world. Perhaps it gave my overall perspective of this world more clarity. For many years I've held the belief that the external world might be very different from how I perceived it. Now I know it's at least somewhat different.

This, in a way, is a great freedom. I am no longer bound by the preconceptions of this world most people develop as children. My surroundings are no longer definite; they are now subjective. The way I see the world is inaccurate so I'm free to explore its physical inhabitants without the boundaries of these preconceived ideas. Maybe my eyes cannot see the world as they used to because my brain now refuses to accept the world I've seen around me since my earliest memory is real. A healthy pair of eyes will see something near to them as two images if they are looking past it, at something in the distance. Perhaps I cannot focus on this world because my mind is desperately trying to see past it.

I recall an experience from my adolescence when the world around me was not what it recently seemed to be. It was after sundown and I was lying in my twin sized bed, in my room at my parent's house. I had barely closed my eyes when my body started to stretch. I imagined the physical incarnation of my feet as though they were miles away. My fingers stretched out away from my body. This was likely the product of a malfunctioning body schema. One's body schema is his or her sub-conscious mind's idea of his or her physical body. If my body schema typically behaves in the manner it's supposed to, then it was, on this occasion, malfunctioning. There have been several examples of body schemas behaving in unexpected ways. I believe my experience to be what has been dubbed Alice in Wonderland syndrome. Alice in Won-derland (or Todd's) syndrome is often brought on by migraine headaches or brain tumors.[1]

This was something like four years before I was even diagnosed with the tumor. The only problem with the title of this phenomenon is the term syndrome tends to imply something is not as it should be. The term syndrome is used to describe symptoms of a disease, disorder, or illness. If I did have the tumor at that point, then the use of the word is accurate. I guess the problem is the stigma things like disease have in our society. I believe there is purpose to everything. If I was intended to have the brain tumor and the experience of Alice in Wonderland Syndrome was in fact a product of the tumor's presence, then I was intended to experience it. Perhaps this experience was a lesson in perspective. It was likely one of the first times I suspected my perspective was inaccurate. This was not an isolated incident. I experienced this product of an altered schema several times. Such an experience has been written off as a disorder but perhaps it's not a negative thing. I guess it comes down to one's idea of what is bad. Is pain bad if it makes one stronger? Is death bad if it's only in the physical sense?

---

[1]   Blakeslee, & Blakeslee, 2007

Chapter Twelve

Numbers

Since adolescence, numbers have seemed to hold great significance in the world around me. I've always related myself to the number eleven. I've always related the ex-girlfriend referred to throughout this book as "Nine" to the number nine. When I was in middle school I programmed my closest friends into the speed dial on my portable phone. I made effort to assign each person a number I felt most closely matched my view of him or her. She, of course, was number nine. She was also the ninth person with whom I would share a physical relationship. Like everything else in my life, I've analyzed this to no end. 9-11. 11-9. 9+11=20. I was twenty when we broke up the last time. 9/11=September 11th, a beautiful disaster. It was sad to watch the aftermath of the September 11th attacks but there is beauty in chaos and sometimes even in misery.

Numbers also relate to songs. I've noticed a pattern in the order of songs on their originally released albums. The most obvious to me is track number 8. It usually feels mechanical, like cold metal. Then there's number 3. It's often more approachable than the rest of the album. This could be why track 3 is often a single. I believe colors have number counterparts. This is not an exact science yet but no theory is science until it can be proven. Thanks to the book by Malcom Gladwell entitled *The Tipping Point*, I have recently come to the conclusion that this phenomenon is a form of synesthesia. Synesthesia is an involuntary joining of the senses.[1] Synesthesia could be a simple link in a person's brain founded on personal history. This would explain why, as cited by Phillips, people with synesthesia often do not agree on the color of a letter. It's possible I relate the number 5 to the color orange and my friend

---

[1]   Phillips

Woody, because at one point in my personal history the relationships were formed out of logic. Perhaps Woody had an orange jacket and sat in the fifth desk in the back row of our English class.

Our subconscious minds are like sponges. Our brains are constantly taking in information. Even as you read this, your brain is observing your environment. Your nerves tell your brain whether your environment is too hot or too cold for comfort. Your ears hear the background noise coming from a source you would typically not consciously distinguish, the ceiling fan or voices from the next room. Don't believe me? Try writing while your mother's cat repetitively and incessantly meows nearby.

Even if you could ignore something like the cat, your subconscious is still at bay to your surroundings. This constant taking in of information is the source of a human's ability to realize if his or her body is uncomfortable without consciously forming the inquiry. In other words, we typically don't have to ask ourselves, "Do I feel cold?" We just know we do. We don't have to ask, "Is that music too loud for comfort?" Our bodies tell our brains the volume level could cause physical damage to our ears if the music continues. As our brains collect these observational pieces of information, we form logical relations between them. It is likely my synesthesia is the product of these logical relations.

The physical world would seem to be composed of numbers. Nature is full of geometry. If our entire world was created by the same creator then it makes sense that everything in our world, whether it can be calculated or not, would be made of the same building blocks, numbers.

Chapter Thirteen

Dad, the Aftermath

I would finally speak with my father after months of no communication. After I left my job for the day, I went to my girlfriend's apartment. A stream of tropical storms had been hitting the Texas coast and I lay on her bed and drifted in and out of consciousness as I waited for her to get home. We had planned on driving to Austin so I could play an open mic night but when she got home we decided the danger of the rain swept freeway outweighed our desire to go. We slept for a while and when I woke I found it difficult to get my mind back to the mindset I typically keep in this reality.

The dream I had woken from was so real and felt so good that I had trouble leaving it.

In time there wasn't much that happened during my dream state but I felt innocence all around me. My parents were not divorced but asleep in the next room. It was dusk and the sun's light barely illuminated the room through the blinds in this house that I felt comfortable in but likely have never actually seen in this world. I put the bowl I was holding on a platform near a water spigot. I felt a sense of comfort that I haven't felt in years. Then, in a second, this world started to violently pull away from me as I woke up.

I felt like God wanted me to get something out of the dream; so I asked him, very simply to let me know what he wanted of me. I meditated on it for a few seconds and jokingly thought, "I need to be sure to wash my dishes." Then I thought, "Maybe God wants me to call Dad." I pushed the idea away fairly quickly but it was almost immediately pushed right back into my main focus. I hated the idea. I had written him numerous letters in the past, to which he'd never responded. I felt I had done what I could and that the ball was, figuratively, in his court. But God pushed it on me further, so I left a message on my father's voicemail. It's probably good he didn't answer because I could barely get the words out. When I hit the end button on my cell phone, I let the building emotion overflow and I began to cry. He called back a few minutes later to ensure that there was no emergency and to let me know he would call me later that night.

When we finally spoke, it felt somewhat forced. We talked a few minutes about the usual stuff. I asked why we hadn't spoken in months and he had a few answers. He said he was angry but that the main reason was he was trying to let me know it was time to grow up. The night we shared on the side lawn when I was fifteen was, according to my father, because I was trying to grow up too fast. The second happening between us that has affected me on such a level, this severing of our relationship, was because I was not ready to grow up.

I suppose when I first had this thought I was trying to point out contradictions in his actions. Despite the fact that he couldn't possibly understand my perspective at the time, these situations were divided by several years. He also said that, even though it probably wasn't the best way to handle the situation, his way worked. His smugness made me feel worse. He was referring to the fact that at the time I worked five days a week, and when he severed our relationship, I didn't have a job. At the time of the, "so good luck" conversation, I still felt pretty bad physically, although I had been looking for a job under pressure from my mother. She theorized that I would feel better when I took a more productive approach to life. She was half right.

Activity dulled the pain at times. Having a purpose helped me keep my mind off the pain. When I had somewhere to go, I couldn't remain leaned against the wall, feeling as though a brick was slowly being pressed against each side of my head. My dad wanted me to ignore my pain. I believe I was better for my attempts at progress but I hated that I often had to ignore how I felt physically to get through the day. The distance we shared seemed acceptable to him. I wondered if I had to be as disconnected from him as I imagined he was from his dad to be an adult in his eyes.

He once asked my sister how I, "the son who never spoke to him", was doing. He didn't return my letters and yet showed interest in talking to me. I often questioned my translation of the occurrence. Maybe his idea of the son who never spoke to him was a good thing, or maybe he was just too, in his words, "pissed" and too stubborn to accept my written apologies. Perhaps he didn't respond to my letters because he didn't want to reward me for pitying myself and being self-defeating by acting as though I were already defeated. My tone in the letters was defeated because I felt defeated.

I went through a period when I didn't have much of a life outside of work. It caused distance in my relationships, especially in the one with my girlfriend. I remember understanding when I was younger that my mother didn't care about money. She just wanted my dad around more. Had I become my father?

There was a time I even dressed similarly to the way he dressed me when I worked for him. I wondered if that was what it meant to be an adult or if that was just my dad's experience of adulthood. Did I have to be disconnected and alone to have people accept me? I had thought I had been an adult for a few years but if being an adult meant forgetting about how I felt and going along with what others thought was best for me, I'd have rather not. Besides, I thought having your mind made up for you was something most people left in childhood. Adulthood should be about knowing one's limits, making one's own decisions. Maybe I was wrong; my limits were obviously well beyond where I thought they were but at the time I wasn't willing to go through the discomfort to get here. Maybe being an adult is not so much about knowing your limits but knowing how far you're willing to stretch them.

I love my father, even though it sometimes feels dangerous to do so. I fear rejection from him. I fear I cannot be what he wants in a son. I suppose I also fear rejection for the ways I feel I've wronged him. I don't know how much was actually my fault but I was a large part of a lot of the hurt he's received. I respect him for what he did at the time, marrying my mother for his unborn child's sake. I recently acquired a copy of my birth certificate. Box 9 Reads, "Age (At the time of this birth) 22." My father was twenty-two and my mother was twenty-three. I know these are not, by any means, the youngest recorded parents in history. In fact many families begin around this age. But when I asked what would have become of the situation if I were not conceived, he said he likely would not have married my mother. He also said my existence likely saved him from being a casualty of the reckless lifestyle he'd been living until that point. Just as it did to my sister years later, the laws of society first affected my parents. They married because society said a child should not be raised outside of wedlock.

By the time they divorced he had built a strong angst toward my mother for trying to change him. Had she tried to change him? I certainly can relate to the desire to see growth in one's significant other. But, when I was growing up, his actions seemed to undoubtedly be his own.

I remember helping him move to Arizona when they divorced. We were, for the first time, friends. We drank and listened to 70's rock, the stuff he grew up on. I remember him singing "Free Bird." He told me my mother had tried to change him but, quoting the song, "This bird you cannot change." His tone was celebratory but his actions seemed bitter. I am now older than my father was when I was born and I cannot imagine the change that would come from my child being born to this world now. Mom also included me in the decision to divorce him. She called him an abusive man, which seemed to refer to the scuffle we had on the side lawn when I was fifteen. He once told me she never forgave him for that. It's poetic. I suppose I can't take all the credit but I was a large part of the beginning and I was a large part of the end for them.

Since my recent, I suppose, enlightenment, I have had the desire to apologize to many figures from my past. I have tracked down most of the ones I felt I did serious injustices to but I cannot find the words to apologize for certain trespasses. Perhaps I'm just afraid of the consequences that would result from the potential apologies. On the other hand, it could be the desire not to cause the potential recipient of the apology any more injustice. Still, how does one apologize for something like my situation with my father?

The first of the three major contributions to this post-divorce situation was my conception. It was not an action of my will and therefore the apology should have a different, less consequential, meaning. It should be more sympathetic than apologetic: "I'm sorry that happened." But, I cannot be sympathetic to the fact that I came into existence, and I don't believe either of my parents is regretful for anything but possibly the situation I joined when I was conceived. Still, looking at it now, it makes me sad to think of the way my existence has affected their lives.

The second major contribution I've made to this current situation was a result of an act of will on my part. My father changed in my mother's eyes after he beat me up for taking his car. My mom's problem was with my father's decision, not mine. How does one sympathize with a person's decision without sounding condescending?

The third contribution I've made to the current situation was the decision to support my mother's choice to divorce him. I don't know how much my opinion affected her decision but this contribution seems the most significant. This was the first time I sided against my father. I felt I was delivering justice, just as I, now, suppose every person who commits an act of revenge does but this wasn't out of anger. It was for something good for the majority of my family and with little regard for how it would affect the minority, my father.

As it turns out, he was the only one who seemed to deal with the situation without too much trouble. Still, when I think of him, my inner-monologue insists on uttering the phrase,

"I'm sorry." Perhaps I'm simply not ready to forgive myself. I suspect he would forgive me, if not be dismissive of my remorse, were I to apologize. I'm not so vain as to think I'm solely responsible for the current situation but my attributions are the most significant to my perspective. If I were to receive forgiveness or even that condescending dismissive reaction I expect, then I suspect I would have little remaining reason to hold myself responsible for the trespasses I feel I have committed.

I recently spent some time with my father and his girlfriend in Arizona. Not long ago he offered me a job. After considering the fact that my vision problems along with my lack of experience were making my job more difficult than it seemed to be for most in my position of phlebotomist, I considered it. I decided to take him up on his offer after my girlfriend, in spite of my expectations, committed to accompanying me. I was to make the trip before her and she would follow a few weeks later.

One night shortly into my stay, I found myself sitting in silence, as I often did, in one of the four red chairs surrounding the table on the back porch of the house my father and his girlfriend shared. My father and his girlfriend drank and made conversation. I spoke very little but we did have a few honest moments. I suppose the lack of conversation on my part was simply fueled by fear. For some reason, I've always respected my father's opinion. I have so much so that in the past I've taken his opinion as my own because I saw it to be profound (a word my father voluntarily defined for me years ago). I am hesitant to make any definite statements for fear that my perspective might be seen as unrealistic or silly. I am afraid of giving him fuel to condescend with. His actions would seem to be motivated by a desire to lighten the mood whenever he does this but in trying to lighten the mood, he's pointing out what I believe he sees as my flaws and making a spectacle of them.

Earlier in the day he had asked what kind of beer I drank. I told him I didn't care for beer and that, in fact, I'd noticed myself getting depressed after one sip. He questioned, with a slight sense of suggested absurdity, "A sip?" It's situations like these that make me feel like an alien to this world. I explained I had exaggerated and stated that realistically the feeling didn't start until I'd had a full beer. Now sitting on his back porch with him, he asked his girlfriend to bring him another beer. He then said, "but Phil can't have a sip." In this statement he was insisting on the absurdity of my seemingly poorly thought out statement.

Looking at my personal history, I can point out situations where I behaved in a similar manner with others. I believe my actions, when I spoke to others as my father did to me, were fueled by insecurity. I pointed out the flaws in another to remove what I thought was the focus on my flaws. I wonder if his motivation was similar.

I recently allowed myself a sip of my girlfriend's wine. That familiar buzz in my head returned, followed by the sense of internalization and self-awareness that in my personal history has led to a depressive state. This internalization was very similar to the meditative removal I've willfully imposed on myself as an escape from physical pain. I was right in my statement of "one sip" but my father's confidence in my absurdity changed what I knew to be true about myself.

That night his girlfriend brought up an incident that I believe caused my father to sever communication with my mother. Dad's girlfriend seemed to be angered by the memory as she recalled the incident for the purpose of conversation. When we were all together to be with my dying grandmother, my mother had asked my father if she could borrow his jacket. Dad's girlfriend, seeming somewhat inebriated, repeated the position over and over again. She told me she could have been a good friend with my mother if my mother had not performed this act of testing rank.

I wasn't counting but several beers into the night, my father's speech began to slur. He started talking about his side of the divorce. Would they have divorced if an affair hadn't taken place during the marriage? He was implying my mother had been unfaithful. He said he was, now, the happiest he'd been in years and that his girlfriend needed not fear his return to my mother. He then seemed to take delight in pointing out that I had decided to come to be with him, as if he'd won. He said that my, then fifteen-year-old brother, would be next if my father put together the right string of words toward him. He also said my sister would likely have little problem with moving to Arizona. He said this would leave my mother alone and that we would hear her crying on the phone.

His speech was, at this point, hard to understand, not because of the slurring but because of the random focus of the speech that must have come from an overwhelming number of thoughts. His emotion was clear though. My mother would be sad and in a seemingly hopeless situation and he would not care. From his perspective she'd put herself there. It's sad to see how my father now views my mother. If they did, at one point, love each other, then they certainly have fallen far. If they didn't, then I'm simply the product of a sexual encounter that occurred in 1983. This, somehow, seems as though it would be easier for me to deal with.

Shortly after this conversation we heard yelling in the distance and Dad said something about being sick of "him" beating up on "her." I followed my father through the house to his driveway.

Tires screeched on the street in front of the house. The neighbor's truck stopped in the road as my father reached the end of the driveway. I stopped next to my father a second later. I felt united with him. I'd sided against him before but now I was siding with him. Although I couldn't see the driver, he seemed to be contemplating the challenge my father's presence posed. The truck drove off and, after waiting a few minutes for the truck's return, we retired back to the back porch. He would later ask, in what seemed to be a rhetorical tone, when he got to be so angry. Why was he so eager to confront the neighbor?

He claims to hold no negative feelings over the current situation. He claims he's happier than he has been in years. Yet, he showed surprise at his general state of anger after our near encounter with his abusive neighbor. I believe a part of him is still bitter about the situation with my mother. How can I expect to ever get to know him, beyond what he intentionally shows me, if he refuses to be honest with me? I don't know if the deceit is actually toward me. I don't know if he truly knows his heart when it comes to this. I don't know that I can blame him. When his emotions were not so buried, his wife divorced him. I suppose it's a natural defense. Our brains recognize weakness through being attacked and then fortify the weaknesses with walls of defense.

I dreamed about him again last night. I started my car in the driveway of a house that would not be familiar to me in this world but was familiar in the dream. Then I realized I had forgotten something inside. As I passed, my father was sitting on the living room couch. I told him I'd forgotten something. He said, in a somewhat mocking tone, "Just keep chasing your dream." I was empowered by his words. I verbally unloaded something that is, now, hard to explain. It was not judgmental. It wasn't self-loathing or self-pitying. It was not the statement of a martyr or a person who felt holier than his audience. I told him I was sorry if I had disappointed him but that his condescending was hurtful. In that moment he seemed to understand the trouble his words had caused.

I know these actions I perceive as condescending are not meant to cause the chagrin they sometimes do in me. He believes he's right and any representation of his perspective is presented as fact because he believes it is. Any perspective that's in contrast to his seems absurd to him because he is right. This is how I can feel belittled in my interaction with him and he can feel as though I am being overly sensitive when I feel this way. He's stating fact while I'm hearing contrary opinion.

My perspective has a lot to do with how I perceive these actions. He has little control over my internal reaction. I just wish I could find the words, or the courage, to attempt the words I uttered in this dream state to have him see, for that instant, from my perspective. I have the power to control the way I receive what I now see to be condescending. The motivation that births these actions is not malicious. Then again, my repeated actions become habits become patterns become a part of me. If I were to decide to not respect his actions as strongly as I do now, my image of him would die. These individual decisions would eventually become a part of me and I would no longer respect his perspective. I suppose it comes down to what I value more, the absence of this negative feeling that comes with attempting to see my father's perspective, or the knowledge that I feel I have to gain from him. I suppose I can attempt to filter out the bad and keep the good but I will have to make strong effort not to mentally discredit him completely.

It is difficult to witness someone so similar to me be so dismissive of my perspective. I suppose it's the age-old challenge of coming into one's own. I believe this all could be a product of something much larger, something inbred. As far as nature and the continued existence of humankind are concerned, a man's purpose is to spread his seed. It is theorized this is the force that typically allows a man many more sexual partners than a woman. Theoretically, once the seed becomes an able part of society, there is not social need for the man who conceived the child. Perhaps my father's pointing out of my shortcomings is simply his way of empha-sizing his own still intact usefulness.

Perhaps my mother's representation to me of the will to divorce my father, the question about "such an abusive man" was not intended to show the desire to bring change in my name.

If Mom held the anger she birthed for him because of the physical conflict we shared, this change was likely for her purpose. From the way I see it now, their marriage had been deteriorating for some time. The events surrounding my relationship with my father have altered my mother's view of him but I've been told certain things by both parties that lead me to believe they worked hard enough to destroy their marriage, and their friendship, without my help. I don't know if anybody really knows what went wrong. The two major perspectives involved, my mother's and my father's, when presented to me, seem very different. They each honestly believe the other is to blame.

I realize now, despite my past with my father, that, for a long time, my mother's perspective of the happening was the only perspective I was exposed to. I took her point of view as profound word. I realize now that I cannot blame any one person for their separation, because no one involved has a profound idea of which situations made the strongest contributions to it. I suppose this inability to hold blame applies to myself as well. I do see some of the ways I've affected their lives. Some of which make me sad, despite my inability to control said ways but if the major figures in this complication can't agree on what actually caused the destruction then I certainly cannot take the blame. I suppose the desire to hold the blame comes from the tendency toward martyrdom that, for some reason, has been instilled in me since childhood.

Still, it makes me sad to think of the relationship that gave me life in the state it is in now. I am very much like my father. I don't fully compre-hend how significant these similarities are. I have heard his relationship with his father was no better than mine with him. In fact, our relationship seems like a less explosive copy of theirs. My dad has even shared with me that he took his father's car when he was roughly the age I was when I took his. He said he claimed to have borrowed it while his dad said he'd stolen it. He also claimed this was just as our experience had played out. I never knew I was accused of stealing his car but this is just another example of the different perspectives we hold. He said his dad beat him up, just as he had done to me. From what I've been told, my grandfather was not a bad person. He was dying when I was born so I never got to know him very well but apparently he loved me very much. Still, I wonder, if my dad's father hadn't been abusive, how it would have affected, or not affected, my relationship with mine.

I don't blame my father for our relationship problems. In fact, I see now that he worked very hard for me and I believe he has loved me since I was born but, despite the good I see in our relationship, I am fearful for my future relationship with my child. It is difficult to draw a definite line where the product of one's environment ends and the physical incarnation of one's freewill begins. I just hope my will is strong enough to overcome any remaining trace of this pattern of history dictating its future. It may take less will than I suspect. From what I have heard, my father's relationship with his dad was much worse than mine with him. Hopefully, by the time I have a child, this pattern can afford us a perfectly healthy relationship.

I recently spoke to my father about some of the issues that have been troubling me. I asked if he still had anger toward my mother. He said he never had anger toward her but that he was disappointed. He then expressed anger for the man she allegedly cheated with. How unfortunate is this situation? My father has bad feelings toward my mother's boyfriend. My father's girlfriend has bad feelings toward my mother. It is no wonder they have, for the most part, severed all ties. My father expressed to me that he felt his relationship with my mother ended the night he beat me up on the side lawn of our Austin home. He said, "and you wouldn't fight back." I don't know his exact purpose for bringing up that specific detail but it felt good. It felt complimentary.

I said I wished I hadn't had such power in the destruction of his relationship. He seemed, as I had feared he would be, dismissive. He said, "But you have to love her for doing what she did." He was referring to my mother's refusal to forgive him for the trespasses he committed against me. He was right. My mother's initial intent was pure. It was out of love for me. Still, this attitude of dismissal from my father was hurtful.

My remorse is a product of my analysis of the past as I see it. Even if I'm completely wrong about where the blame should lie, I am still remorseful for my intent when it comes to the conversation about, "such an abusive man." In dismissing my feelings of remorse, he was, with no apparent delay, stating that my analysis of my world was wrong. His intent was good. In his world, the only perspective that matters is his own. This should be the case for every one of us. Despite my high opinion of his perspective, I can no longer take his opinion as profound and infallible. That was something I left when I learned to think for myself. If the only perspective that should matter is one's own, I should be working on forgiving myself.

Perhaps I'm not the son he wanted me to be but maybe this disappointment is not in me but in the decisions I've made. My parents were told I was well above average intelligence. By the time I got to high school, I had pretty much stopped trying. I did wish good grades upon myself but that was about all I did to better my situation. My parents were promised a success and instead got me. If income or even social standing is our measurement of success then I'm not entitled to, nor am I on the path to, this falsely foreseen label of my youth. When I became a certified phlebotomist, he admitted the feeling of pride for me. He said he'd simply floated through life but I'd actually done something to better my situation. It was an effort toward bettering my circumstance but it has since proven to yield little result for my current monetary situation. Then again, I suppose success is a factor of perspective. I am the only person who can measure my success because I'm the only one privileged to my perspective.

I recently found the means to communicate, in my best effort not to be confrontational, actions I saw as condescending on his part. He then, admittedly, intentionally condescended to me. He was trying to give me a contrasting example. When I told him I couldn't tell the difference he seemed livid. He raised his voice and claimed he knew I couldn't tell the difference but that one day I would be able to. He then dismissed himself. I suppose any condescension is the representation of an inaccurate perspective. The condescending perspective is that one is not what he or she should be because he or she is flawed. The flaw represented here is a lack of knowledge or understanding. If no person is perfect, then any flaw cannot make a person less than he or she should be. If we know the act of condescending is belittling to a person and we do it anyway, then we are actively engaging in an act we suspect will cause pain. In this case, condescending seems to be the result of the perspective that one not only is not all he or she could be but should feel bad because he or she is not all he or she could be. If our actions are deliberate and we know the likely outcome, are we not intentionally causing the outcome? Perhaps condescending comes so naturally because our individual perspectives seem so definite to us. We condescend because we have great faith in our own analytical ability but no perspective is flawless.

I've only spoken to him once or twice since. My girlfriend and I still live in Arizona, the place we moved to for my job with my father but he and his girlfriend have since moved out of state. My mother was the one to tell me he had gone. I have no ill will toward him. In fact, I love him very much but I have to say I'm disappointed to have made the two-state move from Texas to maintain the type of relationship I had with him before and to have actually worsened my financial situation, not that either of these are his fault.

Chapter Fourteen

Power in Suggestion

Suggestion is more powerful than we sometimes would like to believe. The story of "The Emperor's New Clothes," is a great illustration of this, despite the story's fictionality. The premise, however stretched for entertainment value, is there in everyday human behavior. The story is that of a king who hires two men to fashion him a suit. When the men present their "fabric" to the king, they claim the fabric is invisible only to dimwitted people. The king goes on parade around the city and his subjects all believe he is, indeed, wearing this incredible suit of fabric that is only invisible to the dumb until a young boy declares the king is in fact naked.[51] The fact that the subjects saw nothing in the place where this wonderful garment was said to be, and believed it to be anyway, expresses some self-doubt on the subjects' part but how powerful to them was the opinion of the voice that told them of this incredible suit? It was powerful enough to cause them to doubt their own physical perspectives and intelligence.

There's a joke I am fond of that uses this power to test a person's willingness to go along with a suggestion. A person asks another, "How many of each animal did Moses bring onto the Ark?" This, of course, refers to the biblical story. When the person responds with little thought, "Two." The asker can correct him or her by reminding the person that the story said that Noah, not Moses, brought animals onto a giant ark.

The power of suggestion can be illustrated in the question, "Does your nose itch?" This suggestion can often be easily dismissed because the person being asked can usually tell the asker is simply trying to evoke a

---

51   Anderson.

response. However, occasionally, the person being asked the question cannot help but scratch his or her nose. This form of suggestion is so powerful because it is the representation of a second perspective.

According to psychologicalscience.org, the very suggestion one is consuming alcohol can alter a person's perspective and behavior. The mind believes the body is ingesting alcohol, so the brain reacts as though the body has. These effects are not just the giggly speech slurring we've come to expect of an inebriated person but include many I believe most of us are rarely aware of.

The test that backs these claims was a test run on two groups of students told they were receiving vodka and tonic water, and students told they were receiving straight tonic water, when in fact both groups received straight tonic water. "Vodka and tonic" test subjects were more easily swayed by false information. Their ideas of their own personal history were not as accurate as those who were told they were consuming straight tonic water. These students were affected in such a way because their personal history led them to believe that, after drinking alcohol, they would feel inebriated. The suggestion, along with their past experiences, made undeniable changes in their perspectives.[52]

I recall a study featured in Malcolm Gladwell's *The Tipping Point* in which the subjects, students of the college performing the study, were recruited for what they were told was a marketing research group to test the quality of new high-tech headphones. They were each given an identical audio recording to listen to in which an argument for higher tuition was made. Some of the students were instructed to constantly nod their heads upwards and downwards. Others were instructed to shake their heads from side to side. Still, others were instructed not to move their heads at all.

At the end of the study each student was given a questionnaire that featured questions about how their head movements impaired or enhanced their listening experience. At the end of the questionnaire was the real question, the reason for the study, the question of how convincing the argument recorded on the tape was. A much greater majority of the students who were instructed to nod their heads up and down agreed with the argument on the recording, that the school should increase how much students paid in tuition. Likewise, the students who were instructed to shake their heads side to side strongly disagreed and the students who didn't move their heads, for the most part, showed indifference.[53]

There is a common practice in subconscious suggestion, meant for the purpose of entertainment that would seem to paint a vivid picture of the

---

52   "Study Finds that Alcohol Placebo Impairs Memory" 2002.
53   2002.

power of suggestion over the brain. One person asks another to spell the word silk several times. After "S I L K" is repeated several times the person conducting the test then asks the participant of said test "What do cows drink?" Often the person will respond "Milk" without much thought. The Quizzer then typically responds with something like "No, cows drink water. Duh."

I have found it particularly humorous to be the person so obviously wrong in his answer. It is a strange feeling to be so sure of something in an instant and then seconds later see the ridiculousness in the idea. But what happened? I believe this is a basic example of habitual patterns. The output becomes less a product of analysis and more a product of basic repetition. Once the brain is in the pattern of repeated "S I L K", which is strongly related to the sound that the word "silk" makes, it's logical response when questioned about a liquid related to the idea of a cow is "Milk. Duh." This practice is meant for entertainment but it would seem to clearly display a common pattern in brain function.

If we can be so sure of a perspective in one moment only to see the absurdity in it the next, how can we ever be completely sure of the validity in our perspectives? If we can be so obviously wrong in our perspectives because of a willfully repeated output then our perspectives can be influenced by past decisions. This seems to illustrate how we form our perspectives through personal history.

Our perspectives of the external world are largely affected by other's perspectives. An individual perspective is often affected a great deal by another person's declaration of belief. In its most basic form, we are told something is a certain way and we believe it but these attempts are often casualties of skepticism. The suggestions more likely to root themselves in another's perspective are typically more devious in nature—even if they are of good intent. They are truly suggestions and not declarations of truth. Remember my father's suggested absurdity of "one sip"? He didn't tell me my perspective was absurd. His tone did.

Look at the placebo. A placebo works because its taker expects it to work, even if only on a subconscious level. The person's expectations alter his or her physical world by altering the symptoms he or she feels from the affliction the placebo is said to cure. We accept the general consensus of different aspects of the world as a product of the power of suggestion.

I have recently noticed a pattern in my father's initiation of inter-action with me. When he desires an action from me but suspects I might be hesitant to perform said act, he challenges me to perform it. Instead of asking me to perform this action, he knowingly suggests I will not voluntarily do so. My thoughts are not "Do I want to perform this ac-tion?" but rather, "Am I willing to perform this action to prove my father wrong for thinking lowly of me?" Usually, it works. I want to prove I'm not as uptight as he seems to think. So, again I prove to myself that my father's opinion, despite my views on perspective, seems to be incredibly significant to me, if only on a subconscious level.

I have to give credit where credit is due. He's very intelligent. He seems to know a lot about psychology and how to get the reaction he desires. I suppose this is the skill that has built his successful career in sales, although, I have trouble deciphering the difference between tactical conversation and manipulation. It's one thing to use this method of altering a person's thought process to obtain a preferred response when it comes to sales. It's another to use this method when it comes to friendly conversation and interaction with loved ones. Then again, I suppose this depends on how a person uses his or her sales ability. Sales can go way beyond the sales floor.

If a person tries to convince another to agree with his or her perspective, he or she is trying to sell the person on it. These methods my father uses to alter my responses are simply sales methods he's used throughout his many years of sales. Still, I suppose I prefer a genuine response from those I interact with. If I alter my delivery of a message or question in the aspiration of changing the person's response, then his or her response is not genuine as it was not solely created by his or her perspective and freewill. My will helped manufacture the response.

If our perspectives, and even our actions of will, can be altered by suggestion, then who is to say which actions are the product of which will? Look at the Tate / LaBianca murders. Most agree Charles Manson was responsible for organizing the murders, yet he took no part in the physical act of these murders. Many say Manson, a very charismatic 34-year old, brainwashed the people who carried out these acts. It's said he actually instructed the "killers" in these acts: "Totally destroy everyone in it" referring to the house in which the Tate murders were to take place, "as gruesome as you can." He did this with his words. With his commandment for action he suggested these people should perform these acts, and they did.[54]

Adolph Hitler convinced Germany to attempt the capture and extermination of many . . .and they did. They did this because Hitler presented his ideas as absolute truths. Germany, in a frail condition, was looking for a path to return its greatness.[55] It was the suggestion of perspective that led to the genocide.

What about the statement I made to my father about the problems in his marriage? I believe, when my mother spoke with me about the lack of communication in her marriage, she was looking for a sympathetic ear as

---

[54] The Ovi Team, 2009.
[55] Stein, 2000.

opposed to an advocate but an advocate was what she got. When I told my father, in my mother's presence, that I saw problems in his marriage, I may have planted the seed in my mother's mind that led to their separation.

Personal problems have seemed very different in my personal history when the problems were represented by another's lips. Suggestion is a very powerful force to which we each have access. We must be sure we aren't sending messages we'll one day regret. This is one of the many reasons we should represent our opinions as opinions and not absolute truths. We may develop advocates for a cause in which we do not truly believe.

When I was younger, my mother enrolled me in a Taekwondo class at the local YMCA. I recall an exercise in meditation that clearly illustrates the power we have over our minds through suggestion. We sat cross-legged on the floor of our practice room with our eyes closed. Our instructor led us through this practice in meditation. He said to imagine the taste of vanilla on our tongues. He said to repetitively press our tongues against the roofs of our mouths while focusing on the taste. We imagined the taste and simultaneously stimulated our tongues' sense of touch. There was no vanilla on my tongue, yet my brain received signals simulating the taste that had previously only been experienced by having something of the vanilla flavor in my mouth.

If our perspectives of the world can be altered in so many ways simply through suggestion, if we can know what we experience is genuine only to dismiss it a moment later, then how can we be sure of anything? These examples work as evidence in support of the theory that no perspective is absolute.

Chapter Fifteen

"Christian," the Adjective III
The Royal Law

I believe sin is not something humans should try to define for anyone other than ourselves. The idea of sin can become very complex when we try to label it, because we all have different perspectives of right and wrong. The Christian Bible has ten basic "Thou shalt nots." It seems pretty simple, doesn't it? What about profanity? It is widely accepted that profanity is a sin against God. Colossians 3:8 says, "But now you must put them all away: anger, wrath, malice, slander, and obscene talk from your mouth." Ephesians 4:29-31 speaks of "corrupting talk" and slander,[56] but what is "obscene" or "corrupting" talk? I know that one can make statements that would seem obscene to most without using what we know as profanity; so profanity would not seem to be the direct focus of the word obscene here. Likewise, "corrupting talk" seems to deal with subjects like honesty and perversion from purity, not profanity.

If these passages were making reference to profanity then it would make sense that it would be a sin to use profanity in one's inner monolog. Popular belief is that God knows every thought we have. Even if he didn't, if there were one aspect of life to which God was blind, would a sin not still be sinful through such an aspect? What about habitual profanity? I've caught myself unintentionally using words considered by most to be profane. I wouldn't encourage the patterns that make profanity habitual; but if I don't make the decision to use profanity, would it still be a sin?

When a cousin of mine was learning how to speak, she had trouble pronouncing the sound a consecutive "T R" made. When she was asked

---

56 English standard version, 2001.

to say the word truck, she said with a big smile "Fuck." She had no idea what she was saying was a "bad" word. Was this a sin? If profanity in one's inner monolog is sinful, then was it a sin when you read the profane word above? I suppose it was not, because a sin is an act of the heart. But if this is so then I can't see how an act with such a lack of malice would be an act against God. Likewise, if we know what is asked of us and refuse to abide, then our actions would be defiant. But what is being asked of us?

There are many interpretations of the scripture. Leviticus 24:10-16 would seem to paint "cursing" in an entirely different light. It says a son of an Israelite woman "blasphemed the Name, and cursed." Then God told Moses, "And speak to the people of Israel, saying, 'Whoever curses his God shall bear his sin.'"[1] The trespass didn't seem to be the use of a "bad" word but of blasphemy. Our consciences are our moral guides but a person's conscience is affected by his or her perspective at the time. So, is what we consider profanity a sin against God?

Profanity is not listed in the big ten. What about stealing? Here we get to the age-old question, "If a man steals bread to feed his starving family, is it a sin?" Depending on what bible you are looking at, either the seventh or eighth commandment is "Thou shalt not steal."[57][58] Morally the man could not let his family starve but by these "laws of God", he is forbidden to steal to remedy the problem.

In my early teen years I worked in the back room of a furniture store my father managed. Once, while talking about an employee, Dad mentioned the man's girlfriend. I was surprised to hear the word girl-friend. I asked why he wasn't married at his age and Dad told me the man couldn't afford to be married.

Premarital sex is widely accepted as a sin and there are several places in the Christian Bible that warn against sexual immorality but would it be immoral for a man to make love to a woman who was not his wife only because he could not afford to be married to her? If we believe in a powerful creator then we must conclude the survival of the human race's dependence upon sexual intercourse was intentional.

Matthew 19:5 says a man should leave his parents to be with his wife and that they should "become one flesh."[1] This is one of the many verses I've heard used to condemn premarital sex but it doesn't seem to actually say anything about it. 1 Corinthians 7:2 says, "But because of the temptation to sexual immorality, each man should have his own wife and each woman her own husband."[1] but this, to me, would seem to suggest we should all be married to avoid the lure of sexual immorality, not that it is immoral to have sexual relations outside of wedlock.

57   "10 Commandments - God's Standards," 2002-2009.
58   "Essential Freedom: Catholic," 2000.

1 Corinthians 7:1-5 says, "Now concerning the matters about which you wrote: 'It is good for a man not to have sexual relations with a woman.' But because of the temptation to sexual immorality, each man should have his own wife and each woman her own husband. The husband should give to his wife her conjugal rights, and likewise the wife to her husband. For the wife does not have authority over her own body but the husband does. Likewise the husband does not have authority over his own body but the wife does. Do not deprive one another, except perhaps by agreement for a limited time, that you may devote yourselves to prayer; but then come together again, so that Satan may not tempt you because of your lack of self-control."[1]

This passage says a lot. It says it's bad for a man and a woman to have sex. It says, in order to avoid the temptation of sexual immorality, we are to willingly give ourselves to each other within the state of marriage. It still doesn't seem to say anything about sex outside of marriage. Common translation of scripture, or analysis of anything for that matter, would seem to gravitate toward the idea that the rightness of one way makes any other way wrong.

Our society has put into place fairly rigid gender definitions. Men are supposed to be strong and fairly emotionless. Women are supposed to be week and sensitive. In spite of the limitations these roles place on us, I believe a child needs to experience what his or her society defines as male and female roles to understand his or her place in society and his or her relationships as he or she develops.

I believe my sixteen year-old brother is struggling right now because he has no real male figure in his life. Our father lives two states away and, from what I have gathered, they rarely talk. I once asked why he was disrespectful to our mother and he said he didn't fear her as he did our father. When I was growing up, my mother took on the role of nurturer and my father assumed the role of enforcer. Since the divorce, my mother has had to play both roles. I suppose this system helped keep me from feeling too horribly whenever I was being punished but the roles would seem to be too conflicting for my mother to play at the same time. This idea of a mother and father figure would seem to be the most convenient way to put these two roles in place but again, the fact that one way works doesn't mean the other ways are wrong.

If my father had not taken on the role of enforcer we might be closer now. I might feel more inclined to share personal feelings with him. Unfortunately, we do not live in a society where this kind of relationship is common practice. These roles of father and mother are common but I have yet to find scripture that says sexual intercourse is something to be reserved for those bound by wedlock. I suppose these roles are often played by different people in a child's life.

Deuteronomy 23:2 speaks of a child's ability to enter the gates of heaven. Depending on your translation, it speaks of a child born from a "forbidden union", a "bastard"[59] or an "illegitimate" child.[60] If you're reading the English standard version, which says, "forbidden union", I suppose this goes back to the question of premarital sex. If premarital sex were not forbidden, then I would have no reason to believe the union was. If you're reading the *New Living Translation*, which uses the word "illegitimate" to describe the child, or the King James version, which says "bastard", then the idea that a child should not be born out of wedlock would seem to hold its ground. But which version is the most accurate?

The New World Translation, which some argue to be the most accurate translation in circulation today, says, "Illegitimate son." This evidence would seem to support the idea that a child born out of wedlock is the subject of the verse but Deuteronomy 23:2 in this version says this child would not enter the "congregation of Jehovah."[61]

Sex does often lead to childbirth and contraceptives are never foolproof, so if we believe a child born out of wedlock, an illegitimate child, would never enter the gates of heaven and be condemned to either hell or purgatory then it would make sense to avoid sexual intercourse for the sake of the potential child but the Bible does not say these are the only options. Revelation 21 depicts a new Earth with no sadness and no death. 1 John 5:28-29 paints a picture of those who have died on Earth rising from their graves, some being resurrected to life and others to judgment. It has been suggested these passages, among others, were meant to depict a world in which humans could live eternally in happiness. This would seem to give a fourth option: to heaven, hell or purgatory. This would seem to change the intended message behind several passages, including the idea of the "illegitimate" child not entering the "congregation of Jehovah."

The Seven Deadly Sins were a creation of humankind and yet they've been used to guide and even condemn people. The idea behind the Seven Deadly Sins came from the Eight Evil Thoughts, the works of fourth century monk, Evagrius Ponticus. They were revised into the Seven Deadly Sins in 590 A.D.[62] What was once viewed as the sin of sloth would seem to have all of the symptoms of modern day depression. According to Ms. Anutza Bellissimo, CAMF of thesamigroup.com, scientists have theorized that sloth was the medieval diagnosis of depression. Today a person suffering from depression is the victim of a disease, not a sinner.

---

59 King James Version.
60 New living translation, 2004.
61 New World Translation, 1984.
62 Aubuchon, 2009.

But what has changed, other than our idea of it? The point is it is not a person's place to pass judgment on another person.

We were given a moral compass to let us know what is right. The "laws" of the Bible seem, to me, more like guidelines. God would not require something of us if we had insufficient understanding of the requirement. The idea of absolute anything is beyond us. Therefore the laws would not likely be as written in stone as they are in the story of the *Ten Commandments*.

It's the conscience every person has that lets us know if we are following the right path. The Christian bible says we are forgiven of all sins if we confess to them. Again I go to 1 John 1:9: "If we confess our sins, he is faithful and just to forgive us our sins and to cleanse us from all unrighteousness." Psalm 7:12 says, "If a man does not repent, God will whet his sword; he has bent and readied his bow." If we forget to ask for forgiveness are we not forgiven?

I believe these passages are supposed to encourage us to try to see the error in our ways. I remember lying in bed at night as a young teenager and asking for absolution of all of the "bad words" I had used that day. I actually remember making the conscious decision to use a "curse word" knowing I would later repent. Although, I suppose it wasn't true repentance unless I was remorseful. At the time it felt more like the "Save" option of a video game. I suspect I felt that if I, for some reason, died in the night, God would allow me to go to heaven because I had confessed and asked for forgiveness. If God is all knowing then he must know every sin we've ever committed. I certainly cannot remember every action in my life that triggered that uneasy feeling we associate with the conscience. I think the objective is for us to attempt to live in a good way, knowing we will occasionally fail to do so but then have the will to try again.

The Bible says we are to honor our parents. As teenagers, coming into our own, we typically believe we know the right path for ourselves whether our parents agree with us or not but we still have that little voice inside. At this stage, many of us ignore the voice—or perhaps are even overwhelmed with emotions to the point that we don't want to hear it—but if we listen, we always have that tool at our disposal.

God has set rules for us much in the way an earthly father sets rules for his children. A child does not always have what is best for him in mind. In fact, many children likely could not make an educated choice in specific situations because they have not had the experience to predict a logical outcome. Children often don't know what's best for them but their parents usually have a better idea.

Likewise, as intelligent as we believe we are, we may not always know what's best for us. If our creator is eternal and all knowing, then it only makes sense that he would. These "laws" are simply to keep us out of trouble. We always have the ability to choose our path for ourselves but if we suffer consequences, they will not be at God's hand but at our own.

That being said, I don't believe God's "laws" to always be the right path. We often cannot see the future consequence of our actions and I believe God has pointed out some of these potential hazards to us. These guidelines meant to protect us are now often viewed as absolute law from which we cannot stray without punishment; but would the god the Christian Bible depicts really want to punish us for doing what we feel is right?

We commonly allow "sin" in society, yet we condemn certain "sin." The mother of a disobedient child may smile while her child clearly disobeys the (depending on your version of the Bible) fourth or fifth commandment. The same mother could feel her stomach turn as she watches a gay couple pass her in the aisle of the local Walmart. It is common belief that all sin is the same in the eyes of the Lord. James 2:10-11 says, "For whoever keeps the whole law but fails in one point has become accountable for all of it. For he who said, "Do not commit adultery," also said, "Do not murder." If you do not commit adultery but do murder, you have become a transgressor of the law."[1] This referral to "the law" is to the "royal law", God's law. To use one part of a religion to condemn a person while ignoring another part is hypocrisy. I believe the Bible was meant as a map to use in ruling oneself, not condemning others. Sin is an act of the heart. Therefore, it is motivation, not action that defines sin.

Matthew 18:18 says, "Truly, I say to you, whatever you bind on earth shall be bound in heaven[63], and whatever you loose on earth shall be loosed in heaven. [64]" The word bind can be defined "to unite by any legal or moral tie: to be bound by a contract." The word loose can be defined "to release, as from constraint, obligation, or penalty." If Jesus died for all of humankind's sins then this statement is directed at all of humankind. So, is a thing like profanity a sin in the eyes of God? According to the book of Matthew, it is up to us.

Titus 3:5 says we are saved by mercy and not by righteous works. If we are not saved from condemnation through actions then could actions condemn us? After all, not performing a "sinful" act is an act of will but John 5:29 talks of judgment for those who have committed acts of evil. James 2:20 says "faith" without "works" is "useless" or "dead." So are we judged by our faith or our actions? I suppose real faith and actions are one in the same. If we have faith, we will do our best to live in a way that

---

[63] Bind.
[64] Loose.

emulates an idea of good that is represented by the ideas that build around the faith.

Chapter Sixteen

The Science of Emotion and God

What is emotion? It has been said emotion makes us human. What we know as emotion could be defined as temporary emotional states that are induced by chemicals in the brain. Emotion is said to be a product of the physical brain but emotion cannot be seen, only felt. What is emotion to everyone outside of me? I will never know because it is a magnolia. It is something with roots in an individual perspective but is never fully understood (the iceberg). There is a strong link between our emotional and physical states. My emotional and physical states mimic each other very closely. I will often sink into a state of feeling physically and emotionally bad so subtly that it's hard to tell which negative feeling came first. The right frontal insula of the brain is active when we experience both physical and emotional sensations. Not only does this illustrate the connection between our physical and emotional states, this activity in the right frontal insula would actually seem to be a physical incarnation of emotion.

I have found that, in my past, perceived emotions have made habit of seeping into my personal emotional state. The most obvious examples of this are the emotional states I experience while listening to music with a melancholy perspective, or watching a film in which the main character experiences significant emotional pain. Mirror neurons are the driving force behind our ability to have a personal experience by simply witnessing another person experience something.[1] If our subconscious brains are constantly absorbing information from the external environment and adjusting our perspectives based on the information they receive, then it makes sense that our emotional states are affected by the information as well.

I receive emotion from ones close to me much in the way a sponge absorbs water. My mind recognizes the pleasant and unpleasant feelings and empathizes. Mirror neurons in the brain are responsible for empathy. These neurons are the reason we can feel so emotionally attached to a character in a movie or why we cringe when we witness another in physical pain

So, if our mirror neurons are functioning properly, we should all be affected by the suggested emotional states of the people around us. These seemingly unforeseeable emotional influences have a great impact on how we, as individual pieces of society, analyze our social surroundings and interact with them.

Our emotional perspectives and the physical world would seem to be connected in a great way. This is how we can manage to "treat" a thing like depression with chemicals. I use quotes with the word treat in the sentence before because we do not really treat depression at all. Modern medical science has yet to cure depression. Antidepressants only remedy the symptoms of depression. In my experience, an anti-depressant put me in a kind of dream state. I was happy but I didn't feel justified in my happiness. I suppose the real problem with anti-depressants is the inevitable awakening that occurs when a dose is forgotten. We are then allowed the opportunity to view the world from that familiar perspective. It's sometimes sad but is clear, unlike the dream like world of a chemically pacified brain.

In the large scale of things, it would seem ridiculous to believe something like love could happen by chance. I'm not necessarily talking about a significant other, soul mate kind of love.

This could be any kind of love. The point is love would seem too mystical and perfect for us to be able to assume it could have spontaneously come into being. Such a system would seem as though it could only have been designed. This holds true for homosexual and plutonic love as well as heterosexual love. Why would God give someone such a feeling if they were not supposed to act on it?

A three part, chemical cocktail is responsible for the feelings we associate with "love": adrenalin, dopamine and serotonin. Does this mean love is a prosthetic feeling because all feelings are prosthetic? I don't think so. I believe our brains are supposed to receive serotonin when we engage in actions that tend to instigate feelings of love. People often try to separate science from spirituality but if you believe in a higher power then you likely believe he is not a magician but the creator of all rules. Why would he make these rules to break them? If God created our world and the laws of our world, not human made laws but the unbreakable kind, laws of nature and physics and of the brain and of the heart, then science is the study of God's work.

The scientist laughs at the Christian for believing he or she is feeling the Holy Spirit when he or she lifts his or her arms to praise God. The tingling feeling in one's arms after they've been raised for some time can be explained by the fact that the majority of the blood has left his or her extremities as a result of gravity's pull. But if you are one who believes God created the world with the intent of an all knowing creator then you must believe gravity was a creation of his, just as the tingly feeling one gets in his or her arms must be. If a miracle can be explained through science, does it cease to be a miracle or does it simply mean we can understand how that miracle was executed? I've heard theories behind the science involved in the ten plagues of the Old Testament. It's been said the ten plagues could have been a chain reaction sparked by the Minoan eruption currently estimated to have occurred between 1627 B.C.E. and 1600 B.C.E.[65]

Even a thing like positive results following prayer could be explained through science. Praying causes optimism and positive thinking, which could yield positive results without the intervention of a higher power. A person, no matter how skeptical, could subconsciously expect healing when being prayed for and, in doing so, relieve emotional stress and allow the body to heal more effectively. When I experienced the threat of recurring cancer, I was told a positive attitude was an essential part of staying cancer free. Somehow, it seemed to be the attitude of the patients before me that caused them to contract the deadly ailment a second time. As unfair as it sounds, I have heard difficult patients are the ones who tend to survive life-threatening illnesses. They refuse to give in and, in their resistance, tend to survive more frequently than the quiet patients. This phenomenon and the positive results that tend to follow prayer could be products of the same source.

I mention in "'Christian', the Adjective II", the insult other religions pose when it comes to personal prayer. If their god is the one true god, then we're simply talking to ourselves. I don't know that prayer to any god is unlike talking to oneself. I have noticed many people like to pray out loud. They like an audible version of their prayers but if there is an all-knowing creator, then our thoughts are not outside of his under-standing. We birth thoughts and he understands them. I don't believe prayer to be this spiritual, direct phone line to God. Although, I suppose if this were the case then John 14:6 would make Jesus the metaphorical telephone operator, ". . . No one comes to the father except through me."[66] but even that's up for interpretation. If you are talking to yourself and the

---

[65]   "The Science of Minoan eruption," 2009
[66]   English standard version, 2001.

higher power, whoever he, she or it may be to you, understands, is it not like talking to him, her or it?

What of the conscience? It's likely our ideas of right and wrong, the superego, as Freud calls it,[67] are simply products of our perspectives. I suppose the formation of a person's conscience is a product of mirror neurons. We really only would seem to experience troubled consciences when we are causing harm to other sentient beings in our world. We experience moral pains only when we cause harm to or witness harm being done to something we expect to feel pain. The consciousness of plants has been debated but common consensus would seem to point to a lack of consciousness. This could explain why some feel comfortable carving their initials into a tree and far fewer are comfortable carving their initials into the chest of a fellow human. We personally experience every experience we witness in the physical world.[1] Why would this phenomenon be limited to our physical experiences of this world and not affect us when we simply know of the experience taking place? Empathy would seem like a likely inspiration for the formation of the Golden rule: "Do unto others . . ." If we personally experience every experience we witness then we, in a sense, are doing to ourselves when we do to others.

I believe these complex patterns of cause and effect we know as science are still miracles. They are patterns set by God. If God set everything in motion then everything is a miracle. I suppose my faith in God's willingness and ability to help me through my struggles could make me work harder, believing I could not fail as long as I tried. My faith in this matter could require I work harder to succeed so I do not give reason to doubt my faith but then would my success be by the power of God or a result of my own power? I believe it would be both. I would have succeeded because of my faith, because I needed to not have reason to doubt it.

In the 1930's and 1940's, Dr. Wilder Penfield conducted several experimental surgeries that led to many discoveries regarding the human body's link to its brain. He found parts of the brain that stimulated movement in parts of the body but I believe his more profound discovery was a part of the brain that could trigger the will to act. His patients were always conscious during the procedures and, with stimulation to certain parts of the brain, reported desires to execute simple functions. Was this discovery the actual physical incarnation of free-will? Possibly but the desired functions were the most basic of actions. The reported desires were not those to build a house or write a symphony but desires to raise a hand or move a leg.[1] If a person's hand is burned by fire, the subconscious reaction is to pull away. These functions were not much more complex than that. I suppose these desires were actually more a part of the

---

[67]   Superego.

subconscious and less a part of the actual freewill. I believe this is just one more example of the power of God's creative hand.

I don't believe the Christian Bible is always meant to be taken literally. I don't imagine many believe Jesus of Nazareth was actually a lamb but I suppose this was not a metaphor created by God but by a man written about in the bible. Many believe the Earth was created in seven of our days and that any ideas contrary to this belief are blasphemous; but what is a day to someone who is infinite? If we consider the creation story of Genesis to be profound truth, our worldly idea of a day didn't exist until God created light and separated it from darkness. This was the first day; but how does an infinite being measure a day?

It is not written that God created light and separated it from darkness in twenty-four hours. Even if it were, what is an hour to an infinite being? I have heard it theorized that one biblical week is seven years in our measurement of time. This does give some room for interpretation but the interpretation is still bound by laws of this world.

It has been said he will not affect freewill and we live in a world seemingly run by humankind. We live in giant buildings we erect ourselves. We drive machines we've created down roads we've designed in cities we've built. It would seem that God is nowhere to be found in modern society. He does, however, have the power of influence. The Christian Bible gives examples of God influencing a person's perspective. In Exodus 4:21, he said he would harden Pharaoh's heart. If he could alter Pharaoh's perspective, why couldn't he do the same in us when we ask for it? What we consider God answering our questions to him and others consider talking to ourselves may be one in the same. We gain new perspective through thought, analysis, and God's placement of it, on us.

A common Christian belief is that our world did not exist before God created it. The Law of Conservation of Matter and Energy says no energy is ever destroyed but simply rearranged to form something else.[68] This would explain how we get heat from consuming a piece of wood with fire. According to worsleyschool.net, Einstein's E=mc squared concludes that matter and energy are two forms of the same thing. This explains why the amount of an object's energy changes in direct relation to its mass, why E (energy) equals mc squared (mass x the square of the speed of light).[69] If the level of energy the physical world holds is constant then it would make sense that every molecule that makes up every pebble that makes up every road on which we travel existed in some form or came into existence when our world came into existence, depending on your beliefs, somewhere between 6,000 and 4.5 billion years ago.[70]

---

[68] Law of Conservation.
[69] Willis, 1999.
[70] Robinson, 2009.

So, what's the difference in 6,000 and 4.5 billion years? One could easily say it's a math equation, $4,500,000,000 - 6,000 = 4,499,994,000$ but time is completely relative to the individual and even to the specific instance. Time moves quickly in some situations and slowly in others and our minds likely could never grasp the idea of such a large amount of time. It's true the sun will set and rise according to a schedule but some days would seem to take a lot longer than others and 1,643,587,704,046 sunrises and sunsets would seem impossible for the human mind to fathom. If time seems to change according to our perspective then we simply cannot measure time without at least the training of an external device and training only allows a person to measure inconsequential amounts of time. There is no way to measure time on a global scale. The billions of years difference in the theory of creation vs. the theory of evolution is miniscule in the human mind because it is simply incomprehensible.

I believe the years represented in the Bible are not the years we humans designate as twelve months but simply ways to signify, not measure, certain lapses of time. Something significant happened each day of the creation period. Could this not simply be a way to label periods of change? This would explain how we can have so much proof of evolution and change in our world and still allow a perspective of legitimacy to those who claim knowledge of a higher power. According to Einstein's Special Theory of Relativity, time is relative to one's velocity.

This is known as gravitational time dilation.[71] So, according to Einstein, time is not a mechanical system but rather one that fluctuates based on circumstance. On what day were the laws of physics created?

It would seem to me modern society almost always tries to separate the idea of God and science. A person can either believe in creation or evolution. I believe a greater mind would see it from both sides. The Christian Bible would seem to be full of metaphors, and nothing in the external world is written in stone. Albert Einstein is, arguably, one of history's greatest minds. His focus was on the sciences of the external world but he also would seem to have held a faith in a higher power: "Before God we are equally wise—and equally foolish."[72] If Albert Einstein's intellect is so respected by the scientific community, do these scientists who see creationism as an absurdity suspect he did not use his great intellect in every aspect of his life?

What of the theory that religion is simply humankind's attempt at defining ourselves? Without the belief of an afterlife or a higher power, this life could seem fairly bleak. There is no way to prove or disprove the existence of God. For the most part, humankind's reality is rooted in the

---

[71] General Relativity, 1995.
[72] "Before God We," 2009.

physical world. How could anything that lives in a world beyond the physical one be proven in the physical world? I have personal evidence of a higher power but this evidence cannot be displayed to anyone but myself. This evidence is an undeniable feeling. This evidence has several times been a profound sense of a presence greater than myself. I remember one specific time I physically felt on my body what I believe to have been what some would call, "The Hand Of God."

I suppose the problem is humankind's undying desire to define ourselves. We have trouble admitting there are things we cannot understand. We would seem like the child who closes his eyes when he is scared. "If I can't see it, it's not there." This form of defense would seem illogical to most adults, yet we often use the same thought process: "If I can't touch it, if I can't prove it, then it does not exist." We use science to measure our advancement. We use science to define ourselves. So, it's not solely religion's burden to define humankind but science's burden as well.

I mentioned before that my father once said he morphs his reality so he is never wrong and that I suspect everyone does this to an extent. I wonder if I do this so much that my world is not as I perceive it at all. There are too many coincidences or "magnolias." If this is not a dream world, these magnolias, and even similarities in the world, are proof to me there is something beyond this physical world. There is geometry in everything. Math is the foundation of our world. But this proof of a world outside of ours goes beyond physical similarities in our world.

There's proof in the habits of everything. If a rock spends enough time in the dirt, a hole will build around it. It roots itself in the ground and becomes more difficult to move. It stays in the ground because it's been in the ground for some time. I have noticed self-sabotaging habits motivated by the fact that, until recently, I was comfortable being sad because it was familiar. I stayed where I was emotionally because I'd been there for some time. Physical pain is a signal to the brain that something is wrong with the body. Emotional pain is a sign to the brain that something is wrong with patterns of input. So, these patterns over-lap between the laws of physics and the human perspective.

Physics is "the science that deals with matter, energy, motion, and force."[73] Science is defined as "a branch of knowledge or study dealing with a body of facts or truths systematically arranged and showing the operation of general laws: the mathematical sciences."[74] Nothing can be studied without something to contrast it. The best way to study a creator would seem to be to study his creation. If the study of a creation is a useful tool for studying a creator then the study of physics is the study of God.

---

[73] Physics.
[74] Science.

It would seem to be common theory that numerology is evil and something one of faith should not dabble in. If numbers are the building blocks of our world, then the study of numbers in any form is the study of our creator.

Many are taught to do as they are told, not ask questions, and "fear" God. It's my opinion that God does not want us to fear him and that he created us to be inquisitive creatures on purpose. So many people would seem to believe God likes a quiet, submissive child but if you agree people are naturally inquisitive and God is flawless then you must conclude God wants us to ask questions, to go against the grain, and to think for ourselves.

There is a fine line between taking bits of a religion that fit into your idea of how people should live while ignoring other parts and thinking for yourself. 1 John 4:1 says, "Beloved, do not believe every spirit but test the spirits to see whether they are from God, for many false prophets have gone out into the world."[4] I believe those who accept the scientific explanation of miracles, as opposed to ignoring the facts, because explaining them would be blasphemous, would have to actually be of greater faith. When something can be explained without using the idea of a higher power, it takes a greater faith to still believe.

Nothing is supposed to be considered fact until it can be proven but science does not disprove the existence of a higher power. To me, science supports the idea of the existence of a higher power who has applied unbreakable laws to the world he created. The search for the answer always brings me back to math but God is an artist as well. Take the circle for example. The circle is the perfect geometrical form. If a circle's circumference is divided by its diameter we get pi. To our knowledge, pi is an infinite number. It never ends and never repeats sequence. If God is perfect, the study of our world is the study of God, and the circle is the perfect geometrical form, then pi is infinite because God is infinite. Perhaps we can't understand infinity because we can't see it and we can't understand what we can't study. Maybe we can't see infinity because God is infinite and to view infinity would be like viewing the face of God.

I've theorized this world is not as genuine as most would seem to believe it to be. It's possible my theories of an artificial external world could come from the sense of other things in the world we as humans do not normally sense and likely could not understand. I've heard stories of hallucinogenic experiences that hit home when it comes to this topic. I have never taken hallucinogens and I take every story with a grain of salt. But it would make sense to me that certain chemicals could alter our perspectives in ways that enable us to see the world from levels difficult to reach otherwise. I am not condoning the use of any mind-altering substance. It's possible we are not supposed to understand the potential of the world around us.

I have heard, once one has used these substances, he or she perceives certain things differently than he or she did before. It is possible that mind-altering drugs can open the takers' eyes to things in the world not seen by the naked eye but it's likely the trip is so distracting the taker cannot understand what he or she is experiencing. If the study of our world is the study of our creator then we likely could not understand what we observe when given a glimpse whether our minds have been altered or not. Again, we cannot grasp the idea of infinity.

Chapter Seventeen

"Christian," the Adjective IV la palabra, le mot, das Wort, la parola, a palavra, **слово**, het woord, **η λέξη**, uttrycka, «·fl·... 単語, 낱말, 词, the word

The Christian Bible makes reference to false gods or idols. I give you Psalm 40:4 of the New Living Translation, "Oh, the joys of those who trust the Lord, who have no confidence in the proud or in those who worship idols." [75] Of course the English standard Version says, "Blessed is the man who makes the LORD his trust, who does not turn to the proud, to those who go astray after a lie!" [76]

How about 2 Kings 17:15: "They despised his statutes and his covenant that he made with their fathers and the warnings that he gave them. They went after false idols and became false, and they followed the nations that were around them, concerning whom the LORD had commanded them that they should not do like them."[2]

I believe these "idols" are not as distant to modern American society as we would like to think. We are blind to modern incarnations of these idols that were so warned against because we often take the Christian Bible at its literal translation. We don't see any giant golden calves in our society but we fail to see our obsession with things of the superficial world. A true modern incarnation of a false idol would seem to be something that takes our focus away from living as God intends us to live.

---

[75]   2004.
[76]   English Standard Version, 2001.

I believe even a thing like the Christian bible can become a false idol when used in support of any perspective contrary to love. I know the Christian Bible has been translated many times for different reasons. Thomas Linacre once wrote, after learning Greek and comparing the Greek translations of the Bible to the Latin that was in circulation at the time, "Either this (the original Greek) is not the Gospel . . . or we are not Christians."[77]

I believe, in its original form, the Christian Bible might have been very different. It has always bothered me we are taught to "fear" God. The Christian bible mentions the "fear" of God several times in a positive way. It says the righteous fear God. I have looked at the text and found it would be easy to replace the word fear with another word. When the word fear is used to express a feeling toward God, it can easily be replaced with the word respect. Genesis 22:12: "He said, 'Do not lay your hand on the boy or do anything to him, for now I know that you fear God, seeing you have not withheld your son, your only son, from me.'" Genesis 42:18: "On the third day Joseph said to them, 'Do this and you will live, for I fear God:'"

Exodus 18:21: "Moreover, look for able men from all the people, men who fear God, who are trustworthy and hate a bribe, and place such men over the people as chiefs of thousands, of hundreds, of fifties, and of tens."[78]

Fear is defined as, "a distressing emotion aroused by impending danger, evil, pain, etc., whether the threat is real or imagined; the feeling or condition of being afraid."[4] This does not seem like a characteristic the loving deity of Christianity would desire from his followers. In the Christian Bible, fear is painted as a good thing. The emotion we know as fear, and the fear in the Christian Bible would seem contrary.

The Christian Bible makes many references to slaves. It even explains proper procedure when it comes to slaves. Leviticus 25:44 says, "As for your male and female slaves whom you may have: you may buy male and female slaves from among the nations that are around you." Again I believe something was lost in translation with the presented idea of "buying" a person. I believe the word slave may have, in many cases in the original text, been very similar to our modern ideas of an indentured servant. Exodus 21:16 says, "Whoever steals a man and sells him, and anyone found in possession of him, shall be put to death." Surely our modern definitions of slave fit this verse better than they fit the verses that use the word "slave."

---

[77] English bible history, 1997-2008.
[78] Fear, 2009.
4

In certain versions of Genesis 47:19-25 men offer themselves to be Pharaoh's slaves;[79] other versions use the word servants. Genesis 47:19 says, "Why should we die before your eyes, both we and our land? Buy us and our land for food, and we with our land, will be servants to Pharaoh. And give us seed that we may live and not die, and that the land may not be desolate." In Greek, the word Doulos means slave. It has been claimed that, in Biblical text, the word was meant to mean servant, as it is represented in some verses of other versions of the bible but according to *ntwords.com,* there is a specific Greek word for a servant who is not a slave: Diakonos.[80] Why would the Greek read Doulos and not Diakonos if this was meant to mean servant instead of slave? One could conclude that, either the Greek was mistranslated when the New American Standard and New World Translation versions were being composed, or the word's representation in Greek was Doulos.

Exodus 21:2 says, "When you buy a Hebrew slave, he shall serve six years, and in the seventh he shall go out free, for nothing." Leviticus 25:42 says, "For they are my servants, whom I brought out of the land of Egypt; they shall not be sold as slaves."[2] These two verses would seem to contradict each other. They were commandments to the Hebrew people about the Hebrew people, after they were delivered from the Egyptians, with one book of separation in the modern incarnation of the Christian Bible.

I believe the Christian Bible was inspired by God but we have little doubt it was written and translated by humans. Any creation of human-kind is subject to humankind's flawed perspective. In the "New World Translation of the Holy Scriptures" this passage is worded slightly differently. It says, "For they are my slaves whom I brought out of the land of Egypt. They must not sell themselves the way a slave is sold."[81] I have heard this was to mean that, because the Hebrew people were bought out of slavery in Egypt, they were the property of God and therefore could not sell themselves, because they were not their own to sell. Still, this interpretation does not make the two passages seem less contradictory. In Exodus Hebrew slaves are permitted. In Leviticus they are not, theoretically, because they are the property of God. Were they not the property of God before? They had already been delivered from slavery in Egypt. Perhaps our translation would seem to contradict itself because it is not true to the original text.

Luke 14:26 says, "If anyone comes to me and does not hate his own father and mother and wife and children and brothers and sisters, yes, and even his own life, he cannot be my disciple."[2] What was the word hate

---

[79] New American Standard, 1995, New World Translation, 1984.
[80] Slave.
[81] 1984.

supposed to mean here? It has been said that God allows evil but does not cause the evil himself. Exodus 32:35 says God sent a plague to the Hebrew people for building a Golden Calf.[2] Modern incarnations of the Christian Bible wouldn't seem to be perfect interpretations of God's will. Still, they would seem to present helpful insight into his desires for us. If the Christian Bible was written by humans then it is subject to flawed perspective, just as humankind is. Even with its flaws, the Christian Bible may be used to govern our own actions. Still, the actions in which we choose to engage will always be weighed against our own personal perspectives, our analytical abilities and what we believe to be morally right. We can choose to blindly follow the book or be guided by our minds and our hearts. The latter would seem like the path which Christianity's namesake would take.

Chapter Eighteen

God in the Dream World

There are constantly happenings in our world that would seem too specific to the situation to be coincidence. They may not be "miracles" but if these magnolias are not the product of the world I create, they definitely show a system, a connection in our world. The other day, I was flipping through a magazine and came across a small section about a toy gun that could kill a fly from across the room. I didn't give it much thought. Two of my cousins were visiting and when I got out of bed the next day my younger cousin was shooting flies with that same gun. Isolated, this would seem like a coincidence but phenomena like this occur regularly. Often, I make a reference to a specific episode of a television show only to find that it airs later that night on television. This happens too often to be coincidence. They say art imitates life. Maybe this is an example of life imitating art.

When I was at work the other day, I logged onto the Internet. The home page set on that computer often displays several news stories or magazine articles, scrolling one by one. The first one I saw was an article giving some relationship advice that seemed interesting. The article was a person's views of what lies are okay in an intimate relationship. I tried to read it but my eyes got the better of me. The next day I turned on the TV before work and watched a sitcom episode with a theme of "what secrets are okay to keep from your significant other." I think God wanted me to learn that lesson and, when I didn't get it from the Internet article, he used my morning ritual to expose me to the idea.

Allen and I lived in apartment number 212. When we first moved in, I wrote a poem called Genesis 212. The idea was that I was starting a new life in this apartment numbered 212. When I moved out, I wrote one called Exodus 212. This very bitter poem eventually turned into an even more bitter song. This was the song Jo asked me to record for her years later. It was about what I painted as an inevitability: his killing himself: "*Has he fallen yet? Is he falling yet?*" I don't know that I've ever experienced so much regret over the realization of a correct prediction on my part.

If you look in the Christian Bible under Genesis 2:12 you will find something along the lines of, "And the gold of that land is good; bdellium and onyx stone are there."[1] If you look in the Christian Bible under Exodus 2:12 you'll find something similar to, "He looked this way and that, and seeing no one, he struck down the Egyptian and hid him in the sand."[1] I had not read either of these scriptures when I wrote the two poems but their contents would seem to fit the ideas behind the poems well.

This would appear to be evidence in support of the idea that everything is connected in some way. It's possible that everything seems to be connected because I never woke up from that tumor surgery and the world around me is an elaborate creation of my subconscious. The undeniable feeling of a higher power could be a sense of my subconscious brain guiding me through this dream world. In a world where all is created by the brain, like a dream, the brain would seem to be god. Then again, my brain creates my perspective of the world whether this is a dream or not. I suppose that, in a sense, the brain creates the world outside of it because it creates our perspectives of it.

When I awoke after the surgery, I was in a room that had a great feeling of sterility. Everything was white and I was propped up in some kind of chair. My legs were bent and my thighs were spread apart. There was something indefinable extending from my genitals. What if this world was the world outside of mine? If perspective is a physical incarnation in the brain then disruption of the physical structure of the brain could cause a vast change in perspective. It has been suggested that we are blind to things we cannot understand. I know my experience of the world is based on past experiences of it. We have already established that what is real is based on perspective. What if this world I only spent a few minutes in was what others would consider the "real" world?

Another possible explanation for everything being connected is the idea that our creator made systems around which this world revolves, like math. The systems of this world are so detailed that what seems like chaos is actually detailed intricacies in vast systems. It's the "butterfly effect" (or Chaos Theory). The butterfly effect gets its name from the idea that a butterfly could flap its wings on one side of the globe and cause a storm on the other side. *The Chaos Theory* states that a system with finely defined laws can eventually take the form of something that appears to be random by the cause of the systems sensitivity.[82] Everything has a

---

[02] Paul, 1900.

purpose. Take a look at a basic food chain. A bug eats a plant. A bird eats the bug. A man eats the bird. The man dies and turns into food for another plant. This is a simple example of the sometimes very complex systems on earth.

It is likely that, by constantly deconstructing the world around me, I'm trying to understand God. I have heard that, since the beginning, humankind has been trying to figure out why we are here. What makes me any different?

I'm no longer afraid of death. When I was first told of my brain tumor I accepted the fact that I might die. Since then, the world around me has felt very distant. Maybe the reason I don't fear death is because I'm not sure of the reality of this world. The only absolute truth I have is the way I feel. I now believe in an afterlife that far surpasses any kind of joy I could feel in this life.

Sometimes, when my physical pains become more than a welcome challenge, I consider the reasons God might not take me home. I'm still here for a reason. They say what doesn't kill you makes you stronger and that God allows trials to come into our lives to build strength. Whether it is to make the world a better place in my day-to-day efforts or simply to learn and grow, I have to have faith that he has a plan for me.

Both the physical and spiritual worlds are God's creations. There is beauty in everything because everything is God's artistic creation. I believe we are spoiled to the world's beauty because we are too close to view it from an external perspective. When we can't see the beauty of the world, we're like the child of wealthy parents who is bored with his new toys. The child isn't ungrateful. His boredom is simply a product of the perspective he was given. We often can't see the beauty because we're constantly exposed to it.

If everything in the world is God's creation then there's beauty even in pain. I've seen the beauty in my own pain. Why is it we can see the fragile beauty in a thing like a flower but when it comes to the fragile side of our own nature, we often deny it? In order to be happy with one's situation in life he or she has to remember that, no matter how much seemingly evil there is in the world, there is also beauty and love, and innocence and good, all around.

I was awakened the other morning by my phone's alarm clock. When I looked at the screen on the face of my phone, I saw something that looked like a familiar text messaging screen. At the top of the screen was my girlfriend's name. At the bottom, written under a white tint, in a way I'd never seen before, was "only 'and now I repent' can be added to it."

I read the message aloud and then closed it so I could disarm the still ringing alarm. When I went back to find the message it wasn't saved in any of the texting files. Perhaps I had hallucinated but this doesn't mean it wasn't real. It was real to me, and mine is the only reality that defines what's real in the first place.

Chapter Nineteen

Limbo and the Lull behind the Wheel

Perhaps I'm simply in a limbo state. I'm not dead but I'm not alive. A coma is defined as "a state of prolonged unconsciousness, including a lack of response to stimuli, from which it is impossible to rouse a person." I would imagine the first person perspective of a coma is very much a state of limbo. Years can go by from a first person perspective in a dream state. Maybe I'm still in surgery. If this is, by how others would perceive it, the "real world", then this is still somewhat of a limbo state for me. I'm still healing. I spend my weekdays mostly working or asleep. I do go out of my way to have fun but it's unlikely my fun will result in anything consequential. Maybe life on Earth for everyone is a time of insignificance. It could be viewed as filler between the two big events in life, birth and death. However, this view of the world is likely inaccurate and far too bleak. I still feel I should be doing more with my life.

My purpose in most aspects of my life has become more to stay alive and less to actually live. There are certain aspects of my life I thoroughly enjoy; but it would seem I spend more time doing unenjoyable things as means to those enjoyable experiences. Maybe we all are born in debt to ourselves. Maybe being an adult is about accepting this debt. Maybe my lack of enthusiasm for the majority of my life after the tumor explains this feeling of inconsequence, of being in a limbo state. I believe I was put here by God to learn and become better and more spiritually evolved. So, I need to be looking for my purpose. I need to be pulling myself out of limbo.

I don't have to treat this inescapable sense of a lack of consequence as a burden. There's freedom in a world without consequence, even if it's only my world. The sense that nothing I'm doing right now will make any major difference in the long run often plagues me but in the big scheme of things nothing of humankind is really consequential. We could destroy our planet and not majorly affect anything in the vast scheme of all; but I suppose this view is too bleak. After all, the world is what we make it. Even if I were in a somewhat literal state of limbo, it would still be up to me how I wanted to respond to the situation.

The heat I feel in my head and the eventual pain I feel in my eyes often seem to be trying to manhandle me into sleep. Almost every day on my drive home from work, my eyes start to roll closed. I have to really focus to stay awake. Perhaps it's death that couldn't reach me during the tumor problems coming back to set things right. I don't know by what motivation it would be sent or even by what force. Could this be God prepping me for something, or even setting in place the science that will eventually take my life? Could this experience be the product of a power of evil intent and means to spiritual growth through my resistance? Could this simply be fate or an internal mechanism that cannot release the idea of a destined early death for me?

Perhaps it's just science. I nearly fall asleep on my drive home from work every day because I spend a lot of time at the computer at work and my eyes are just too tired to remain open but my eyes tend to roll closed during the drive home even when I've spent very little time at the computer.

Maybe this is just one of the many lingering problems that come with post brain tumor life. I have to convince myself this is the case to keep on trying to succeed in finding happiness in life and to not give into the lull behind the wheel. When I was working for my father, I wrote a poem called "Asleep at the Wheel." The idea behind it was the fear that I would become this emotionless slave to money I saw others to be. I dressed like and often resembled them. I now spend more time at work than anywhere else. I usually enjoy my job but there's not much else in my life and I'm now nearly falling asleep at the wheel on my drive home. Maybe this poem is just another addition to the theory that time is limitless.

I suppose we fear death because the afterlife is unknown. I don't believe death is something we should fear. It is inevitable. Why should we fear something we cannot avoid? Death can be a beautiful thing. If we believe the afterlife is happy, which I do, then we should be happy for the people we love who pass on. If we truly believe the afterlife is better than life on Earth then we should not fear death but embrace it. It is strange to me people can say they know, without a doubt they're going to heaven and still behave in a cowardly manner when their own lives are threatened.

I suppose we're all victims of doubt. It has recently been suggested that Mother Teresa questioned her faith at one point. I suppose it doesn't matter how strong our faith is, no one can be absolutely certain what happens when we die. If we have doubt then we cannot judge others for disbelief. If we don't have doubt then we can no longer fear death. Death can be a very beautiful thing. It may very well be the conduit to that person's first face-to-face meeting with his or her creator. If I mindlessly, blindly follow anything, even ideas of religion, then I'm not living up to the full potential God has planned for me.

We as humans desire to give up when we feel we're not making progress. It makes sense. We don't want to spend time on something fruitless. Am I making progress? I can't honestly say

I see progression in myself. If I were not, would it be alright to give up? Giving up on oneself is harder than giving up a goal. Once one has given up on him or herself there is nothing keeping him or her on Earth and there is always the uncertainty of an afterlife. I believe very strongly that there is an afterlife and a God. I have felt his presence but I've been wrong about things I was certain about before. If I'm correct in believing there is a higher power who wants what is best for me, then I have to remember I am here for a reason, for a purpose beyond my vision. If I were to take my earthly life it would be returning the gift God has given to me, more time on Earth. I would not want to fail to fulfill my purpose, the reason God has for keeping me here.

In Roman Catholic theology limbo is defined as a border area of heaven or hell.[2] The Christian religion is a group of beliefs built around the stories of the bible, a book that is, arguably, often not literal in its stories. If the idea of limbo being the edge of heaven or hell came from a book that's not always meant to be taken literally, then what is limbo? Maybe the common idea of being in limbo, the idea of being in between things and the Roman Catholic idea are one in the same. At a very young age I grew to see hell as a place that was without the presence of God. The pain described was the emotional pain of never knowing one's creator. What if hell is simply the absence of God? We can never completely understand our creator. Perhaps what we feel as distance from God and a lack of consequence is the Roman Catholic, metaphoric limbo.

---

[2] 2010

Chapter Twenty

Condemnation Among Humans

It is commonly believed the act of stereotyping inspires inaccurate perspectives. Still, we would all seem to be guilty of this act in one way or another. We stereotype because we all have the need to simplify and categorize the information our minds take in. Recent analogies compare the human brain to a very intricate computer system. Imagine you are looking at the desktop screen of a computer. The page is full of Icons. These Icons will take you to different folders. Inside these folders are more folders. In what we generally think of as a computer, there might be a few files inside a folder maybe inside another folder. The human brain has to recognize and analyze everything we see, hear, smell, taste, or feel, and be able to reference and analyze many of these perceptions at a later date. This means one hundred files inside one thousand folders inside one million folders and links to related files.

Stereotypes can be particularly problematic when we are dealing with human data. I believe a stereotype is placed when we recognize a pattern in a specific group of people and, for the purposes of simplification and prediction, we make a generalization instead of filing the attribute in the specific file for the person who holds it. Some stereo-types hold true in specific cases. But a stereotype states that most, if not all of the people to whom this stereotype is assigned share the attribute. Therefore, if a stereotype is based on fact, all or most of the group to which the stereotype is assigned should behave or look accordingly. This is rarely the case. It is unfair and irrational to assume a stereotype will hold true before we have evidence of its truth. Even if the stereotype is completely accurate when it comes to the majority, there would always seem to be exceptions.

A stereotype is a product of a person's personal history. If the person did not witness evidence of the stereotype's validity in the physical world him or herself, he or she most likely witnessed it represented by another perspective. It was then up to his or her analytical ability to justify or discredit it. If we make exceptions in our expectations of the mentally challenged instead of condemn them, then we should do the same for those who have lower than average analytical ability.

I suppose the bigot's need to generalize is not very different from a child's inability to give more than one name to a physical incarnation in the external world as cited in *The Tipping Point*.[83] If a horse is presented to a child and the presenting adult explains the horse's name is Abby. From then on, the child may often give the name "Abby" to all horses. The child has yet to learn to recognize the difference in a proper noun and a common noun but more applicably, has trouble attributing more than one name to the "Abby." The child sees every horse as an "Abby." In a similar way, the bigot sees all a stereotype encompasses as the original representation of the stereotype.

We all make generalizations. We have to. The human brain would not seem capable of analyzing and filing all of the information it is constantly receiving. Judgment is still judgment no matter who is being judged. If we blindly judge the bigot when he or she judges for superficial reasons, without trying to see his or her perspective, we are practicing the same social actions we're judging him or her for. After all, judgment from a bigot's perspective is not a moral issue. He or she believes him or herself to be morally right. It is, like any other issue putting distance between us, the product of a difference in perspectives.

No person tries to do evil. Even if he or she engages in behavior the entire world sees as evil, he or she is doing what he or she rationalizes as being moral. Let's start with "The Axis of Evil." On September 11th, 2001 "Terrorists" attacked the United States' World Trade Center. It's common knowledge in the United States that these people believed the United States to be a great evil in the world but many expressed anger toward them. Many who claimed Christianity as their support for feelings of hate for their fellow Americans expressed feelings of anger toward these people identified as terrorists. It baffles me how a person who believes we, as a country, are so lost in our ways with things like homosexuality and abortion can be so blindly angered toward someone who is trying to hurt our country.

What would you give to be able to sacrifice yourself for the greater good? These men took actions they viewed as being morally right. Many United States citizens have morals that could be questioned as easily as the morals of our attackers have been. I was raised to believe one should always do what he or she feels is right and to not go along with the crowd or give in to peer pressure. If we assume perspectives solely because we

---

[83]   Gladwell, 2000.

view them as the most popular, how is this any different? Either way, even when we are doing something we know is said to be wrong, the end justifies the means, or we wouldn't do it.

Take prostitution. It is said we live in a democratic-republic, which means we have representatives, who we vote into office, to vote on anything we don't vote on ourselves. Prostitution is illegal. The governing lord of morality and public wellness that is our government has said prostitution should not exist. Prostitutes and those who solicit them know it's illegal but the end justifies the means. For the prostitute, it's worth the many risks the act presents to have the money that results in the act, and I think we know what the John gets out of it.

I've always had an especially strong repulsion toward rape but from a perspective, I was the committer of said act when I took the virginity of my friend's sister. Rape, murder, molestation, even the most heinous of acts, are justified in the actor's mind. Even when a person takes action for no purpose other than to cause hurt to another, he or she feels justified in his or her actions. Does it make someone a bad person if he or she performs a malicious act? When we commit a malicious act we feel justified in performing the act for one of a number of reasons. Revenge is a common theme. We feel we are delivering justice. Perhaps the motivation is jealousy. In this case we feel bad about our own situations and want to make things seem fair from our perspectives. This would be the attempted dispatching of fairness, which certainly does not seem to be a condemnable act.

Consider mirror neurons. Remember, these make empathy in the brain possible.[84] If mirror neurons enable empathy, then perhaps a person who does not feel empathy for the target of his or her inflicted pain does not have the mirror neuron capability to do so.

Amoralism is defined as, "having no moral standards, restraints, or principles; unaware of or indifferent to questions of right or wrong: a completely amoral person."[85] If empathy is the product of physical cells in our brains and empathy is responsible for morality then amoralism is the product of a malfunctioning system in the brain. Once a person's perspective is broken down into science, it makes it somewhat difficult to pass judgment on the person for his or her actions because it is no longer a question of his or her will but an inconsistency in what makes his or her perspective, a rarity, a key to individualism.

Even when we say to ourselves, "I know I'm going to regret this", what we are really saying is, "Even though this is justifiable now, I know my view will change and I will come to see my actions in a new light." We often create moral views of certain actions based on our past beliefs,

---

84   Blakeslee & Blakeslee, 2007.
85   Amoralism.

based on the beliefs that have been instilled in us all of our lives. If we allow our perspectives to grow then we know our original perspectives are not always correct. This is how it's possible to have beliefs in place that say an action is wrong and still be right in feeling it's justified. I believe no person acts in a way that is unjustifiable to him or her. Even if we are being forced or just obligated to do something, the wrath of the power that causes this force or obligation is our justification. Even if we know our actions are wrong or regret our actions in the future, at this moment everyone in the world is acting in a way that is justifiable to them.

The only inhabitants of this world we are accountable to are ourselves. Humankind can try to punish us but in this life we only have to answer to ourselves, our moral compasses. If I ended up in jail tomorrow, it would be up to me whether I felt bad about what I had done. Outside forces, like government, can try to sway the way we feel about our actions but in the end we are our own jury. If you don't feel bad about your actions until someone tells you you should, then you shouldn't feel bad at all. Each person has a moral compass. Some don't always point to our ideas of North but who says our ideas of North are right?

The term Insane is generally defined as "not sane; not of sound mind; mentally deranged",[86] but, according to Ryan Howes, Ph.D., Insane is not listed as a diagnosis in the Diagnostic and Statistical Manual of Mental Disorders.[87] The field that deals most with what we know as insanity, Psychology, has yet to define the term. There are too many different specifications and levels of derangement to draw a definite line around what should be considered insane. For that matter, what does a term like "mental health" mean? When any outside party has diagnosed a person as having mental health issues, all they are really saying is the person's perspective and/or behavior is different from their idea of a commonly accepted standard.

What we view as inaccurate or even stupid is often just a perspective that is not grounded in our idea of reality. We all constantly have to justify our actions to ourselves, even if it's on a subconscious level. If we truly felt like we willfully acted in an unfair manner to another, then we could not feel justified in expecting others to behave fairly toward us. So, do we think we're bad people or just that we are better than others? I believe we are each born unique but I also believe we all could be capable of even the most heinous acts, given the right circumstance.

We don't even understand when life starts, yet we are so opinionated that we have laws about abortion. I am not condoning abortion or an outlawing of the act. The point is we should hold ourselves to our moral obligation, to not allow ourselves to invent and then regulate laws about

---

86   Insane.
87   "The Definition of Insanity Is . . .," 2009.

things we don't even understand. After all, when life begins would seem to be the true argument behind the abortion dispute. The prolife side argues that abortion is murder while the prochoice side says it's the body of the woman in question and she should be able to do what she wants with it. We are ignoring the one major variable in the argument. We don't know what defines life within a mother's womb.

I think we all can agree it's not right to kill a baby, born or not but at the same time most of us would agree if abortion were simply a prevention of life and not a destruction of it, then it would be a feasible alternative to bearing a child into other than ideal circumstances. We fight because we don't understand and yet refuse to see any side but our own.

Most disagreements come down to speculation or misunderstanding. Some know that to be gay is wrong because it's a choice and the Christian Bible condemns such actions. Others know that homosexuals are born having such tendencies and are not rejecting ideas of Christian faith by being gay but rather often reject such ideas because such ideas first rejected them.

Emotion can temporarily empower a person to take action of which he or she would normally not be capable. A person's first reaction to an emotional situation is usually fueled by emotion. We should attempt to only react to a situation after we have had time to analyze all perspectives and not act out of emotion but this is often easier said than done. Often these rash acts become "crimes of passion." A person who would otherwise not cause damage to any living thing could be guilty of a crime of passion. Should he or she, in turn, be punished?

No person can fully comprehend another's motives; so the first should not pass judgment on the second. Judgment from a governing body is another matter. No one can be morally judged, so no punishment should be dealt for any crime no matter how severe but actions to ensure the prevention of future damages would seem necessary. It is a question of the judge's heart. Repercussions should be reserved for prevention, not for wrath or punishment. If we as the authoritative body, for the purpose of revenge, decide to end someone's life after they end someone else's life, then we are engaging in the same act for which we are dealing punishment.

Murder is defined as, "Law. the killing of another human being under conditions specifically covered in law. In the U.S., special statutory definitions include murder committed with malice aforethought, characterized by deliberation or premeditation or occurring during the commission of another serious crime, as robbery or arson (first-degree murder), and murder by intent but without deliberation or premeditation (second-degree murder)."[88] So common definition of the term murder states that the law is what defines the word.

I have a different definition for the term murder. I believe murder is the willful and unjust, premature ending of a person's physical life. This would include death by a legal ruling motivated by emotion and not analysis.

I believe the forced death of another person motivated by anger is always murder; but the people who commit these crimes are spreading unfairness to the people affected by their crimes. The forced death of another person motivated by the will to prevent future acts of the same tone would seem just and necessary for us to put forth our best effort at giving everyone in this world a chance at equality. We must always remember to try to see things from the other party's point of view.

What of the common idea of an "eye for an eye"? Leviticus 24:19-20 in the Christian Bible says, "If anyone injures his neighbor, as he has done it shall be done to him, fracture for fracture, eye for eye, tooth for tooth; whatever injury he has given a person shall be given to him." The idea of the punishment fitting the crime would seem a just one. I believe taking from someone what he or she has taken from someone else is a fair solution but this poses an awkward question: What is an eye? To the sculptor an eye is very important. He or she needs both eyes to truly understand depth in the world around him or her, which is an important part of sculpting but to the writer, one eye would seem far less important to his or her craft.

What if one eye has already been taken and the loss of a second eye would mean complete blindness? Surely the loss of one's depth perception is not equal to the loss of one's sight. I don't see how this idea of "eye for an eye" could possibly be regulated by humankind. No person tries to do evil and most of the time motives are not even malicious ones. The fact that we can't always understand someone's motives does not make their motives malicious. But when we feel we have done wrong, we should be the first to hold us responsible.

I recently found myself in an auto-lube station waiting room. I sat in a plastic chair next to a small magazine table. The "Boerne Star" newspaper rested on the table. Beside it, a magazine folded open to a page full of black words on a white background. Without removing either from their resting positions I read the stories on the front page of the paper. Lightning had set fire to a house. In a small town, this kind of news is typically the default for a front-page story. A few moments later a customer removed the newspaper for his reading pleasure.

Again I noticed the magazine. I have found it to be a habit of mine to first read the larger quotes that are normally planted somewhere in the

---

[00] Murder.

body of the text to get an idea of the topic of the article. It was about hypocrisy. I dove deeper. The article explained a psychological experiment in which half of a group of people was given two tasks. One was a task with the potential of ease and fun; the other was a slightly more challenging math problem. Each subject in this half of the group was then asked to designate responsibility for the two tasks between him or herself and another member of the group as he or she saw fit. A vast majority chose the easier more playful challenge for themselves. They were then asked to rate on a scale of one to ten how fair they were in delegating responsibility for the two tasks. A majority of the subjects deemed themselves reasonably fair in their delegation. Then the roles were reversed. When the same subjects were asked how fairly they were treated when they received the harder of the two tasks, they responded with considerably lower ratings of fairness. This is hypocrisy in its most basic form.

The experiment was then run again. This time the subjects, before being asked to distribute the tasks, were asked to memorize a group of numbers. When time came to rate the fairness of the distributions the subjects almost always reported they were equally as fair in assigning the harder task as the person assigning the harder task to them was. In keeping the brain occupied with the memorization of the numbers, the subjects blocked the use of their higher brain functions. In the original test the participants' analytical minds were altered by their emotions. In the second, the participants' emotions could not alter their analytical abilities. I have, since reading this article, discovered an online version. This study was performed by psychologists David DeSteno and Piercarlo Valdesolo of Northeastern University and sighted by Sharon Begley in her 2008 article for *Newsweek, Do as I Say, Not as I Do, Hypocrisy requires high-level thinking. In our heart and gut, we're more moral, honest and fair*. If our brains can be manipulated to think analytically, without letting our emotions affect the outcome then we should be able to willfully do the same.

I often hold myself to an unattainable standard but condemnation of oneself is even more ridiculous than condemnation of others. After all, we are the only ones privileged to our specific perspectives. I am often frustrated with myself for not rising to my greatest potential but I need to remember to see things from the perspective I had at the time. I put forth the effort I was willing to. It might have been my best effort or I might have been able to do better but the effort was the product of the conditions preceding and surrounding the effort. My level of effort is a direct product of the inconvenience my effort causes compared to the benefit my personal history has led me to believe I will reap. I will likely endure more inconvenience for a benefit I truly value.

Our personal histories have the potential to affect our will. Personal history builds perspective. We always have a choice of how to use our personal histories to form our perspectives but without personal history our perspectives would be nonexistent. If personal history affects our perspectives and our moral views are based on our perspectives, then there is never a universal right or wrong. Our personal histories change by the second and our perspectives change with them. There is only right and wrong in the moment.

I believe the movie "Memento" illustrates this idea pretty well. The main character wakes each morning with no memory of how he got there or where his many tattoos came from. He uses his tattoos to build a new perspective and a new motivation each morning. He builds his perspective on the personal history he has drawn out for himself on his body. He then develops a will from his recently acquired map of personal history.[89]

No one is perfect, and perfection would seem to be an unrealistic expectation for anyone. Unlike other's actions, we have a much better idea of the motivation behind our own actions. If we can be open mind-ed enough to try to see another person's actions for the motivation behind them then we should have no problem understanding our innocent intensions. Even if our motives were only selfish ones, even if our intent was to do nothing other than cause hurt to another person, the actions were justified in our minds or we wouldn't have performed them.

I believe we are each capable of acts for which we would have no trouble condemning others. I like to think I would be strong enough to perform any act if I knew it to be an act of true justice. I like to think I would be strong enough to perform any act if I knew it to be God's will. I am not talking about murder because "God told me to." The God I believe in would not make such a request. I am talking about acts that would typically be condemned by society but may be justified in a specific setting. We are capable of what we currently view as immoral, because our justification will inevitably change with our perspectives. If no perspective is absolute, then no person can be morally judged for anything in his or her past. This includes actions, ideas and points of view. This includes my own previous perspective and the trouble and pain it caused.

---

[89] 2000.

Chapter Twenty-One

Our Law

I've noticed that different opinions on specific human-made laws are usually accompanied by a difference in moral views. We don't feel we're being unjustifiably selfish. Each person believes his or her way is the only correct way and that the opposing party is being irrational. Laws are meant to rule an entire group of people, not just those who believe in the ideas behind the laws. Many laws are formed out of a desire to govern others actions as a result of moral perspective. But should we allow ourselves to be ruled by laws inspired by moral views? The answer comes down to one's definition of morality. If morality is what is good for us all, then morality should rule. If morality is based on beliefs we adopt out of any desire other than justice then morality should not rule; but who can say what is good for us? We each have different goals and our goals are bound to compete on occasion.

Standing up for what we believe in is necessary. We should not worry about the disagreements we're bound to have with each other. Disagreement is not the problem. Disagreement is the product of diversity and difference. The problem is intolerance and anger over difference. I am not saying there's no absolute right or wrong. There is; but it is internal and specific to the individual. These ideas are products of perspective and therefore, not absolute to anyone but the person who birthed this perspective. The only true measure of morality comes from within.

A human's judgment is flawed and the only absolutely just judgment would be that of an infallible higher power. Our opinions are subject to flaw because they are birthed by an imperfect creator, the human. I cannot definitely state that any opinion is incorrect because I cannot possibly share the exact perspective of the person who birthed the opinion but the idea that there is no wrong opinion is an opinion and therefore, subject to flaw.

Many views on morality are similar but as history has shown, what is popular is not always right. There was a time in the United States when owning another person was socially acceptable. There was a time when the extermination of Germany's Jewish citizens seemed like the correct path for many. There was a time when the majority of the known world knew the globe to be flat. Likewise, what's unpopular is never automatically wrong simply for being unpopular.

Perspective changes a person's idea of what is justifiable. The action may still be labeled "wrong" in his or her mind but when something is justifiable it is simply right, or acceptable in the moment. Because perspective is internal, we can never judge a person as a result of personal views of right and wrong. He or she might see the issue differently.

Still, members of a society affect each other in significant ways. The saying, "No man is an island," was crafted by John Donne in the 1600's,[90] but it is now often sighted as common knowledge. Each of us is connected through our decisions. Even if the offending party feels completely justified in his or her actions, he or she may affect another in a negative way.

I believe in the idea of "live and let live" but a person may, even unknowingly, cause pain or inconvenience. We cannot judge a person for his or her actions; however, we can judge a person's actions as a result of how the actions affect us. When judgment is of a person's actions and not of the person him or herself, the judgment is not of morality but of how we are affected. The difference is the action, as opposed to the person, is the offender.

Judgment of a person inspires anger, while judgment of an action does not. Moral judgment causes pain to the person who does the judging. We can empathize with a perspective. We cannot empathize with an inanimate force like action. Steps may need to be taken to ensure an offender does not take such action in the future but the repercussions are no longer based on judgment for what we view as immorality.

This is why society must have laws but these laws should solely be based on the most common idea of a person's rights. If a person's decisions pose a threat to another person's rights then the person who posed the threat should be deterred from doing something of similar form in the future. Aristotle said, "The law is reason, free from passion."[91] To me this means laws, and repercussions for them, should be formed and carried out solely through logic and not through emotion. Repercussions should not be about exacting revenge but about future prevention of the problematic act. Let's go back to my idea of murder; "the willful and unjust, premature ending of a person's physical life." I believe unjust is the key word. An act can be personally justifiable without being an act of justice by the

---

90   Martin, 1996 – 2008.
91   Aristotle Quotes, 2009.

majority's standpoint. The law is supposed to be a representation of the majority's common moral ideas; therefore, the law should typically be able to define what is just for the majority it is meant to rule. It is the law that should determine repercussions for an outlawed act, not the emotions of the person assigned to carry out the law.

Not all humanmade law is enforced by a judicial system. Social law is not as finite as judicial law. But social law plays an important role in shaping our interactions with each other. Members of a society would seem to put social law in place in an attempt to ensure social fairness to every party. These laws are typically not written anywhere but our brains, and because perspectives differ when it comes to individuals, we each have varied ideas of what is appropriate. Because there is no social police force, because there is no concrete social law, we must attempt to regulate our ideas of social justice for ourselves, not by forcing our opinions on others but by bringing into focus the discomfort certain actions cause. When we bring to light the inconvenience certain actions cause, we should remember the actions that caused the offense were justifiable to the actor. We should not be accusing or condemning but patient and understanding.

These laws are birthed to ensure we all know where the line is and not to cross it; but if these laws worked as they were designed to, so many others and I would not feel uncomfortable as regularly as we do in social situations. I suppose this discomfort comes from the fact that our perspectives differ. The knowledge of these laws without the understanding of where the line is can be burdensome.

We often condemn people for acting in ways we view as inappropriate. The rules have been set out for us and we each have an obligation to those rules. People who act differently are viewed as outsiders. What makes us think normality is necessarily correct? We typically condemn people for behaving in these manners we have deemed inappropriate. Some of the world's greatest minds were considered radicals in their times and yet there is little forgiveness for an adult who behaves differently. Since the beginning of time we have tried to govern ourselves. The flaw in human-made law is the fact that it is absolute. We cannot possibly understand everything in our world; so, what makes us think we can govern what we can't understand?

As a society, we often claim to appreciate individuality and yet we fear anything different. This sounds somewhat contradictory but makes sense. Difference takes us out of our comfort zones. I suppose it is only natural to be uncomfortable with something with which we are unfamiliar. It would make sense that we naturally find comfort in familiar things because, if past events dictate future ones, things of familiarity are more predictable.

By the same logic, things that are unfamiliar are harder to predict. What is unfamiliar is uncomfortable. At the same time I understand why we appreciate individuality. Its history's individuals who have made some of the largest contributions to society. Even so, they were likely ostracized at the time for their seemingly radical thinking to only be celebrated after their theories came to be known as fact.

We, as a society, must learn to use our analytical minds. On March 23, 1933 the German people elected to pass Adolf Hitler's Enabling Act, which, in turn, would make Adolf Hitler dictator of Germany.[92] Our laws are designed to protect the majority members of society from potential discomfort. This could be how we can feel justified in causing certain members discomfort in an attempt to insure the majority is protected; but we often protect ourselves from forces that would never become threats. When we choose to think for ourselves, we should be able to distinguish the Einstein's from the Hitler's.

---

[92]   Gavin, 1996.

Chapter Twenty-Two

Interaction with Other Perspectives

No matter how alone we feel or how much we try to distance our-selves from others, we affect others' lives. Again, no person is an island. Even a person who lives outside of society, miles separated from any other person, has affected another in some way. Most of us are born into a family structure of some kind. If we survived to be adults, we likely had someone care for us at one point in our lives. Even if every person we once knew was now deceased, those people affected people who affected people. We are all connected. Remember the Chaos Theory? This theory is based on aspects of the physical world but it applies to human interaction as well.

If we all have the potential to affect the world around us in significant ways without even the desire to do so then we must decide how we are willing to affect our world. If my effects are inevitable then I am forced to choose whether to attempt a positive effect or a negative one. By product of the Chaos Theory, I could hypothesize that every decision I make today will affect someone, possibly in a significant way. I like the common story originally featured in Loren Eiseley's, *The Star Thrower*. The story tells of a boy throwing beached starfish back to the sea. When another witnesses his efforts in comparison to the huge number of starfish still on the beach, he suggests an apparent futility in the boy's efforts. The boy replies, "It made a difference to that one," as he throws another back to the ocean.[93] If no person is an island then we all have an effect on the world around us.

In the "Condemnation among Humans" section of this writing I recalled finding an article about hypocrisy in a magazine while waiting in an auto-lube station waiting room. When I was in my commute from work to this place of business I was involved in a minor car collision. I was rear-ended while stopped in traffic a few car lengths from a traffic light. When the other driver and I pulled into the nearest parking lot to check

---

93   "The Starfish Story", 2004-2009.

for injuries and damages, I recalled the last minor collision in which I was involved. From my point of view it was no fault of my own but because I had faith in the other driver's goodwill, I didn't bother to call the police. On this occasion we exchanged insurance and continued upon our merry ways. I learned shortly after the incident the other driver was claiming the accident was the result of an error on my part.

Now, over one hundred miles away from the site of that original fender bender, I was cautious enough to request an officer come out to file a report. The other driver was very understanding. We talked while we waited. She apologized several times until I told her I believed everything happened for a reason. She reciprocated. After we exchanged phone numbers and hugged goodbye, I made my way home to Boerne to get my car inspected. When I first sat down, I noticed the magazine and ignored it. It took an act of another's freewill (the removal of the newspaper) to bring my attention to the article. If the man in the auto-lube station had not taken an interest in the newspaper atop the magazine, I likely would not have given the magazine a second glance. This action intertwined our lives. His choice affected my discovery.

I cannot imagine the magazine article that caused such inspiration would have been presented in the way it was when I arrived in the waiting room had I not spent that time beside the busy thoroughfare after the accident. If I hadn't experienced the collision with the person who claimed I was at fault that time before, I likely would not have insisted the other driver involved in this day's collision and I wait for an officer to arrive. This article has yet to be life changing but it was inspiring. I believe we affect each other in less apparent but just as significant ways every day. The only difference in this day and every other day is I was looking for the connection. Perhaps the true power in the happening is in the fact that I can see the connection. It is powerful because I can see the power. This, to me, is a very obvious representation of a magnolia. It is something inside itself.

I believe our connections with other people seep deeper than we would like to believe. The inhabitants of this world, animate and inanimate alike all have energy. Einstein's E=mc2, energy equals mass times the square of the speed of light,[94] would seem to prove this. This equation would seem to state that if an object has mass and we can see it, then it has energy. This is a way of measuring energy by measuring an object's mass. If the physical world is made up of molecules, each having energy, who is to say the energies are not connected? If these energies are connected, this might explain these things like premonition, empathy and coincidence. Premonition, empathy and coincidence may all be products of

---

[94] Willis, 1999.

connection in the physical world. This connection would explain morality through powers of empathy.

Although we often don't understand how we affect each other, we would, at times, seem very aware of others' effects on us. We form systems of categorization in order to more readily deal with other members of our societies. Labels would seem to naturally form as a result of our need to categorize when we are trying to understand others but we apply these labels to ourselves as well. Perhaps this is a way for us to validate our roles by confirming what's expected of us.

We all would seem to do it whether we realize it or not. The most obvious examples of these labels would seem to be the cliques from our high school and middle school days. It would seem common practice for a young person to assume the attributes of a stereotype as a form of identity. The terminology is constantly changing but the self-inflicted stereotypes have not changed much. These stereotypes made statements about what extra-curricular activities we participated in or what kind of music we listened to. Whether we intended it or not, these titles inspired us to distance ourselves from each other.

We, as an adult society, have long outgrown such basic labels but we adults still stereotype and conform to stereotypes. I suppose we all intentionally assume some characteristics of certain stereotypes. We present ourselves and behave in ways representative of things we relate to. To an extent, we even choose our interactions with other members of society in this way. If we recognize most of us make assumptions about a person based on superficial things, then how we present ourselves is a choice about how we want to be received. We don't waste our time on people to whom we feel we could not relate. Often, this judgment is made at first glance.

We adults would seem to place labels on people as well. Maybe it's not as obvious as the teenage labels of geek or stoner but we do it all the same. I suppose, in a way, this subtlety makes the labels more powerful. They are more likely to be viewed as absolute truth, and less likely to be viewed as speculation. The most prevalent adult label used today would seem to be "successful." This label is usually assigned to one who has a rather sizable income. The term "successful" would seem to be short for "successful in business." In modern society, a person's success often determines his or her value and dictates social interaction.

Humans communicate our perspectives, mostly through language. The Shannon-Weaver model of communication identifies five basic parts for audible communication: the source, the transmitter, the channel, the receiver and the destination. In other words, I form my words, I speak them, they travel as sound waves, your brain translates the waves and you understand my intended communication. There is something to be said about nonverbal communication but it would seem that anything more than a very basic perspective typically requires some form of language based communication to be understood. We give power to our words. We birth words and their meanings, so a word only has the power we give it. Any presented perspective is subject to our power of interpretation, because we choose what power to give it. I suppose we give such power to words because language is typically our chosen form of communication. We give words power because we desire the power we give them.

It's been suggested the one thing humankind is most afraid of is public speaking; not something that might be a physical threat, like flying or spiders or even death but public speaking. If we know perspective is flawed, why do we care how others view us? Maybe we care about others' perspectives because we are constantly searching for validation. After all, the only thing that makes our opinions feel validated is a second perspective. But we can never prove to ourselves the second perspective is correct.

Look at Nazism. The ideas of National Socialism (Nazism) were widely accepted when Adolph Hitler was head of the German government from 1933 to 1945. Around 6,000,000 Jewish people were executed for the greater good of Germany. Now Nazism is considered by most to have been absolute evil; so a second perspective would seem to differ greatly from the first. We need validation because knowing we could be wrong makes us uncertain in our actions. So, why do we feel we always need to be right? Perhaps our potential to be wrong causes us to feel helpless against forces in our world. After all, if we cannot understand something, we certainly cannot control it.

Why do we as humans care so deeply about represented opinions of ourselves? Represented opinions are really just strings of words and social interaction to which we give power. When I was in middle school I believed I didn't care what anyone thought of me but I made myself feel this way because this was how my peers told me I should feel. I wanted to not care what others thought of me because the people I looked up to told me I shouldn't. If no person is an island then every person is affected by another's actions. If other's opinions affect how they treat us then it would be wise to try to ensure other's opinions are not negative ones.

We all base our views of the world on our own pasts. We know a certain action will most likely cause a certain reaction. We know from past experience, if we behave in a certain way, we will likely be treated a certain way. We also know, from our own personal histories, that a person's opinion of us affects how they treat us. If we plan to be a part of society, this seems like good motivation to care what others think of us. Still, we must not sacrifice ourselves, our uniqueness in order to fit more readily into our places in society.

Chapter Twenty-Three

Lies

I try my hardest not to put myself in a situation in which I have to lie. It can be very difficult but I've noticed that lies tend to build on top of each other. If I've gotten anything significant about life out of the sitcom, it is the reinforcement of this belief. If art is said to imitate life then we can learn about life by observing art. It may not be the most efficient method of learning but the execution of lies in sitcoms is almost an exaggeration of reality.

Many sitcom stories are formulaic. Many of the formulas are based on the idea of a lie growing out of control. Typically, in my experience of the sitcom, it's the main male character that formulates the initial lie. Then he spends the rest of the episode going to extravagances to avoid honesty. It's entertaining because we viewers see the absurdity in the situation, yet we put ourselves in similar situations when the subject of the lie seems less trivial. I suppose we empathize so easily with the characters because we see ourselves in them.

I believe, when we are dealing with our loved ones, honesty would be the idealistic course of action for any situation. The problem is, as much as honesty is said to be valued in our society, most people don't want absolute honesty. I do see the difference in honesty and bluntness. We can usually be honest about our feelings without being hurtful to others but at the same time, if we want true honesty, we cannot be defensive when the honesty delivers an unflattering view of us. Unfortunately it comes down to the fact that we have trouble accepting a perspective if it differs from our own.

It makes more sense to me to censor my thoughts than to censor my words. If I feel bad for saying something, I should probably feel bad for thinking it, just as, if I don't feel bad for thinking something, I should probably not feel bad for saying it. Too often we are persuaded by the reaction we expect.

Often, we lie to spare someone's feelings and then have to keep lying to keep that first lie valid. These patterns of untruthfulness can lead to distrust and ultimately the destruction of a relationship. On the other hand, telling the truth can be a huge burden too. Most people are happy with their ideas of the world; telling absolute truths from one's point of view can take others out of their comfort zones and even cause insult and regret. I believe careful and sensitive truths are a better alternative than lying to spare everyone's feelings.

Despite my attempts, I still lie to save face. I lie in situations to spare myself from embarrassment. There was a time when I was required to lie on a daily basis for my employer.

Sometimes I was even encouraged to create my own falsity to help them avoid someone or to keep them in other's good graces. I had to be dishonest because others allowed themselves to act dishonestly.

Lies in the business world do seem to make sense from a business standpoint. I once worked as a sales representative for a wholesale furniture company. It was my job to service my accounts based on how much business they gave us. But each account was the most important to its owner.

Most owners or managers would seem to have understood their individual places in my list of priorities. At the same time, they tended to get frustrated or even angry when I could not respond quickly enough. I often had to lie about my priorities to avoid my clients coming to view me as apathetic to their problems. It is a salesperson's job to make a potential buyer feel important. If my inevitable priorities were revealed, these business people would likely have been more inclined to buy from one who made them feel as if they were larger priorities than they actually were. Don't misunderstand, every account was important to me but it seemed like a matter of much more importance to check on an account that did $50,000 worth of business a year as opposed to one that did $6,000.

It's hard sometimes not to lie. Most of the time, in this adult world, when we lie, we are doing so as to not cause conflict. It is rare to lie with malicious intent. But lying, even with good intentions, can reap severe consequences. From what I have learned about sales, a large majority of it would seem dishonest. It's hopefully not dishonesty about the product but a kind of dishonesty that creates a false self. If sales is truly the selling of oneself, then it was my job to make myself as sellable as possible.

As a result of the confidence issues I experienced at the time, this forced charisma sometimes felt very dishonest but then I suppose it would have felt deceitful even if my view of myself were much greater. I had been directed to display a beyond common positive attitude. It was the falsifying of this positive attitude that felt deceitful. But of course, who wants to buy something from a person who seems unsure of him or herself?

I sometimes lie in a purely selfless manner. I lie about my own situation in an effort to avoid inspiring others to pity me. Much of society's courtesy is based on lies. To me, the most apparent incarnation of this can be observed when one asks, "How are you?" In most circumstances, if the question is not answered with the socially imprint-ed, "Good. You?" or a slight modification of the phrase, we don't know how to respond. (It is almost laughable that this socially imprinted response is incorrect when it comes to the laws of grammar. "Good" would be a shortened version of "I am doing good." The correct form would be "I am doing well.")

I recall a period, shortly after having the tumor removed, when I was in a measurable amount of pain throughout the day. I often wanted to respond to the question as honestly as possible without sounding like I was complaining. Then I realized, after a few attempts, I did seem to be complaining. Even if the person asking was truly sympathetic, an honest expression of a less than desirable state was usually not wanted. In our society, the question, "How are you?" is more of a greeting than an inquiry.

So, what is a lie? Most of us were raised to believe lies were bad. This was a very black and white way of looking at things. As we got older we learned about things known as "little white lies"—acceptable if they didn't hurt anyone or if they spared a person's feelings.

The word lie is defined as, "a false statement made with deliberate intent to deceive; an intentional untruth; a falsehood."[95] So, by its def-inition, if the intent to deceive is backed by the intent to spare a per-son's feelings, it's still a lie. If the false statement is made because it's expected by society and is not of the intent to deceive but to be polite, then I suppose the known false statement would not be a lie. We must force ourselves to make efforts to recognize personal motivation behind a false statement. I would like to live in a world where no one lied but until we learn to accept other's beliefs and flaws, and start living honestly, I suppose it's an ideological and unrealistic idea.

---

[95] Lie.

Chapter Twenty-Four

The Competition and Happiness

I suppose life was simpler when it was a competition. When we were young, we always knew where we stood because our quest was for things of this world. He or she who had the most, the newest, or the coolest was the winner. Now we often like to think what we search for is emotional fulfillment. Maybe this search for the intangible is just means to feeling like winners; but those who work for the superficial are petty, aren't they? I consider myself an intelligent person and I believe intelligence often births the desire for things beyond the physical world but I have noticed patterns of materialism in myself.

The term "consumer" can represent two very different ideas. The first of these is illustrated in the following definition: "a person or thing that consumes." The second is illustrated in this second, very different definition: "a person or organization that uses a commodity or service."[96] We often think of the term consumer as it is represented in the second definition but I think the first definition has a lot to do with consumerism. The state of the physical world is temporary. Things of the physical world will inevitably dissolve over time. If we live for things of the physical world, we tend to consume at a higher rate than those of us who do not. If our love is for food, we will eat more. If our love is for television, we will watch more frequently and retire our television set sooner. In this case, the consumer truly consumes.

We are all consumers at one point or another. This doesn't mean we live to destroy; but people who live for money and things of the physical world, inevitably end up becoming consumers (those who consume). The

---

96   2009.

Christian Bible says in 1 Timothy 6:10, "For the love of money is a root of all kinds of evils. It is through this craving that some have wandered away from the faith and pierced themselves with many pangs."[2] If you don't subscribe to the Christian faith, you can still see the wisdom in the passage. When money becomes one's sole purpose, he or she loses sight of anything else. Still, I wonder if these people who focus on physical desires know something I don't. They always know who's winning but more importantly, what they have to do to win.

My attachment to material possessions is bothersome to me but these patterns have become second nature to me now. I believe most things of the physical world are fairly insignificant but we often form emotional attachments to physical things. Even things without sentiment can become a part of our emotional well-beings. We make emotional attachments to that which we desire most and, if physical things are what we desire, these things link to our emotional states. When things of the physical world become a part of our emotional well-beings, they have the power to alter our emotions. We often measure our worth by what we own and a sense of self-worth can have a strong impact on one's emotional state. If we become emotionally attached to things of the physical world, as we inevitably do, then things of the physical world have the potential to be emotionally gratifying.

One definition of "Consumerism" is, "Attachment to materialistic values or possessions: deplored the rampant consumerism of contemporary society."[3] Although a certain attachment to material things would seem necessary to our survival (We cannot survive without sustenance.), excessive attachment to material things would seem to emotionally handicap us. I believe my gravitation toward materialism inhibits me from being all I could be. My desires are that of the spiritual world but I often catch myself thinking of things in the superficial sense, "What will I gain by this? Could I have better than what I have? Am I winning?" I constantly have to remind myself of the lack of fulfillment these things have brought me in the past but I suppose it is easier to measure success in tangible things than it is to measure it in fulfillment. Still, if we desire happiness then we should focus on things that truly make us happy and not on ones that simply pacify an emotional void.

Another definition of "Consumerism" is, "The theory that a progressively greater consumption of goods is economically beneficial."[97] This definition tickles me a little bit. To me, this means consumerism exists only to enable itself to exist. A more stable economy means more jobs means more purchasing means more jobs. Although, I suppose

---

[2]   English standard version, 2001
[3]   2009
[97] 2009.

without a stable economy, it becomes harder to afford the physical things we need to survive. The threat of nonexistence would seem to have the potential to make most people emotionally uneasy. Still, there's a fine line between survival and gluttony.

When I was in my teens, my father had me listen to a series of motivational tapes authored by the speaker Tony Robbins. The most prevalent bit of knowledge I absorbed was represented by a sentence he repeated rather frequently, "Repetition is the mother of skill." It really seemed to be a new representation of the much older and well-known saying "Practice makes perfect." Our actions become habits. Our habits become a part of who we are. We live for what we care about and we care about what we live for. If our focus is in the superficial world and we surround ourselves with superficial things, we become superficial beings. If we focus on things that can't be measured as easily as one's monetary success then these things become a part of who we are.

I suppose, if we plan to be a part of our society and must worry about outside perspectives we should be priming our lives with the attitudes and ways of the things we desire. If we are dealing with someone who cares about superficial things, then it's beneficial to be wealthy in the superficial. I suppose it really comes down to our goals, what we feel will make us happy. If we want things of the superficial world then, logically, we should focus on superficial things, so we will have something superficial to offer in exchange for superficial things we desire. Likewise, if we want things that can't be bought, like enlightenment or faith, then we should focus on these things to encourage growth in these areas.

I can only truly know what will make me happy and I have yet to really understand that completely. "The Competition", to me, may seem insignificant and even illogical at times but my perspective allows me these opinions. Other's perspectives may not inspire the same conclusions.

Chapter Twenty-Five

Rocky and the Punch Drunk Consequence

Shortly after the tumor experience the understanding that I had little control over my life was reinforced. I learned, in this state, to accept things as they were because I truly felt powerless against the forces that put these consequences in place. My motivations were not those of the people close to me and my desires seemed to be taking a backseat to the desires of the ones I loved. This was when my unfortunate condition stopped being a reason for special care on the parts of others and became the inconvenience it caused.

Sometime after my very brief, "so good luck" conversation with my father, my sister moved into a house with some friends and took my dog Rocky for a little while but she didn't have funds for the pet deposit so he ended up back with me at my mother's house, in the cage and very lonely. I was forced to make flyers to see if I could find a home for him. I didn't want to give him up. He was my only friend during a very bad time but he was not happy.

I found blood on the carpet near his cage at one point. There was a night a couple weeks after that when I released him from the backyard into the house to put his incessant barking to rest. We went to my bedroom and I opened his cage door. He gratefully walked in and I closed the door behind him. When I left the room, he started crying almost immediately. It went against the patterns I had formed but I learned to ignore him. He was either crying in his cage inside or outside barking to be let in. The suburban neighborhood my mother lived in was not the ideal place to have a loud pet.

One evening I heard a quick scratching sound coming from my bedroom. I went in to see if I could remedy the situation. Rocky was in a panic, frantically digging at the plastic floor of his kennel. I tried to comfort him with words but he wouldn't calm down. As much as I wanted to ease his frantic state, I had little power to do so. He couldn't spend more than a moment on my mother's floor and he wouldn't be the quiet pet of suburbia I would need him to be to allow him to occupy the backyard at that moment. When he finally put the tantrum to rest, he immediately reverted to wearing a smile. I believe the blood I noticed before on the carpet near his cage must have been from an injury he acquired while trying to dig himself out on some other night.

He was my friend but more importantly I was his dad. I had to do what was best for him no matter how badly I would miss him. For a little over a month, I had been looking, at a somewhat casual pace, for a home for him. All at once, my girlfriend offered to keep him at her apartment. She had been talking about getting a dog so I didn't impose my need for Rocky on her but she had offered to keep him instead of getting one of her own.

The next day she went to a "no kill" shelter with her mother "just to look" and fell in love. She called me and told me she had a new puppy. "Shink" my defensive walls shot up. What would happen to my friend? She would later tell me she assumed there wouldn't be a problem with keeping both of them there. After a closer observation of her lease agreement she realized her dog along with her roommate's cat put them at the maximum pet occupancy for their apartment. Luckily, her landlady understood my situation and decided he could stay anyway. My desires seemed to be going by the wayside. They only seemed to be considered in situations like this when they didn't interfere with another's desires.

One night I woke my mother after realizing my younger brother and his even younger friend were nowhere to be found. I first, of course, called my brother's cell phone. He didn't answer. When I finally resorted to waking my mother, I approached her with love but my softened actions still startled her. I told her everything was fine and that I was only wondering where my brother was. She confirmed he and his friend weren't supposed to be in the house, as they were staying at the friend's house that night and I apologized.

The next morning she woke me. The first thing I remember was, "I'm very mad at you!" I looked up and said with a certain nonchalance, "I'm sorry." I had yet to understand my offense. She explained that I had no reason to wake her and that she could not manage to go back to sleep afterward. I wasn't drawn in by her anger but explained my perspective, that I wanted to ensure my brother and his younger friend were not roaming the streets. She dismissed herself and I returned to my slumber. The huge consequence I'd recently faced trivialized anything of this smaller magnitude.

Before he went to stay with my girlfriend, Rocky's panic from behind his cage door had become an unexpected part of life. I empathized but was still very disconnected from any negative feeling that accompanied my empathy. I was punch-drunk and immune to the consequence of daily life. I experienced this lack of consequence when I ended my relationship with Nine. I decided one day that I was done. I felt like I was neglected and, though the assumed neglect caused hurt, it was somewhat expected and not nearly as hurtful as it was in the world before the tumor.

A few months ago Rocky became very ill. He vomited quite a bit. Not to mention the bloody stools he passed. When his wellness finally won over the money we didn't have, he could no longer willingly use his legs. We carried him to the back seat of my car by the corners of the blanket on which he had been lying. The doctor suggested we have him hospitalized but this was definitely not in our budget. My girlfriend and I had been living in Arizona, away from the family, and I'd recently lost my job. The doctor called after running some tests and told me that

Rocky had developed pancreatitis. The doctor said that such a condition really did require hospitalization but that, if I couldn't afford it, a boiled rice and hamburger diet would have to suffice. We changed his diet and he seemed to be doing better.

A week ago today, he began showing the same symptoms. He vomited up his rice breakfast, so I put him out on the porch. When I went to check on him I noticed pools of bloody fecal matter. I brought him inside to the blanket he'd used many times before and he lay there while I worked on this book. I thought this was simply a symptom of his pancreatitis and hoped it would pass soon. I tried finding information about his symptoms but little was available. I did speak with a vet who stated he needed to be seen in a professional setting but I had less than

$100 in my bank account and knew I would have no way of paying the bill.

Up to this point he had been panting and didn't seem to be in any pain. Then the signs of pain started. We couldn't afford to make him better and wondered if euthanasia would be the best option. I sat on the floor stroking his head as I waited for my girlfriend to get off work. Rocky tried to stand and, almost immediately, toppled into the nearby TV stand. I saw myself in him. His will and his body were disconnecting. I had tried to fight it but at that point my empathy took hold. This had been me those few years before when I dealt with symptoms of the tumor.

I apologized for waiting so long and hurried to my car. I pulled up to the curb outside of our apartment and left the back door of the car cracked in hopes I could swing it open when I got back with Rocky. I would have to carry him. In a panic I rushed back into the room where he lay. I realized I couldn't possibly open the car door while carrying him. I knocked on the neighbor's door but got no answer. Then I went back to the car and opened the door as wide as it would go. I rushed back in to gather him up.

His eyes were open and his tongue was protruding. I said his name and stroked his head. He had died in my scramble for the car.

What a whimsical innovation, the pet. Originally the animal served as either friend or food to the human. Now we pay money for the unconditional love they give; that is until it becomes an inconvenient relationship. Then we often discard this living being as the burdening thing we've grown to see it as. Having a pet is a way of owning an intimate relationship. Perhaps we feel we have to own our relationships for fear of being hurt by one. I've heard of people who would seem to prefer the company of animals, people with twenty cats and no human family. Maybe these relationships are just easier. The only expected return on the animal's love is food and occasional affection.

We decided that, because we would one day return to Texas, we could not leave him here, so we had him cremated. He's now sitting on the shelf in the living room. It's interesting to me now that his loneliness was such an impactful influence on his state of happiness. He was physically cut off from the world outside of his cage. I, on the other hand, have cut myself off socially. The belief that most others view my perspective of the world as absurd has caused me to distance myself from others. This only proved to strengthen my empathy for my friend.

Chapter Twenty-Six

My Own Personal God

Once, during my rebellious stage of adolescence, my father encouraged me to explore my copy of the Christian Bible. I was not too eager to comply, considering my recent proclamation of Atheism. My father knew I no longer carried the strong faith I had as a young child. He told me that, despite my views of theology, the moral lessons in the Bible were still right. I believe he was right and now, despite the many problems with the modern incarnation of the Christian church, I still believe the basic teachings of Christianity are good. While I cannot say with absolute certainty that anything other than my perspective exists, I have great personal proof of the existence of a higher power.

The tendency toward familiarity I mentioned earlier in this book works as personal evidence of the existence of a creator. Let's go back to the rock in the ground. It becomes rooted in the ground as a result of the time it has spent there. This very closely mimics the idea that humans become comfortable and become rooted in common feelings or habits, even if they're negative feelings or habits. These two examples would seem to be the products of two unrelated systems behaving in a very similar way. If these systems were the products of a single creator then their similarities should be no surprise. It would make sense that a creator's works would resemble each other at times.

I mentioned earlier in this writing that I have physically felt what some would call "the hand of God". I am reluctant to use phrases like "hand of God" because of the stigma that comes with any commonly used phrase. A phrase like that often loses the meaning of its original reference and becomes the ideas we relate to it. Still, what I felt was a physical incarnation of God's will moving in me.

My grandmother saw that I was depressed and prayed with me to remove the "spirit of depression." As she expelled the spirit, "in the name of Jesus Christ", I felt it physically leave me. After the extracting feeling of this spirit leaving me, I felt instantly, physically lighter. She explained to me that in order to keep the spirit away I had to change my habits. She said these spirits are constantly looking for a home and that, unless I took measures, it would be back.

Whether this was a spirit in the sense that we like to think of them or simply a physical, chemical incarnation of emotion, the experience affected me greatly. There is no greater proof to me that the spiritual and physical worlds are connected. I have heard we are not supposed to need proof of a higher power's existence, that we are supposed to rely on faith alone but I am a scientist by nature. This incident is my greatest personal proof that God is not a creation of the human mind. Of course we will always have freewill and this includes the will to ignore any personal evidence of the existence of God.

I suppose, knowing what I know about the human brain, I could theorize that what I perceived as the physical incarnation of God's will was simply a psychosomatic feeling. I felt it because I wanted and expected to feel it. This could be no different from a recovering heroin addict going into a psychosomatic high after being stuck with a syringe needle containing no heroin—which I've heard happens—or a group of college students becoming inebriated from imbibing tonic water.

I suppose it all comes down to will. I want to use the information I have as evidence that I am not talking to myself when I talk to God. It's not manipulation. The information is open to interpretation because there is no profoundly correct perspective. A feeling does not amount to be evidence as anything to anyone but the person who has the feeling.

Look at premonition. A person can have an undeniable feeling without any proof of its validity and know in his heart that the feeling is accurate. In a world where nothing is absolutely absolute, feelings, ideas, and perspective are all we have. I suppose I came about the need for belief in a higher power when I thought I might die but now I can't imagine my perspective without it. I could choose to dismiss any belief in a higher power, excusing it as a product of suggestion but I am not as alone and purposeless now as I felt without it.

I have found the statement about spirits returning if habits are not changed to resist them to be true in situations that I don't necessarily consider to be spirit-driven situations as well. I smoked cigarettes for years. I started smoking on "special occasions" as a treat when I was thirteen and fourteen. I started smoking habitually when I was fifteen. In February of 2007, when I was twenty-two, I had my last cigarette to date.

I believe I accomplished this through a few channels. Shortly after my health problems my grandparents were incredibly gracious and bought me a new car. I was a smoker at the time but would not smoke in it for hope of resale value. Since the tumor operation, the first cigarette of each day tended to make me dizzy and sick to my stomach. When I started my new job in January of 2007, I wanted to try my absolute hardest to succeed. Part of me wanted to be the man my dad was trying to make me. I wouldn't allow myself to smoke while at work. Eventually I spent enough time not smoking that the majority of my cigarettes were the first of the day.

After that I still stubbornly tried to continue smoking, despite the fact that I had so recently survived cancer. It was a part of who I was. Eventually I ended up with what I would assume was an aphthous ulcer (canker sore) in my mouth and decided to take it one cigarette at a time. I convinced myself I didn't want that next one because it would likely cause discomfort and probably make me sick. I changed my physical habits as well as my thinking habits; but the canker sore almost feels like a loving father's slap upside the head, "You already had cancer. You enjoyed it enough to try it again?"

We often treat the idea of God as the kid with the trampoline in the neighborhood where we grew up. We subscribe and adhere in an effort to win favor and earn our way to a happy afterlife. I often hear people talking about "getting into heaven" and even rating a person's heaven or hell-worthiness. We can't willfully buy good will from God through our actions because he, she, or it knows our motivation. If our actions could buy good will from God, it would be the actions without the intent of creating good will that would do so. My purpose in this world is out of love for others and a debt I feel I owe. I am grateful for every insignificant hour that I have been given. It's my job to make these hours significant.

I occasionally consider ending my life in an arguably rational way. I have weighed some of the pros and cons of living and dying. There are great parts of my life of which I will enjoy seeing the future incarnation but at the same time, the inescapable, physical pain accompanied by this feeling of inconsequent and monotony in my daily life has me looking for an escape.

Somewhere between moving out of my parent's house when I was seventeen and moving in to my mother's house after the tumor, I lost my sense of home. Home used to be where my parents lived. It was the place I sometimes hated but knew I was always welcome. I suppose this loss is just a part of growing up but it was also likely the power behind the dream I mentioned in "Dad, The Aftermath." I was home in this dream state.

I believe my true home is waiting for me when I die. I have occasionally considered the possibilities of willingly going to my true home. Sometimes the troubles of my own mind accompanied by the troubles of my damaged body have felt like they were all too much for me.

I usually store ideas for this writing in my phone. I usually use the T9WORD function when I am entering these but it does not always work the way I want it to. The other day I was driving home and had an idea. The sentence I was trying to spell was "The absence of a feeling of home makes me want to go home." The sentence I started writing was "The absence of a feeling of home makes of want to in" I deleted the word "in" and tried again without the T9WORD. This time it capitalized the "g" in "Go." I left it and finished the sentence. A few minutes ago I had just finished writing about and deleting another idea when another headache came on. I closed my eyes in an attempt to dull the pain and thought, "I am so tired of this." When I opened them I saw the words "Go home." The automatic scroller under the notepad option of my phone had frozen.

Was this a sign from God? I don't agree with the popular theory that suicide automatically deems a person hell-worthy. I believe God's understanding is too vast for us to comprehend; but I understand where the theory of automatic condemnation for the taking of one's own life came from. "Thou shalt not murder" is one of the big ten. If a person breaks a commandment while dying, he or she does not have the ability to ask for forgiveness for his or her actions; but I don't believe we have to ask for forgiveness to avoid an afterlife of torment.

In "Christian", the Adjective III (The Royal Law) I mention the "Save" option I used daily when making my awkward transition from childhood to my teenage years. I swore every day, because I thought it sounded cool, and then asked for God's forgiveness every night. If God counted every supposed sin against us, I suspect not one of us would avoid an afterlife of torture.

As for now, I cannot be certain the "Go home" incident was an act of God. I would hate to be wrong and not live out the plan in place for me. Still it's strange that a group of people who claim to know that the afterlife is a happy one can view people who have the desire to end their worldly lives as mentally ill.

A while back I wrote a song called "Spectacle Of Misery." At the climax of the chorus are the lines "The sun is always in my eyes. If only I could see the son." The other day I was driving to my mother's house and feeling very alone. I spoke to my idea of God, expressing the presence of this lonely feeling and as I pulled into my mother's neighborhood, the trees covering my view cleared and the vast sky filled with bright pink clouds lined with white. The beauty filled me and I no longer felt alone. I think that, along with easing my loneliness, God was giving me new perspective. The two lines from "Spectacle of Misery" mentioned above no longer have the meaning they did when I wrote them. The "sun" was the offender, while the "son", or evidence of the presence of God, was the object of my desire. In the moment I broke free of the trees' obstruction, the two, the sun and the son, became one positive thing.

Recently I was witness to something I feel was proof of something beyond this world. I have always felt very close to one of my cousins. I've been in her presence when she claimed to visually witness things that are not of this world. I was told that the night my grandmother passed away, this cousin, for no apparent reason, began to bawl around 1:30 in the morning. Around 3:30 the house received a telephone call letting them know our grandmother had had an accident.

Grandma passed away shortly after that.

Then there was debate about what to do with her remains. The remaining at home cousin spoke with her father via telephone. She calmly expressed that Grandma acknowledged "the necklace." My grandmother's daughter knew right away that she was referring to the necklace she had on, the one Grandma had given her as a gift. She also said Grandma had no preference regarding where her remains were to be kept. According to her mother, my cousin had no way of knowing she was wearing that necklace. This is not absolute proof something beyond this world exists.

The skeptic could find many "What if's" in my story but this was proof for me. This was proof because I felt it to be authentic. Really, this is the only form of proof that exists. In their most basic forms, the only truths we have are personal truths.

I have recently been exposed to the idea that this was not my grandmother's spirit but was, in fact, a demon. This theory comes from translation of biblical verses like Ecclesiastes 9:5, which would seem to say that the dead are not conscious of anything. I have only heard this idea expressed alongside the idea that a day of judgment is coming and the Earth will be restored to perfection as portrayed in John 5:28-29 and Revelation 21.[1] Perhaps this is true. The spirit did say she was trying to figure out where she was supposed to go. I can see how this statement could bring doubt about what a person has heard about the afterlife.

If it is true the dead are not conscious of anything then "home" will have to wait; but what is time to one who cannot think and is not conscious of anything? The transition from this life to an afterlife would likely seem instantaneous.

To add to the proof that a person with a scientific mind, such as myself, desires, a while back I witnessed another happening that seemed to be a product of God's will. I had spent a lot of time analyzing my situation with my father. Our communication problems are just one factor that has led to this great void between us. Another factor that contributes to this void is the fact that my father's form of shown love is usually monetary. Because my eye problems make it difficult to read for extended periods of time, I often use the "Speech" option in my word processor. I

---

[1] English standard version, 2001

was editing an article before this one when I noticed something inaccurate with the spoken voice. Where there was clearly typed "Proverbs 20:21", I heard the voice say "Proverbs 8:21 p.m." I stopped the speech program and had it reread it several times. Each time it said, "Proverbs 8:21." I understand now that the computer was simply reading the numbers as military time and converting them to the 12-hour clock. Still it was perplexing to me at the time. I looked up the verse and this is what was written, "That I may cause those that love me to inherit substance; and I will fill their treasures."[2]

I suppose verses mean different things to us at different times. This verse would seem to clearly be talking about love for God but it seemed like more than a coincidence that I would be led to this verse at this time. It said, ."..those that love me to inherit substance . . ." This seemed to be referring to physical inheritance for love. I have recently come to realize that I had cited the wrong verse in the spot my word processor misread. I was quoting 18:21 but wrote 20:21. It is interesting that this particular verse would be the focus of this quandary and the words spoken by my computer would so closely resemble the verse number I meant to record.

I recently experienced another happening that seemed to be a work of God. Again, I was using the Speech option to review my work. This time it misread a Romans passage number. I looked up the passage that it read, Romans 2:10 and, before I was done editing for the day, stumbled across the exact place it fit in my line of reasoning in "Christian, the Adjective II." I was struggling with the message featured in Exodus 34:13, the idea that God would want us to act with such disregard for other's beliefs. Then I was faced with Romans 2:10, which would seem to state that peace should be with everyone, despite their beliefs.

It really comes down to what we're willing to believe. If we're not willing to believe something, we always have the ability to morph our view of it. This holds especially true for a thing as abstract as the Christian Bible can seem to be. We are always left with our speculation and skepticism. It will always come down to personal proof; and personal proof can be manipulated by desire.

---

[2] King James Version

Chapter Twenty-Seven

An Intended Beautiful End

A friend of mine, whom we'll call Buckley, has an admitted romance with the idea of using heroin. He's a huge fan of music and is an aspiring musician as well. He once said he believes this "romance" exists because many of his idols have died from heroin use. What will come of my memory when I pass? If I die young, I will be missed. I suppose whether I will be missed if I live to be old will depend on what I do with the rest of my life.

I've heard love is unconditional. Is time a condition? Maybe the theory that love is unconditional comes from the idea that we can't help but still feel love for someone we once loved when we think of him or her. If love were truly unconditional we would not be able to distance ourselves from those we once loved.

How do we grow to love someone? It is strange to think an emotional permanence can have a beginning in the constantly fluctuating chemicals of the human brain. I don't suppose love ever really fades but I know it changes. I believe my mother's love for my father changed the moment she realized he hit me. I also believe my father's love for my mother changed the moment he found out she wanted a divorce.

Maybe, if we become distant from those who love us, it's not because they love us less but because the love between us has changed. I have lost what feels like many loves in my life and I suspect I will lose more before I leave this Earth. Many of the people I once had love for don't even seem now like the people I knew. Over time they added pieces to make up who they are today, as I have done for myself . . .and the love between us changed. They are still the same people I love; I just receive them differently now.

I've recently come to the realization that this writing has been, in a big way, a confession of my sins and a declaration of my beliefs. I have admitted to the trespasses I've found most significant, the past misdeeds over which I have really agonized. Perhaps the only sins that really matter in the eyes of our creator are the sins we feel bad about. If other so called sins were a problem, I believe God would let them weigh on my conscience. I've suggested the world I live in is a state of limbo. What if this is a much more literal limbo, the limbo of Catholicism? Maybe this is my chance to confess my sins and hold myself accountable before I move into the afterlife.

I've started to experience problems that could very well be signs of a recurring tumor. The other night I was driving on the freeway when my equilibrium violently and suddenly shifted, telling me the road was on a sharp incline. After a few seconds, the feeling receded. I have been in a fairly dizzy state for the past two days. When standing I am hesitant to close my eyes for fear I'll lose my perspective of up and down and end up falling victim to gravity. Once gravity takes control, it can be hard to reverse it.

I have experienced similar symptoms since my experience with cancer began but these feelings are lately more insistent. I'm not in more pain. These feelings just seem more profound. Perhaps this idea of "limbo" is more closely related to its common use. Maybe I am almost done with my work here. I've heard a person who has had cancer is more likely to develop cancer a second time than a person who hasn't had cancer is to develop cancer at all.

Since I first theorized the growth of a second tumor I've noticed a rare occurrence in myself, a smile on my face. My random spurts of pain have caused happiness. At first I thought this was simply the effect of self-destructive habits. Then I supposed the joy in my pain was for the potential opportunity to go home. Even if this world were not a creation of my overactive imagination, a tumor to end the life a tumor began, the life I started living after the tumor, would be great symmetry. God, the artist, has created beauty in symmetry. Whether this world is "the real world" or a fabricated one, it would be a beautiful ending.

I've been told the first tumor couldn't have killed me; it only made life difficult. It's likely the development of another will not end my stay on Earth; but why the happiness if it will only cause more pain? Perhaps this smile is much like the enthusiastic "Yes!" I gave when I was originally diagnosed. If I can't stop it then I'm not going to fight it. If I'm not going home then I welcome the challenge. I will do my best. Also, when I was in the hospital with the first tumor everyone, including my recently divorced parents, came together for my sake. My flaws didn't matter. I felt truly unconditional love from everyone close to me, including the loved ones who otherwise seemed judgmental.

In spite of my theorizing, my most recent MRI shows no signs of a recurring tumor. These seemingly profound signs of oncoming trouble are, apparently, just aftermath of the tumor from 2004. It's been several years and I'm still dealing with lingering problems. Still, I suppose it was selfish of me to want to go home. I blinded myself with my own pain. I didn't want to see the pain it would have caused.

I felt I was alone in this world. My connections with everyone I loved were distant. I suppose my self-esteem distanced me. I thought I was protecting the people I loved by not allowing them to be connected to me. I still feel I don't have much to offer. It's not that I'm not a good person, or even worth the love of others, it's the fact that I would not enjoy being with someone like me in a social setting. I tend to, at times, live inside my brain. I often have little to say in a social situation. I'm lost in a sea of thought, melancholy, and/or, pain but despite my efforts and view of myself I would have been missed.

It would seem, when we die, we all turn into saints in the eyes of the living. People's views of the recently deceased, in my experience, can be much greater than the views held when the person was alive. The day I attended Allen's funeral, I hadn't talked to him in years. I hadn't wanted to hear from him. When we parted ways years before, he seemed like too much drama for me to want to deal with. I didn't really even respect him but shortly after he died I felt I would miss him.

If I were to die, especially of a force I couldn't control, I would be, not only missed but, in a way, glorified for my acts when I was living. Perhaps my sometimes-welcoming attitude toward death is backed by the desire to be bigger than I otherwise could be. I suppose the star of a funeral is always the one in the casket. I thought I was done but I believe I'm still here for a reason. I suppose I still have more to learn. I could go at any time but anyone could. I have faith in God's judgment. I am here to grow.

Chapter Twenty-Eight

The Incredible Human Brain
(Change your Mind)

Our brains form our perspectives, and our brains are much more competent than our analytical perspectives would often lead us to believe. Our analytical perspectives tend to view the world in the metaphorical black and white; but I have personal proof that my perspective is capable of several shades of grey.

I have quite a bit of control over my brain function. There are things of the subconscious mind that can be harder to control but I'm the master of my brain. I stopped eating what I would consider "fast food" a few years ago. Its appeal left me much in the way the appeal of cigarettes was removed from my brain. The motivation behind the removal of fast food from my diet was partly health related. I also found I tended to feel better physically and emotionally without it as a part of my diet. I still eat at sandwich shops and places of that nature but I've erased that fried, grease-drenched food we often relate to fast food from my diet.

A few months after my banishment of the food, I ate at one of these establishments out of the necessity that sometimes comes with a busy schedule. It tasted of grease and chemicals. My brain had refiled the food. Recall the brain files I discuss in "Condemnation among Humans", "one hundred files inside one thousand folders inside one million folders." After a time of avoiding fast food, it moved to another folder in my brain. No longer is fast food viewed as a remedy for hunger. These buildings have become, for the most part, faceless in my mind. They are like specialty shops dealing with hobbies that are of little interest to me.

I awoke this morning with the memory of a dream I'd experienced in the early morning hours. Like many of my dreams, I was in a school-like setting but this setting had a strong feeling of prison as well. I was in a small room in what seemed to be the rear yard of the facility. There were several people with me in this small enclosure. We didn't seem to have a purpose for being there other than to socialize. Woody was there with me. He had arranged for me to trade a, now dysfunctional gun I owned and some cash for a working gun with a person there about whom I felt somewhat uneasy.

Woody and I talked about the exchange to be when I realized I didn't have sufficient funds in my wallet. The person with whom I was trading would surely kill me if I were unable to honor our agreement. I told Woody I needed to get to an ATM. He showed me a line of ATMs but none belonged to my bank.

I blacked out and regained consciousness walking around inside the main building, in a giant courtroom area. I was in a huge daze. I knew I'd planned on shooting someone with the gun that I'd planned on trading for. I also knew the gun was supposed to be hidden in the trashcan I was heading toward. As I pulled off the lid, my mother was standing beside me. She wanted to know what I was looking for. I said someone was supposed to leave a book for me. So, to keep up appearances, I dug around in the trashcan with my right hand. Meanwhile the gun was concealed, fixed to the bottom of the trashcan lid in my left hand.

She turned to look in another direction but stayed near me as to keep an authoritative presence. I reached into the lid and pulled out the gun. The handle felt of plastic. I was still in too much of a daze to give it any thought. I saw the person I was to kill in the lower level of the room. It was surrounded by a metal fence. He walked toward another man, gun drawn. I raised my weapon and pulled the trigger twice but my ears were deaf to the shots. I walked around the enclosed area to the other side to see that the job had been done. Both men were lying on the floor, one face down and one on his back. A gun lay on the floor next to them.

In my dream state, I knew I'd shot the first man, despite the fact that I was wielding a plastic gun that did not fire audible shots. The reality of my perspective within this dream was very real.

So what is real? Our realities are based on how we interpret signals sent to our brains. In this dream I was capable of murder. This was not one of those dreams in which I saw myself acting out unmotivated acts. Even though I couldn't understand my motivation, I was motivated. I believe that, under the right circumstances, anyone could take a life.

The human mind is constantly changing. As mentioned in "Christian", the Adjective I (Homosexuality is Gay), parts of our brains grow and shrink as a result of how we use them. This ability to form a human's brain through action in the physical world would seem to be the force behind certain actions in everyday society. Physical repercussions following a willful act on our part, like the spankings most of us remember from childhood, would seem to be meant as a deterrent for future acts of a similar nature. Presumably, the brain relates the act with the pain that followed it. If the administered pain did its job then the brain has built a link between the action and the pain.

I'm reminded of Aldous Huxley's "Brave New World." In the second chapter he paints the picture of a futuristic, dystopian nursery. Nurses are, under the command of the D.H.C (Director of Hatcheries and Conditioning), setting out tightly packed bowls of roses and open books which present vividly colored pictures of nature between the bowls. Then, again under the command of the D.H.C., nurses bring in several eight-month-old infants. When they are turned to face the books and flowers, the babies light up with excitement and scurry toward the bright objects. The babies' rewards for such interest are a sudden deafening alarm and an electric shock through the very floor on which their bodies rest. When the bells and electrical shock stop they are offered the flowers and books. This time the babies cower from them and scream. The purpose of this system was to ensure the children would grow into adults who cared little for nature.[1] Of course this is a fictitious example but it would seem to be true to a widely accepted view of mental conditioning.

A person who is suddenly separated from the comforts of society may experience a significantly altered perspective. If the brain changes shape and size when it's made to focus on certain tasks then it likely creates new links to aid survival as the brain analyzes new experiences that relate to survival. The brain is no longer focused on the daily hurdles of society but how to survive. Its patterns are changed in order to sustain life and to even maintain sanity.

I've heard of cannibalistic acts committed by people who would otherwise seem incapable of such things. Their minds were simply in a different state from that of their minds while they filled their place in society. In circumstances that exceed a person's perception of normalcy, the human brain is capable of extraordinary things. This, in turn, can make the body capable of foreign behavior. I've heard adrenaline can cause superhuman strength. I know from personal experience that the body can behave differently when it's the focus of physical strain.

Emotions affect our perspectives. Emotions are inspired by physical influences in the brain, like serotonin and dopamine. If our perspectives form in our physical brains, then perspective is a physical thing. The physical incarnations of our freewill are our physical bodies, which allow us to manipulate the physical world. If we are accustomed to the ability to manipulate the physical world then why would we not be able to manipulate our perspectives, which have physical incarnations in the physical world?

---

[1] 1932

If our perspectives are so malleable and our perspectives define the world for us, what is it that makes us so confident our individual ideas of the world are accurate?

Chapter Twenty-Nine

Anger and Sadness

In my mind, rebellion stands against something. There is purpose behind it. Many young people would seem to get lost in the anger associated with rebellious ideas they are taught and don't see the rebellion is usually spawned by love. If someone is rebelling, it is usually against oppression of some kind. Therefore the act of rebellion is an act of love for freedom and for oneself.

Anger behaves like a disease. There is a source, a host, and a recipient (potential host). I have found that, when we let anger grow enough in ourselves, there's little room for any other emotion. Just as cancer does, anger tends to take over anything that was there before it, if we let it. Anger often blinds us from other's innocence. Emotion, good and bad, affects our analytical abilities and changes our perspectives. Emotion is often absent of rationality and yet it affects our analytical perspectives a great deal. Just as cancer behaves, anger spreads, first affecting our perspectives then our analytical abilities, our abilities to form perspective.

To be angry about a person's mistakes, shortcomings, or point of view would seem absurd but we do it. Not one of us is perfect but for some reason, we are often filled with anger when a person makes a mistake. Maybe it's because we assume carelessness is to blame but this mistake could easily have been our own in a different situation. No matter how I try, I will mess up but remorse for imperfection is as unfounded as condemnation for imperfection.

Anger only hurts the person who is angered and the people who empathize with the angered person. I recently found myself working as a phlebotomist in a doctor's office. She rarely seemed happy. She put on a smile for her patients but I believe she was probably just generally unhappy. I suppose this could go without saying but something significant happened the last day I worked for her.

I was trying to process the samples I'd just collected the moment before so I wouldn't confuse them with the samples I was about to collect. Perhaps I was taking longer than others before me had. She was furious, and while she didn't yell, I physically felt her anger. This was a jump from one person's emotional energy to another's physical sense of touch. The sensation could be excused simply as a rush of adrenaline but this was not typical of my previous experiences with adrenaline. This physically felt dirty. Common reaction to an interaction like this is to become angered but I refused to be offended. I saw the pain her anger seemed to cause her and felt pity instead.

If I can understand it, I can choose not to be angry or sad about anything outside myself. Perhaps my ability to dismiss these negative feelings is the product of the fact that the world since the tumor was removed would seem to pose little consequence. If nothing in my world is of serious consequence then nothing really matters. If nothing matters then the experience of pain over a happening in this world would seem illogical. Our temporary emotional states are largely based on our reactions to and interpretations of past events. We may be sad for expected future events as well but our emotion is in this moment.

I know I affect my emotional state simply by the power of memory. A happy memory inspires the release of chemicals in the brain that evoke a sense of euphoria. Happiness is accomplished without any provocation from the external world. If I choose to remember a happy memory then I can choose to be happy in the moment.

We have programmed automatic emotional responses to occurrences outside of ourselves. Different occurrences inspire different emotional responses. These things that affect our emotional states are largely based on perspective and personal history. If perspective affects our emotional responses and we can alter our perspectives then our emotional responses to any situation are the products of choice. If the problem at hand doesn't really matter when we look at the big picture then we can choose to be happy in this moment. We are often unaware of the influential power we give external forces. But happenings rarely make us sad or angry. They only inspire us to be angered or saddened.

The world is only what we make it. The only tool of measurement we have for the external world is perspective. If we can change our perspectives, then we can change the world. Some people remain happy in situations most of us would view as desperate. Our happiness in any given situation is often based on our ideas of the world — on whether we think we're being treated fairly or not. Even though our many views of fairness are similar, no one general idea of fairness is absolutely correct for anyone but the person who holds that idea. Perceived unfairness would often seem to lead to anger with others, God, or oneself.

Though it can be birthed by a person's view of a situation, anger is often transmitted from person to person. We usually feel a person is being irrational when he or she is mad at us and therefore unfair in his or her anger. We, in turn, become angry as a result of the person's unfairness toward us. And so the anger spreads but anger is also spread without confrontation or feelings of mistreatment. We empathize and mentally emulate experiences and perceived emotions. If we perceive anger, a part of us will feel it but anger can be consuming.

We have the ability to choose how to deal with emotional influences. We can react on impulse or analysis. We can identify the cause of negative feelings and, in doing so, dismiss the negative feelings as the products of something over which we have little control. Once the responsibility for a happening is released there is no reason to hold onto the negative emotion. If I can change something that is problematic in the world outside myself, I will try my hardest to remedy the situation. If I cannot, I will not find the means to remedy the problem in negative emotion.

Some people in my world would seem easily disturbed by things that wouldn't affect me in the slightest way. Some people deal with what I would consider abusive actions with a smile. Our personal histories have a tendency to determine our level of contentment in any setting. This could explain why children in a less wealthy country may find joy in kicking an empty can down the street while many American children would be devastated without all of the commodities of modern living. If we can justify our experiences of the external world then negative emotion over an experience would seem irrational. Issues like poverty and even physical pain are dismissible in the eyes of the individual.

Sometimes negative emotion would seem completely unmotivated. This emotion could be a product of the strong connection between our physical and emotional states. It could be a very obviously physical problem, a problem of a lack of serotonin or some other imbalance in our brains. The problem with these physical incarnations of emotional pain is they are harder to rationalize into nonexistence. Then again, if the physical world is based on my perspective, I should be able to remove anything that ails me. I suppose it comes down to the power of my subconscious mind. If I expect to find pain then I will. This emotion with no acknowledgeable source or motive is the negative emotion that has proven problematic for me. If I cannot identify a source for this negative emotion, I have trouble using reason and analysis against it. Still, I've been able to recognize these negative emotions as irrational and remove them as a result.

Unfortunately this excusing of negative emotion can be problematic when it comes to being a part of society. This excusing of negative emotion without resolution of its cause dismisses the necessity to fix the problem that inspired the emotion to begin with. When the negative emotion is inspired by the actions of one who is inconsequential to our emotional well-being's, as the doctor mentioned before was for me, then the voicing of one's grief can easily be made a casualty of civility. I can assume the other party's perspective makes his or her actions personally justifiable.

Negative emotions inspired by loved ones can be trickier. This act of dismissing emotion cannot remedy the problem of social interaction that initially inspired emotional pain, be it the conduct of the person who caused the offense or the personal translation of the conduct by the offended party. If no middle ground is found, if no perspective is gained, then we will inevitably relive the same offenses.

Often our failure to portray the emotions others expect us to feel causes offense. If I have made a mistake and another bore the consequence of my mistake, I either show signs of remorse or display apathy for the problem. If I don't show signs of sadness at a loved one's funeral, other loved ones of the recently deceased may take great offense.

If we know others are right in their actions from their points of view, being angry at them for their choices is illogical. If we disagree with a perspective, this simply means the perspective is different from ours. Our inability to comprehend the thought process that enables a person to reach a perspective does not make the perspective wrong. Our inability to understand simply means the thought process is different from thought processes that are familiar to us. I believe one of our favorite sentences is, "That's stupid." Somehow our minds identify a point of view we don't understand as an unrealistic idea of the topic. In our minds the perspective in question lacked the proper analysis.

What would happen if we held every person responsible for his or her mistakes or miscommunications? What would happen if every person took an eye for an eye, refusing to see the other side of any issue? A person fails to see a situation from my perspective and acts accordingly. I see his acts as unfair and act without consideration for his perspective. He sees this as unfair and retaliates. If we consider the tendency for hypocrisy, we could conclude the punishment would likely be greater than the original trespass. If we never stopped to see other's perspectives, there would be a constantly escalating war between every one of us.

An individual is often angered when someone fails to see his or her perspective. In this situation one of two things is being perceived. Either the individual believes his or her opposition is choosing to disagree and, considering the individual's perspective is right, the opposition is intentionally being difficult, or he or she believes the opposition simply cannot understand the one and only correct logic that supports his or her perspective. I believe anger over the latter often starts with frustration in the inability to express one's perspective convincingly enough to alter the opposition's perspective.

If we truly see the other party's perspective then anger should be impossible. What are we angry at—the situation? A situation is simply the product of a preset inanimate set of laws. Being angry at a situation is silly, even if the situation is birthed by another human. At the root, our anger toward a situation caused by a human, is simply anger toward the human. If the situation isn't caused by a human then it's caused by natural laws and, if you believe in a higher power, by the laws God has set and, as a result, by God him, her, or itself.

Anger toward God is more difficult but I believe in a divine plan and that we face trials to make us stronger. Even if the situation seems unjust, it's part of the plan and has purpose. I've heard anger defined as, "the desire for vengeance." If we believe in a higher power, then is anger over a situation the desire for vengeance on the higher power? If we don't believe in a higher power, then is anger over a situation the desire for vengeance on something indefinable? In most emotional situations, if we allow ourselves to use rationality, as opposed to acting impulsively, we can dismiss these uneasy feelings.

The usefulness of anger has been debated. Malcolm X is quoted as having said, "Usually when people are sad, they don't do anything. They just cry over their condition. But when they get angry, they bring about a change."[1] I do agree sadness would seem useless in inspiring change but I don't believe anger inspires change either. In this situation, it's the will to bring change without the perceived ability to bring it that causes anger. Anger can inspire a sense of urgency to act but it's not the anger but the will that brings forth change. We need to teach ourselves how to be motivated by the will to cause change and not the anger that comes from the hopelessness that forms when change seems out of our reach.

I've found that sadness from a situation not birthed by another person but simply by circumstance, can be more difficult to dismiss through analysis. We are naturally emotional creatures and emotion is often birthed without the use of rationality. A human perspective is typically easier to understand than these natural occurrences against which we feel helpless. After all, the human perspective is something we all have grown accustomed to, while very few of us have ever been a deity. We tend to be sad for circumstances that surround us and the ones we love. Situational sadness comes from the desire for something without the foreseeable ability to attain it.

I suppose it's inevitable to feel unhappy about a situation. I believe sadness can be a beautiful experience as long as we don't allow ourselves

---

1   "Usually when People," 2009

to dwell in the unhappiness. If we live in a world of negative emotion, we become negative beings.

If we know our subconscious brains are constantly taking in information then we can conclude we should try to surround ourselves with influences we are fond of, influences we aspire to. If we surround ourselves with positive things then these things will become bigger parts of our lives. The same can be said about negative things. Our environments and our conscious decisions of focus build our brains and alter our perspectives. If we focus on things we like then these desirable focuses will become larger parts of our lives. If we focus on things we dislike then these undesirable influences will become a part of us. If we allow ourselves to dwell in an unhappy feeling then our brains absorb more of the unhappy influence than if we released the unhappy influence, refusing to dwell in it in the first place.

I do get angry with people despite the conclusions I've reached about anger. But when I explore the reasons for my anger, I find that either it was premature and not fully founded, or my anger was based on feelings of my own inadequacy. If I hadn't completely tried to see the situation from the other party's perspective then my feelings were premature. When I can see things through the other party's eyes, I realize their motives were not malicious but at the most their actions were misguided. This is a forgivable act and does not warrant anger. Anger over my own inadequacy is more difficult to conquer. The most obvious incarnation of this is when I feel someone is judging me as a result of something I feel is a weakness. But these are my own problems and the second party should not be burdened by them.

I often catch myself becoming angered as a result of a person's acting out of ignorance. Condemnation for ignorance is absurd no matter how illogical and even insolent a person's actions seem. Our anger blinds us to reason. When we are angry, our actions often become instinctual and we are more likely to make mistakes. When we are dealing with anger spawned by our own feelings of inadequacy, this failure as a result of the anger only works to inspire further displeasure. We have to remember, when we start to feel angry about something, to try to see the situation from all related perspectives.

We are often offended or even angered by things that would have no power over us if we didn't give in to them. A person's perspective is his or her own and most of the time it does not affect me. We allow hurt to come to us just by the way we perceive other's actions or even words. As mentioned in "Interaction with Other Perspectives", words only have the meaning we give them and therefore only have the power we allow them to have. Language is not universal. It's typically not even constantly consistent within specific areas of the Earth. So, what is it that makes us accept language as something definite? Language is only one expression of perspective and perspective is constantly changing. Even if the language is intended to cause hurt, it's based on perspective and nothing more.

These differences in perspective that cause anger are not so different from the differences that would seem to be the source of much humor in our world. Humor in the American culture is based largely on a difference in perspective. The punch line comes when the difference in perspective is revealed. Probably the most commonly known joke in the United States, if not the world, is "Why did the chicken cross the road?" Most can answer without any thought because they've heard the joke several times but imagine if you'd never heard it. You hear "Why" and look for motivation, a plan or a purpose. You hear, "Why is the chicken trying to get to the other side of the road?" When you hear the answer to, "Why did the chicken cross the road?" is "to get to the other side" you are forced to reevaluate how you interpreted the question.

Perhaps this can better be illustrated with the aid of another chicken joke. The joke is featured in the Woody Allen movie "Annie Hall." "This...this guy goes to a psychiatrist and says, 'Doc, uh, my brother's crazy; he thinks he's a chicken.' And, uh, the doctor says, 'Well, why don't you turn him in?' The guy says, 'I would but I need the eggs.'"[2] This joke holds humorous powers because the perspective of the "guy" in the joke is very different from the perspectives of most who hear the joke. It inspires laughter because the perspective is peculiar.

Let's go back to revenge for a second. According to the Latin proverb, "Revenge is a confession of pain."[3] Perhaps this is just an action intended to relieve our pain; but do we honestly believe causing pain to another, be it physical or emotional, releases our pain? Even people who claim to believe in, and even practice, the forgiveness of Jesus Christ, believe in Old Testament ideas of an "Eye for an Eye." The idea is not so much "Do to others as you would like them to do to you",[4] but "Do to others as they have done to you."

I suppose we romanticize the idea of revenge. We believe our inflic-tion of pain on the soul that recently did the inflicting to us will somehow relieve us of ours. Perhaps it's the idea that the inflicted pain can act as a deterrent for future acts of insolence. Remember the mental conditioning we talked about in "The Incredible Human Brain (Change your Mind)" but it still does not remedy the conflict of the past. I believe the problem is that acts of revenge do relieve our pain in the moment because they relieve our aggression toward the person but this is like treating the symptoms of a disease while it silently destroys the host from within.

---

2 "Memorable quotes for," 1990-2009

3 "Revenge is a," 1999-2009

4 Luke 6:31, New living translation, 2004

It's natural to feel hurt when we feel wronged but if revenge is our intended release of the pain then the thought pattern that caused the initial pain is allowed to remain. This pattern is the refusal to see other perspectives and to be hurt rather than inquisitive, about perspectives that differ from one's own. After all, our actions are justified in our own minds. We are an analytical species and we should be able to choose to rise above our initial instincts for, if nothing else, our own purposes of peace and understanding. Sometimes hurt or anger comes from not being able to understand an opposing perspective rather than the refusal to but we have to remember that in his or her own mind, a person's actions are personally justifiable.

We often feel like screaming when engaged in an angry conversation. I believe, in its most basic form, we raise our voices because we feel we're not being understood. Unfortunately this common social habit is often destructive to the situation. Yelling out of anger expresses that we are feeling anger to the person we are yelling at. Our understanding of this often encourages us to become more frustrated if the yelling yields little or no result. Aside from the fact that it can anger us even more, the thought that the best way to fix the problem is to speak more loudly and even more angrily, would seem irrational. If the problem is that we feel we're not being understood then we should change our words or even our perspectives, not our tone.

Perhaps screaming out of anger is a less violent action for us to take to relieve the pain caused by anger. Some of us inflict pain on others, some of us inflict pain on ourselves and some of us scream. Then again, the least evasive form of release would be to never form negative feelings in the first place. I believe anger is a valid emotion and a reasonable perspective. At the same time, if we desire happiness, I believe we should be in constant search of the greater good: peace and love.

Chapter Thirty

Romeo's Bleeding Egg

I have always been infatuated with the idea of love for a significant other. By the time I was in the eighth grade, attending Covington Middle School, I was ready for my first love-like relationship. She was a seventh grader. We talked on the phone almost every night. She was number seven in the speed dial of my portable phone. This was the same phone into which I would program Nine's phone number and assign the number nine. My grandparents and I had purchased the phone at a garage sale and the battery would only last a short while before it needed to be put back on the charging cradle.

At the end of every conversation there was a slight pause followed by "I love you" from one of us. I remember when she told me she wanted to be friends and that she loved me like a friend. I still said, "I love you" after every conversation. She always replied with a hesitant, "I love you too, as a friend."

After I recuperated from my relationship with her, I dated a girl who was more a part of my social group. Again I knew in my mind I was in love. I was so eager to love. I remember a night a mutual friend of ours threw a Halloween party at her mother's boyfriend's house. By the end of the night, my friend Jo, my girlfriend, and I had made our way to the second story balcony of the party house. The girlfriend, with a very apathetic attitude had announced her plan to throw herself off the balcony to take her own life. We talked for a while but it was like most conversations of attempted reason were with her, like talking to an unresponsive wall. She made conversational responses but she wouldn't let any reason enter. Because she didn't want to see my reason, her responses had little relevance to what I said. I told her again, like I'd told her before, that if she went I would go, too. I began to sob and Jo was there in a second to comfort me.

After a few minutes of sitting there in near silence, I heard my father's voice coming from the bedroom on the other side of the glass door next to the chair in which I sat. "You're all busted!" he said. I was so solemn and yet I managed to feel a little mortified. My father was trying to get a reaction from these people I wanted so desperately to like me. He asked me with that same tone if I was ready to go. On the drive home he mentioned my "friends" had told him my "crazy" girlfriend and I were trying to kill ourselves. I denied any intent rather quickly.

A while after that relationship ended I began the relationship that would end my streak of somewhat innocent relationships. It's strange to think of suicide as innocent but it was. I would have blindly followed her because despite what I felt at the time, I had a child's love for her. My next significant relationship began shortly after that infamous and yet well-guarded secret of a night when my father stood over me in the side lawn of our Austin home. This relationship would do less easily repairable damage.

After dabbling in some heavy petting with various love interests the months before, I found a girl who was ready for sex. I was fifteen. She had been adopted as an infant and after a while of sleeping together regularly she told me she had become pregnant and had had an abortion. I still remember the picture she painted for me. She had had a friend of her mother's take her to the clinic. She had lain in her bed that night, crying as she swallowed "the pill", killing the child that was part me and part her.

She saw a therapist regularly. Her father approached me the one time she had me come to her therapy session. He said very bluntly, "So, I under-stand you've had sexual intercourse with my daughter." He said it was okay and he wasn't mad at me. I think he was trying to reassure me he wasn't going to do to me what his daughter had told him my father had done months before.

Eventually I ended things with her; we lost touch shortly after that. Several years later, we somehow reconnected. I talked to her on the phone a lot after I got out of the hospital. We empathized with each other, having both had our hearts broken in recent history. In one conversation, I brought up the fact that she was once pregnant with my child. She explained she was never really pregnant but wanted to feel what her birth mother must have felt when she gave her up for adoption. I felt conflicted, torn between feeling betrayed and relieved. In the end, I hardly felt either. This fifteen year-old boy, her ex-fiance, as she liked to call me, was hardly a part of the person I'd become.

One impactful encounter of potential love fell upon one of the gaps in my relationship with Nine. Again, I was blind to my lover's perspective. It's interesting to me that Allen's sister was in love with me when I used her for sex and then I loved a girl with the same first name years later and she used me for sex. She lived in Boerne and I was living in Austin at the time.

I received a "Minor in Possession" ticket on the way to pick her up. I was stopped for speeding and the police officer noticed a full can of beer in the box of empties I'd forgotten to drop at the dumpster as I left my apartment complex on my way to Boerne. This should have been a sign to me but for some reason I took the ticket with a smile and continued. I was just happy to be driving to see her. On the drive back to Austin I was flying high.

We stopped for gas on our way to Austin and she got out of the car with me. I told her I had an ex-girlfriend who lived in the town. She said just what I was thinking, "Let's make her jealous." We hugged deeply. When we got to my apartment she said she was going to take a shower. I asked if I could come with. She said, "yes", that it would be beautiful, two friends naked, nothing sexual. I adored her.

In the shower, I ever so gently kissed her on the lips. I asked her if it was okay and she made a joke about not being a foreign exchange student. We left the shower and she laid herself down naked, on my bed. I lovingly made love to her. On the drive home I was giddy. I had loved her for so long. She once told me her mom had asked her why she couldn't find someone like me to be with, and now I thought we were starting that relationship. I flipped through my CD collection, playing different songs for her, telling her how I related them to her. Many of them I hadn't related to her before that night but I thought I was in love. Then she fell asleep. If Nine had done that I would have been angry that she made me make the drive alone but I was happy just to be in this girl's presence.

One day years later, when I lived with my mother in Boerne after my experience with cancer, I found myself making eye contact with this girl as she busily passed in the local WalMart. I said hello with some surprise in my voice. She said she was busy, as if to say she couldn't talk at that moment. She hurriedly carried on as to not interrupt her seemingly fast-paced momentary occupation of placing customer's purchases into bags. Her reaction to this random encounter should have been expected.

When I spoke to her shortly after that silent drive back to Boerne, she made me realize I was attributing much more significance to the encounter than it was due. She said her thought process was that she couldn't have sex with the person she'd been seeing and she "needed" to have sex. That felt like such a copout to me but she was right. There was no chemistry other than that which was going on inside my head. I remember her body quivering afterward. I thought it was something special. Her attitude toward our physical relationship was the attitude toward sex I'd had when I went to high school in Boerne. It was sex for the purpose of sex despite the unforeseen consequences.

I have had quite a few significant others in my life thus far. At the time, I felt I loved most of them. All we have is perspective so we can't think we are feeling something unless we actually are. My idea of love has changed over the years but each relationship fit the idea of love I had at the time. Love is something undeniably based on perspective. I felt I was in love, therefore I was. It might have been different from the love I've grown to expect from adult relationships but it was still love. If love is truly unconditional then we can never stop loving anyone. I still have love for each of these different figures in my personal history. If nothing else, the love I have for them is a love for who they were to me at the time.

We often use the word love as a label. We each have specific ideas of what "love" is supposed to be, which is are usually ideas we have grown up with, ideas we acquired from watching children's movies. It is common for an individual to believe his or her idea of love is the only idea of love. Yet we know there are different kinds of love. Hebrew has a different word for several different kinds of love.[1]

A few years after our final breakup Nine expressed a desire to have me be a part of her life again. For the first time in years I felt a love I'd forgotten. It wasn't that of a lover, even during this heartfelt conversation I was reminded of reasons our relationship didn't work but that of an old friend I somehow lost along the way. I had completely forgotten the unconditional love she'd held for me, even before we dated. My present love for each of my past intimate attempts is different but it's love all the same.

---

[1] Hilla, 2007

Purpose in Evil and Pain

What is evil? We all have moral compasses that would tend to direct us in manners of right and wrong. Is infringement of human rights evil? How do we define "human rights"? Human rights are not the same as rights granted by human-made law. Human rights are the basic rights we're supposed to all be born with, like the right to life and the right to freedom but when does freedom cease to be a right and become a privilege? Absolute freedom would mean any one person could do anything he or she wanted without repercussions.

If true freedom were a right with which we were all born then we would each be born with the right to end the life of another human. If true freedom were a right with which we were all born then we could not expect to have the right to live. I believe we are born with some freedoms but in some cases, execution of absolute freedom would make for an unlivable setting and ultimately lead to the downfall of society.

My first position of employment after the tumor was for a drug-testing lab. We did other things but the company survived on the money we earned for ensuring other company's employees weren't using illegal substances. I was okay with that. I know of effects that mind-altering substances can take on a person that might inhibit his or her ability to do his or her job or cause him or her to behave in an inappropriate or dangerous manner. Even though it would be unfounded to assume people who use mind-altering substances in their free time would use them while being paid for their time; it's an assumption many companies feel they have to make.

The company would be held responsible if behavior associated with drug use caused a problem with a patron or a co-worker. At this time, the only way an employer can ensure his or her employees aren't using mind-altering substances while at work is to ensure they don't use them at all. Technology has only come so far in the field of drug testing. I couldn't blame them for trying to protect themselves. People in our society would seem very eager to sue, especially if they can take on a large corporation that has deep pockets.

We also did private drug testing. Again, I was okay with this. I couldn't see a problem with a parent wanting to know if his or her child could be in danger. I don't consider marijuana to be a "drug" as the word is commonly used, although I do believe it can have negative effects on people, especially teenagers. The biggest problem I see with marijuana when it comes to teenage use—as one who smoked marijuana on a somewhat regular basis as a teenager—is it makes a person content with doing nothing. A person can allow him or herself to become immersed in the habit if he or she is not mature enough to know when enough is enough; but a mature adult should have a good enough understanding of his or her life and him or herself to know when his or her patterns of smoking pot are negatively affecting his or her life.

I personally don't enjoy marijuana anymore. There was a point in my life when I smoked pot regularly throughout the week. After I hadn't touched it for a few years I decided to try it again. It wasn't the same. I felt stupid and couldn't control my thoughts. I was giddy and paranoid all at the same time. I tried it again later because I had friends who enjoyed it and I really wanted to understand what they saw in the experience. It was the same story. I don't know what I once enjoyed about marijuana use but it would be lost on me now.

Despite how marijuana affects me, I do understand other people enjoy it and I believe it should be none of the governing body's concern if these adults decide to take advantage of the way it makes them feel. Extensive habitual use can, arguably, eventually result in the inability to care for oneself and ultimately cause a person to require assistance in everyday life but it's up to the individual to take the measures or precautions to not end up in assisted living. Hopefully, a responsible adult wouldn't end up in that situation but if he or she did, the resulting life could not be any worse than that which can be accomplished a number of different legal ways.

I believe it's somewhat of a copout to acknowledge one thing is bad but cite the continued allowing of worse things as justification for the first. We should be in search of absolute right knowing we can never achieve it and not settle for the lesser evil. At the same time, the last time I checked, we were living in a democratic republic, which leads me to believe the common consensus is that adults are capable of running their own lives.

Most would agree it's evil to remove a person's rights. I believe we all have the right to do what we wish as long as it doesn't hurt anyone else but look at suicide. In the past, suicide has been viewed as a common law felony in the U.S. This view of suicide as a criminal act has diminished and now suicide is no longer viewed as a federal crime. However, some states still view attempted suicide as a criminal act.[1] I guess it's like the old joke:

Q: What's the punishment for suicide?
A: Life imprisonment.
Q: What's the punishment for attempted suicide?
A: Hanging.[2]

The United States government often acts as a parent who knows what's best for his or her child whether he or she does or not but that's not the job of a government. If I understand the reasons our country was founded in the first place, I would say the United States government is actually supposed to do somewhat the opposite. Our government is supposed to ensure we retain the freedom to make up our own minds.

So the infringement of a human's rights is wrong but interfering with one's ability to do as he or she wishes to him or herself would seem justified in certain circumstances. Is evil no longer evil if the end justifies the means? The problem is the labels mentioned in "Interaction With Other Perspectives." We, as humans, categorize everything in our world. We can't analyze every individual piece of our world. Our brains are just not capable. There is no absolute anything in this world and, if we are going to stand for something, we should try to see every angle.

Often, forces viewed as evil don't cause sadness. There's happiness in situations that would seem to be void of what most would consider human rights. Should an outsider who can see a person's lack of freedom help him or her gain freedom despite the fact that he or she is content with his or her situation? Perhaps. But, if he or she is blind to the idea that he or she should be unhappy, it would seem to me to be an evil act to introduce the idea of unhappiness in his or her situation. If we can be happy in some of the most difficult situations known to humankind then even evil is about perspective.

It often feels as though we are born in debt to the world by being indebted to our own well-beings. We cannot simply live. Often we have to do things we wouldn't voluntarily do in order to remain content with our states in life. Then again, this could simply be a product of "The Competition." Still, my limitations in the world in which I was raised are apparent. There are actions that cause me pain that wouldn't physically affect most people, yet I am hesitant to say I'm disabled, because I can

---

[1] "Suicide," 2008
[2] Adams, 2004

perform these actions. In order to feel as though I'm giving my fair share, or in some cases, just to function, I now have to give more than I used to. But I'm not a victim of my situation. I still can choose how to deal with my pain.

Perhaps the story of the "Original Sin" can explain this feeling of debt. The story would seem to narrate a drastic change in our place in the physical world. The physical world would seem to have become a somewhat unfriendly place to humankind after the first humans ate from the tree of the knowledge of good and evil.[3] In its literal form, this story would seem to present a certain paradox. It says sin is wrong even if we don't see it as sin. Can something be morally objectionable if we don't understand the moral implications? If this is so, then we should not be dealing children less severe punishments than we deal adults for the same crime. If knowledge doesn't define what is wrong then all consequences for all members of society should be equal. According to the story, the first sin involved the discovery of sin and we know we learn from experience. If we look at the "Original Sin" as the discovery of sin then perhaps the fruit is not as literal as we often like to think. Perhaps the knowledge wasn't an instant opening of eyes as it is painted but a familiarity.

I believe the most common argument for the idea of a world without a higher power is that a just god would not allow the severity of pain some people feel while others go through little in their lives. Since the brain tumor affected my life, my pain has fluctuated but even a thing like pain is relative to the perspective. I have experienced debilitating head pain, so our ideas of pain might differ greatly. Join me in an experiment. A researcher uses an electrode to induce monitored levels of negative stimulation in our bodies. We are instructed to rate the amount of pain we experience. You might rate a 9 to what I would rate as a 6, or vice versa. Our responses would be based on amounts of pain we've experienced in the past but they would also be related to how recent our experiences of pain were. I might rate a present experience of pain as an 8 while I might have rated the same amount of pain as a 5 when I was in the hospital.

In "The False World" I mentioned the distance from the physical world this pain has seemed to cause. I theorized my method of coping with this pain, the retreating of my perspective into myself, could be responsible for the apparent falseness of this world. The distance this method has caused has given reason for the discovery of ways of dealing with my physical pain other than retreating from it. I can often will it away. I have learned how to mentally push the pain out of my head. I focus on it and, often, I can dissolve it but this release has only proven a temporary one so far. I interrupt the signal to my brain and the pain ceases.

---

[3] English standard version, 2001

When I stop focusing on blocking the signal, the pain returns. This would seem to illustrate the power of will over the physical world but it hasn't yet proven to free me of my pain completely. This pattern of removing physical pain could have been the cause for the birth of my ability to push emotional pain away as well. I don't believe I'm denying my emotional pain. I use rationality and will to dissolve it the same way I use what some would call "mind over matter" to dissolve my physical pain.

God has a way of making good things come from bad situations. If we consider our powers of perspective then I suppose we all have that power if we try hard enough. I believe God used Allen's pain for good in me. Despite the fact that I have regret about Allen's trouble and the way I treated it, I gained perspective from the experience. It's hard to justify the loss with the gain but I don't think it necessarily needs to be justified. The point is that I have seen good result from an obvious evil.

I try to give more than I would have to in every setting of my life. We're born in debt to ourselves but like anything else, we can choose how to deal with the personal need that comes from this world. We can choose to feed the debt or to deal with the consequences of depriving it.

It's interesting to me that some people use pain as a way to excuse the idea of God. I use it as a reminder of what God has in store for me. I just have to have the courage to do what I think he, she, or it wants and not what I want for myself. I have already gained from my pain. I have had to accept that pain is inevitable for me, at least on a short-term scale. This expectation of pain makes the pain less powerful. I am now more equipped to deal with future pain.

In "Perspective" I said there's a strong link in physical and emotional states. I'm now less afraid of being hurt emotionally because I know physical pain is inevitable. The pain I once felt from a lost love is now miniaturized by the physical pain I've endured. I'm already emotionally stronger because of it. While the view that some people go through more pain than others would seem to be accurate, the idea that pain is the only way to measure someone's feeling of contentment in this world would seem irrational.

There's a lot of pain in the world but there's also great joy in the release of pain. In fact, the greater the pain and the longer the pain endures, the more pleasurable the release is. A person who hadn't felt that pain wouldn't be able to experience the joy of its release. But what of those who never escape pain?

Since a cancerous growth formed in my brain, I've been in mild to extreme physical pain most of the time I've been awake. I don't expect the pain to stop any time in the near future. It may never stop but I'm still affected by the balance of pain and pleasure. When my intense, sometimes instantaneous headaches pass, I feel a sense of release. The amount of constant struggle inhibiting a person's life can positively affect the amount that person can enjoy in simple pleasures. When we live with our heads facing downward it can be liberating to lift them.

My pain often encourages me to remind myself I have reason to believe in a higher power who has a plan. Physical pain forces us to live more in the spiritual world than we would without it. We tend to withdraw from the physical world in pursuit of other pleasures. For this reason, I believe my limited vision and dizziness might all be blessings. They provide personal proof the world outside of me is not as I perceive it. My random dizzy spells inspire question for "reality." I get headaches simply from using my eyes. The amount of pain is directly related to the intense focus I demand of my eyes, so actions like reading would seem to be the most efficient in producing such pain.

Shortly after the surgical attempt to correct my vision, my eye surgeon expressed the opinion that my brain was simply not strong enough to fuse the two images my eyes send to my brain. I wonder if it's not lack of strength but lack of desire to force the two images into one. My conscious perspective would be grateful for the ability to see one physical object as one image but I do recognize that, mentally, I'm not fully grounded in this physical reality. I use my eyes to establish a point of view of the outside world and my brain punishes me for it.

This action-reaction pattern of pain for perspective I've grown to know only furthers the belief that the world is not as I perceive it. According to theories of mental conditioning, I should be rejecting the very source of my perspective because it causes me pain. No matter how you look at it, this is exactly what I'm doing. Whether the source of my pain is the external world, my eyes, or my brain, I have chosen not to take the product at face value. I am a Huxley's infants, rejecting the brightly colored flowers and books because of the pain I associate with them.

If this pain is Godsent, then I do, indeed, believe it to be a gift. I suppose it's conditioning. I'm not supposed to take this world at face value. If my eyes or my brain were altered in ways I haven't yet defined for myself then perhaps they're altered for a purpose. The designs I saw in the sky outside of the glasses shop, the pit of blue spheres I experienced, make it almost necessary for me to question my reality. My vision doubles when my eyes get sore and I choose not to attempt to focus on any particular distance. My double vision would seem to be the product of mentally distancing myself from the world.

This distancing from the physical world has made me much more objective in my analysis of it but the vision problems have affected me in other positive ways as well. When I look up, out the upper areas of the lenses in my glasses; I tend to be more likely to see a double representation of a single object in the external world. When I look down, out the bottom areas of the lenses, my brain is usually more successful at making the two images one.

With the self-esteem problems I have borne for a large part of my life, I often feel a tendency to let my head hang facing downward. With the tendency to face downward comes the necessity to point one's eyes upward, to perceive and analyze the physical world. In my situation, this act often leads to headaches from my mind's inability to fuse the separated images. Realizing this, I now make an effort to hold my head higher. This new postural habit has led to a measurable increase in positive self-esteem. I suppose it goes back to the idea that emotional perspective is strongly influenced by the physical world, and vice versa.

When one is denied the ability to perform common tasks for any lengthened period of time the question one asks oneself becomes "Can I do this?" not "Am I willing to?" Because I was incapable of performing many tasks without an experience of great pain for some time, I now find motivation more easily. The performing of many tasks now seems effortless in comparison to the great pain I had to endure and effort I had to put forth to perform these tasks those few years ago.

Although most would seem to disagree, I do not believe absolute evil exists within humankind. There are only vast differences in perspective. The idea of evil among humankind would seem to be the product of differences in opinion. There are many people on Earth who've acted in ways others would consider evil but I suspect no person tries to do evil. His or her actions are always personally justifiable. Difference is what makes this world such an interesting place. Without what we consider evil we would be without purpose. With no difference we would have nothing to stand for.

I believe our desires are a part of God's plan. We all have the ability to make choices but I believe God knows the choices we will make, and has a greater plan for our good that will use our choices for good. Even seemingly evil desires can be used for good. The biblical story of Joseph illustrates this. His brothers sell him into slavery with evil intent. As a result, he is made a ruler in the land of Egypt.3 The actions of humans would seem to be the ones that affect humankind in the greatest capacity but we are not all-powerful and often cannot control the outcomes of our actions.

In the first chapter of this book, I wrote about the emotional anguish my brother experienced as a result of the absence of our father. I felt my presence was helpful to him. This, in my mind, is clearly a representation of the use of evil for a good outcome. I likely wouldn't have been present if it weren't for the recent experience with cancer. We gain perspective from experience and I believe I'm more enlightened now as a result of my experience of pain.

If nothing else, we're stronger for our misfortunes. We become better equipped to deal with future pain within ourselves or within others. But that brings us to the root of our question:

Why do we feel pain in the first place? I've heard it theorized that pain exists so we could choose it. It is said humankind chose sin and disobedience with the "Original Sin" and now we are living our ancestors' choices - Genesis 2:16 - Genesis 3:19.3 I suppose the relativity of this theory is dependent upon your spiritual beliefs; but if this verse was not meant to be taken literally—just as many other verses would seem—then the choice to experience pain in everyday life would seem to be represented here. I have grown to understand ways around my pain, ways to not experience it. If I don't experience the pain then it ceases to be. In a true utopia, no pain would exist but perhaps a true utopian society would understand how to not experience the pain to which most of us have grown accustomed.

Nearly all religions share the same basic ideas of heaven and hell. I think most people who grew up in the United States are familiar with the idea of a city with streets of gold that is heaven and the idea of a sea of flames that is hell. Revelation 21:8: "But as for the cowardly, the faithless, the detestable, as for murderers, the sexually immoral, sorcerers, idolaters, and all liars, their portion will be in the lake that burns with fire and sulfur, which is the second death."3 Revelation 21:21 says, "And the twelve gates were twelve pearls, each of the gates made of a single pearl, and the street of the city was pure gold, transparent as glass."[3] I believe we have the ability to choose, not necessarily through our actions but through our self-imposed perspectives of the world. We can choose happiness as represented by ideas of Heaven or we can choose unhappiness as represented by ideas of Hell. The actual forms of these ideas may vary as much as reality varies from person to person.

If I believe in God, or fate, then I can stop obsessing over my choices. If there's a divine plan then I don't want to fight it. I can only do my best and let the great plan take its course. This also enables the release of any feelings of guilt. If the attempt to act in the perceived, most correct manner is made then we cannot judge ourselves for past mistakes. If we believe God uses a bad occurrence for a good result then we can only do the best we can with each circumstance. If we believe in fate then we must simply learn to let go of any control we might think we have over our lives. We can always make an effort to achieve success in any situation but should not be disappointed when success is not obtained. As hard as we may try, not all things can be in our control. At the same time, we choose how to receive our worlds. If we believe in any kind of predestination then the pain we experience is the means to our predestined end.

Chapter Thirty-Two

Thirteen

As impossible as the relationship with Nine was, I believe it prepared me somewhat for the relationship that would follow. I often felt forgotten when Nine failed to return my phone calls or didn't call when she said she would. It's kind of funny now but at the time the song, "Build Me Up Buttercup", by The Foundations was almost painful to hear; although I remember laughing at myself, even then.

Thirteen is much more independent than I am. I still feel neglected sometimes but I can usually remedy this feeling of neglect by reminding myself she is very independent and wouldn't intentionally hurt me. I try not to make her sacrifice or even compromise any more than she would have to if she were with someone else.

My physical limitations accompanied by my emotional baggage can make it difficult. If I don't give as much as I comfortably can to my relationship I end up feeling neglected more often than I would if I had. Do other people have to give this much just to be comfortable in their own skin? Maybe the idea that I have to give as much as I can to this relationship is simply the product of a lack in confidence. I'm not confident enough in myself to know she would want me if I weren't trying as hard as I do.

Realistically, I know she's with me because she wants to be and not because of something like obligation. I probably have these fears because Nine admitted she was done with me a long time before we separated. She said she didn't end the relationship because she felt obligated to stay with me after I got sick.

It's not that I owe Thirteen or that she owes me. Our relationship isn't about debt. My constant attempts to tally debt in my last relationship contributed a great deal to its end. I suppose I give as much as I can because I want her to have anything I can afford to give her. I give out of love not debt. I once wrote a message in my phone to remind me of how much I truly value her. I wrote, "You're worth the headache."

It's true; as much as I have wished for something else, as much as I have almost given up on life, she's worth any pain I have to go through to stay here. It makes me afraid to say this because I know how independent she is. She once told me something I had said made her feel I needed her more than she needed me. She said she didn't want that because she wanted us to be equal. Now, I fear anytime I think something like, "You're worth the headache", that I'm needing her more than she needs me.

In all actuality, her independence is probably a good thing. Despite the fact that I tend to feel neglected on occasion, I know I often distance myself from the world in which she lives. I bury myself in my brain in an attempt to distance myself from my physical pain. I know that when I am buried in my thoughts, in this distant reality, I can't be all I would like to be for her. I also still battle daily with my self-esteem. If I were attempting a more codependent relationship, it likely wouldn't last very long.

When it comes down to it, love isn't supposed to be the constant scale I've tried to make it in the past. I believe effort in a relationship is necessary but in the end, the amount of effort we put forth is a direct result of how badly we want to make the relationship work. I suppose I've devoted as much as I comfortably can because I want this relationship to work more than I want anything else. Maybe part of being an adult is knowing how much we're willing to give to get or keep what we really want. There is no room for "The Competition" when it comes to love. I doubt one could ever truly feel compensated for the effort he or she puts forth in an intimate relationship, because he or she is the only witness to his or her effort. When it comes to love, we give out of love, not an attempt at equality or fairness.

Shortly after we began this attempt at intimacy, our conflicting work schedules caused us to rarely see each other. My weeks had become too cluttered to get anything accomplished, so my weekends were the only time I had to do things like laundry or get the oil in my car changed. She often worked on the weekend and, with my busy schedule, even if I spent the night with her, we didn't see much of each other. It's hard to feel so emotionally connected to someone and be so disconnected from them in the physical world.

When Thirteen and I first started dating, we didn't spend much time alone. She was my connection to anything social in the town where I lived, the town my parents moved me to when

I was seventeen. We spent most of our free time with mutual friends. These mutual friends were for the most part acquaintances from whom I kept a pretty fair distance before we started dating. These friends were, for the most part, her friends who accepted me into their social group.

Despite what she said, I believed, if we were to have separated, most of them would've demoted me back to "acquaintance" as quickly as they accepted me. I suppose, despite the love I found in and for these people, I would've demoted them back to distant friends before they could've demoted me.

When we first started this attempt, I was still very heartbroken, not necessarily over my experience with Nine but more over the current happenings in my life. I remember a car ride with her. At the time, I was still waiting for my eyes to get well enough that I felt comfortable driving with a passenger at night, so she was driving. We were looking for something in San Antonio. She's told me since that it was a karaoke bar. After not being able to find it, we started the drive back. I, as often, was complaining about something. I believe it was a problem with my father. I held her hand for a while and told her I felt unexplainably connected to her. She reciprocated and we held hands as friends.

Later, while sitting on my mother's couch, I went to kiss her. I'd intended to kiss her in the way I'd been kissed years before by a dear friend. When this friend kissed me, I was not turned on. I didn't try to take it a step further, despite the fact that I'd always found her very beautiful. It was out of love that we already shared as friends. With no deeper intent, I kissed Thirteen with a closed mouth on the lips. A few moments later I did it again and before the end of the night we were really kissing.

I was so smitten, and yet I told her I wanted to take things slowly. I was still very fearful from the hurt of my last relationship and didn't want to jeopardize this friendship I valued so dearly. I also didn't want her to get hurt. I can be unreasonably emotional at times. Somewhere along the way we got closer than I intended. I'm so happy we've gotten to where we are now but, at the same time, I know there would be no turning back if we wanted to. I suppose it all changed the first time I said, "I love you." Those words have been the life and death of me for many years.

I wouldn't go back if I could. She's too much to me now to want to change it. Despite my wariness I know this is not the relationship that caused so much hurt the time before. Still it's scary to be in this box called love in which I've tortured myself before and now not be able to follow back out the road I took to get here in the first place. I once wrote, "I'm stuck in a box I've never even heard of. I'm in love." This was meant to express the overwhelming feeling of young love I experienced years before my relationship with Thirteen. I experienced it but couldn't define it. Despite my fears, I do feel fortunate to be sharing life with her. Just reliving this past experience has been a most enjoyable and emotional one. Her presence in my life and my consciousness has helped me maintain optimism.

My situation shortly after the tumor experience wasn't hopeless but I often felt it was. A person with nothing to lose is capable of things a person otherwise would not be. A person with nothing to lose is much like the person I was when I cheated on Nine. It wasn't that I had nothing. It was my perspective. I was dealing with what I thought was the adult life for the first time. I was living in a friend's living room. I was unemployed and I had stopped caring.

Buckley recently expressed the burden he feels from having something to lose. He's always had anxiety issues but is living without suicidal thoughts for the first time in his life. He is grateful for the newly found desire for life. Still, he's now more fearful of death than ever. I have very little fear for death because I believe in a happy afterlife, so I have less to lose than someone who fears death. I suppose this is a gift. Although, I would imagine it's difficult for my significant other to be connected to someone who's not as attached to this world as she.

I sometimes feel that, these several years later, I'm still waiting to die. I'm not ungrateful. This life is a gift. I'm told the tumor was not a life threatening one but I often cannot escape the feeling that I'm living on borrowed time. Perhaps it won't be cancer. The most recent attribution to this feeling of borrowed time has been chest pains. It would seem like a logical practice to write one's memoirs toward the end of his or her life.

Despite these suspicions, I'm not scared. If this time is a gift, then I should be focused on the reason I have been granted this time. I have a choice of how I want to see these factors. I've heard anxiety can cause chest pains. I don't feel anxious but I know anxiety has often buried itself just below my conscious surface. I cannot very well dissolve it through rationality if I cannot define it.

I suspect it must be difficult for her at times, just as it was difficult for Buckley's wife when he openly considered suicide. Our relationships become our attachments to this world. If Buckley were to quit on life, he would have quit on his relationship with his wife. In theorizing the aspects of my own death, I am, whether I intend it or not, planning on the end of my relationship as I know it. Still, I believe my perspective is too much of a gift to simply dismiss it. Living on borrowed time changes one's priorities. I feel I am more focused on things that are truly important.

It is my perspective but I see many things others concern themselves with as obsolete. I suppose, once one forces him or herself to look at life in a grander scheme, the idea of temporary life on Earth and the little things that come with this life typically don't matter as much. I'm not saying I'm above the emotions of this world. In fact, often the opposite is true. The problem with seeing the inconsequential nature of these trivial things becomes the inevitable pain I experience when I see my most loved ones allowing these things to cause them pain.

I don't know if it is solely a result of my newly found perspective but I've recently begun to feel a great distance between Thirteen and me. Her attitude toward her world seems most apparent when she utters the rhetorical question, "Really?!" when something of negative consequence happens. She refuses to believe she has control over how she feels about her world and instead argues she's justified in being angry. She doesn't seem to understand I'm not arguing the validity of her anger but trying to help her to not experience these negative emotions that have caused me so much pain.

With such different perspectives I find myself wondering what kind of future we could hope for. It's almost like we're speaking different languages. I try to explain how I obtain my perspective through the use of reason and she seems to hear me telling her she's wrong for feeling the way she does. My motivation is a love for her and desire for her to be happy but I suppose I could simply be following old patterns of interaction. I believed Nine was wrong for feeling the way she did and I tried to change her perspective. I could, unknowingly, be doing the same thing here. The song, "I Want You to Want Me", has held significance in this relationship much in the way "Build Me Up Buttercup" did in my last.

I can't imagine an absolute in this world, and she would seem to take great offense to this idea. Could a relationship between two people with so strongly opposing perspectives ever work? Could a person like me, with such a unique perspective, ever maintain a lasting relationship? I've had the desire to seek out intimate relationships since I was very young. I don't believe this desire would be there if I were not supposed to have it. I've tried to put God's will first in my life but it can be difficult when the path causes distress to one who is reliant on me, to one who doesn't see the light at the end of the tunnel because she doesn't believe it's there.

Despite my detached view of the outside world, she does affect me a great deal in an emotional way. When she is sad, I am saddened. When she smiles deeply at me, I am truly touched.

I just have to keep giving as much as I can and hoping I can continue to be what she wants. She once told me I held the incorrect belief that love was a conditional thing. I believed in the idea of unconditional love but never really reviewed the love I felt in my own life to that degree. I believe money was the only way my father knew to show love. Several months after this conversation with my girlfriend, my father called and told me he was revoking any monetary support I had from him. If money was my father's way of showing love and he revoked it, it is easy to see how I got the idea that love was based on conditions.

I no longer believe she might one day stop loving me but I do still believe her view of me, and eventually her love for me, might change. I believe she will always love me, which is something incredible for me to be able to say but I don't know for sure that her love won't one day change, just as mine has changed for the many loves I have had in the past. Despite this possibility, I'm still usually optimistic about our future.

If our ideas of love are based on chemical responses in our brains then love is conditional when it comes to its existence between humans. The variable, or condition is our ability to produce the chemical that produces the desired effects. We can induce these feelings of love through memory of personal history but this poses an interesting question. Are we in love if we are not keeping the object of our affection in our mind's eye? If one allows him or herself to focus on anything but the object of his or her affection, the dopamine-induced euphoria has passed. If love is a feeling, a temporary emotional state, then it too has passed.

We can voluntarily cause the euphoria if we try. In order to stay "in love" we must keep finding ways to release the chemicals in our brains, whether it is by memory or by the occurrence of something present; but it would seem impossible to constantly focus on the desired feelings. It has been said that marriage is the ability to choose the same person over and over again. I believe that true intimate love is the ability to appreciate the euphoric feelings of love even when one is not experiencing them.

Our world is based on our individual perspectives but a large part of what makes those perspectives is our translations of others' declarations of the external world. The perspectives that matter most are those of our loved ones. We have typically grown reason to trust their perspectives but more importantly, we desire to share perspectives so we don't feel alone. If all is relative, as things tend to be in a world defined by perspective, then the only absolutes are our own perspectives. If we can manage to share aspects of perspective with a loved one, we tend to feel more strongly connected to that person.

Thirteen and I recently shared our greatest fears and, while she expressed a fear of the devil, which she would sometimes seem to believe in and other times would not, I expressed a fear of being alone. I hadn't realized this was a fear of mine until I spoke it but it makes sense. I feel alone in my perspective. With no one to share this with, I'm often alone in the world but I suppose I need the hope of companionship she gives me. Maybe it's like Woody Allen said, "I need the eggs."

We go through phases when a long-term relationship seems hopeless and then she smiles at me and I can't imagine the pain I would feel if I lost her. I suppose my grandmother said it best, "Love is blind." If I ruled how I view this relationship with logic, I doubt we would have gotten very far. The emotions we feel when we're in love can be explained through science but the humanity that comes from being in love, the voluntary vulnerability, would seem anything but logical. The origins of love don't seem to be cosmic but the effects of being in love do.

Logic can make me pessimistic about our future. Her occasional lack of joy makes me want to weep. And then she smiles and all doubt is gone. Love is irrational. I don't believe it would function the way it does if it were rational. It's like any other kind of faith. The lack of logic to support it is what makes it so powerful. It is our intentionally self-inflicted vulnerability that makes love so powerful. We crave the inebriated feeling of love, so we forgo the commonly cautious protection of ourselves in pursuit of it.

Chapter Thirty-Three

My Constantly Changing Perspective

Yesterday I woke with a horrible headache. Since the tumor, I've had on occasion what I call rolling headaches. They start with a light, almost as if through several layers of clothing, pain. These layers get thinner as the pain pushes its way to the surface. Within seconds it becomes this very strong, rounded sensation. After a few seconds of intense pain, it buries itself the exact same way it came out.

I usually lose myself in the pain. I stop whatever I'm doing and, even though I rarely close my eyes for it, I focus on riding out the pain. I believe there's strong power in mind over matter but this blinding pain usually catches me off guard. I try to remind myself pain is just information being sent to my brain but, in the time it would take to rationalize this pain away, it has already gone.

That night I went to Austin to play at an open mic. A few things happened to deter me from going to Austin that night. I had the horrible headache off and on all day, and my girlfriend, who was supposed to go, had to work. Buckley, who was supposed to play the open mic with me was not feeling well and didn't have a ride. Perhaps these occurrences were God's way of trying to deter me from going.

My friends, Buckley and another we'll call Monty, were sharing stories when one about me came up. One night I was visiting with Buckley's ex-girlfriend and a mutual male friend at Buckley's house. We often spent time there because his father, who we lovingly called "Old Man", was very accepting. At times, a few of his kids' friends even lived with them. This evening at Buckley's house we were making conversation when someone said something of an observatory nature about voyeurism. Buckley's ex-girlfriend said she didn't have a problem with voyeurism and, for that matter, wouldn't have a problem with someone watching her. Then an opportunity arose.

The other male and I were both in monogamous relationships. His actions could be excused by the fact that he'd been drinking. I think my actions were part of my self-destruction in my relationship with Nine. Buckley's ex-girlfriend attempted to pleasure herself as we looked on. Our dabbling in voyeurism didn't last long because she said she couldn't be in the mood without physical contact from someone else. She seemed to be implying that one of us should physically try to persuade her. I would not and I told my inebriated friend he shouldn't either.

As mentioned before, I grew up in Austin, Texas. My first romantic attempt, the focus of that undying utterance of "I love you" at the end of every call, took place there. I found out several years after I moved away that, for a while Woody ended up sleeping with this object of my first true affection on a pretty regular basis. When I confronted him about it, he was unremorseful. His attitude was that it wasn't as big of a trespass as I saw it to be. So, there I was a short time later, in a romantic relationship I sometimes despised, and an attractive girl, Buckley's ex-girlfriend, was offering to give a friend and me a show. I think I was trying to kill the part of myself that felt empty over this empty relationship, the part of myself that felt remorse.

If Woody could sleep with my first love, then I should be able to watch my friend's ex-girlfriend engage in autoeroticism without remorse. I wasn't technically cheating on Nine but I felt that same disconnected, remorseful feeling I felt when I cheated on her. I probably felt this way because I had an unfaithful heart. I knew Nine would be caused pain by what I was doing if she were to find out. I also empathized with Buckley, who would have to hear from someone other than me about this late night act of disloyalty.

So, in the past, I've engaged in acts most people would find morally objectionable. This incident was one of many but at the time it was reasonable to me. I don't consider myself an evil person. My perspective was different from perspectives held by others but that doesn't mean I was wrong. I felt guilty almost immediately. If we are our only moral judges then the presence of my feelings of guilt does mean I was wrong but it wasn't up to anyone but me to judge me.

Lately my analytical brain is increasingly active. I am constantly making observations in an attempt to better understand my world. I am usually in deep thought about something, constantly adjusting my perspective. This can add a certain difficulty to even the simplest of tasks. When I recently came to this realization, I was on my way to Mc-Donalds, trying to remember my coworker's order. This was a magnolia. I was thinking about the fact that I was trying to remember the order and I was analyzing this. I was thinking about the fact that I was thinking about the fact that I was thinking. It was something inside itself, the idea of the never-ending horizon we perceive when we look into two mirrors.

Fortunately, I did remember my coworker's order. I had enough foresight to go inside instead of using the drive-through. This, I assumed would enable me to take my time and review my purpose there, to remember anything I forgot while waiting. After all of this, I nearly forgot something. It wasn't that I didn't care. I took extra measures to ensure I didn't forget anything, yet, in my experience, apathy is how any absentmindedness is usually perceived. It would almost always seem to be seen either as apathy or stupidity. I believe this inability to deny persistent thoughts isn't the product of stupidity but is the product of passion for the analysis of my world. I also believe that, while my overly active brain can be an inconvenience, it is a gift, not a curse.

My perspective of what is socially appropriate is constantly changing. I will often replace actual heartfelt conversation with over the top, sometimes offensive jokes. I usually feel shameful after one of my jokes doesn't go over well. I fear my friends believe I'm trying to get a rise out of someone but truthfully, even if I know it could offend someone, I'm not trying to cause offense with my off-color humor.

I am still often silent in social settings but the motivation for silence has changed. My desire to see all perspectives before I formulate a conclusion often encourages me to distance myself from the external world. I don't want to be distant, especially to those I love. Still, I suppose I want more for my actions not to represent a position on anything until I truly know how I feel about it. I suspect my perspective to be the minority perspective in almost all social settings. This is typically due to the fact that a large part of social interaction would seem to involve passing judgment on others. The fact that I empathize with the person being judged can make conversations feel unmotivated and empty, which is why I sometimes limit my speech and even eye contact when I'm in certain social situations.

We often say much without meaning to. Even things like body language, posture, or inflection of vocal patterns can send an unintentional message. I don't want to send messages I'll regret but even silence and lack of body language can send messages. If I'm not sending the expected messages, a person might easily assume I've taken a stance of disinterest or even hurt.

Despite the social stigma these deep, analytical, social dream states cause, I do believe they're necessary. I desire to know the truth even if it means seeing from perspectives I've grown a strong distaste for. The ability to see from perspectives we originally disagree with could mean no one is wrong in the eyes of God. To be able to see that no one is wrong would be like seeing through the eyes of God. Everyone is beautiful because, in a way, everyone is perfect. We have these perspectives because we are supposed to. We are doing what we we're created to do: think and grow.

The world is not always completely how I perceive it. My perspective is almost always altered in some way. Occasionally I have moments which I imagine are like an alcoholic's moments of clarity. In these seemingly unprovoked moments, the world is not as dramatic as it often feels. Sometimes in these moments, I can see everyone's perspective without really trying. The world, in all its chaos, is at peace. As irrational as a perspective once seemed, in the moment, I can see it's justified. These moments are so rare and they are gone as quickly as they come. I believe if I could understand the cause of the perspective I hold in these moments, I would understand something that could bring peace to the world.

Is it possible our brains are so cluttered with information and constant signals from our bodies that we can't see the simple truth right in front of us? I can only be sure of what's right for myself. If each perspective is different than morality is up to the individual. That being said, I do believe we all could be much happier if we could look past our impulses and emotions and see other's actions for what they truly are, justifiable to the self, no matter how selfish or thoughtless. We each have the ability to see others' motives. We each have powers of empathy. If we can mentally take the form of another person through the use of mirror neurons and empathize with his or her emotional state then we should be able to empathize with and emulate his or her motivation as well.

If my perspective is constantly changing then how can I judge anyone for his or her perspective? My perspective might, one day, be similar to the perspective I judge. Everyone's perspective will change at some point. If we know our perspectives will one day change then it would be wise not to pass judgment on anyone.

I've recently come to see what I've viewed as my father's negative opinion of me in a new light. Shortly after I moved to be near and work for him, he and I went to an eye appointment he'd set for me. Somehow the topic of my recent employment as a phlebotomist came up and Dad mentioned in a lighthearted manner to my doctor my recent "50% stick rate." He was joking about my failure as a phlebotomist, my inability to hit a vein with a syringe needle. The doctor didn't seem to know how to respond and, in that moment, I saw my socially awkward self in my father.

I have, since writing "Reflection in Limbo and Magnolia (the perfect child)", come to see my reflection as a good thing. I'm reaching to understand new depths of my world. A person's interaction with other humans is probably the most powerful force against this person experiencing feelings of isolation. This fascinates me. I'm the scientist I spoke about in "The Science of Emotion and God." I'm studying God by studying his creation: myself.

Perhaps troubles seem inconsequential to me because I can, and will, adapt. If this is the case, then this perspective of a seemingly inconsequential world could be the first signs of my exit from limbo. I've recently come to the realization that the apparent inconsequential nature of my world is not only the product of choice but also a gift. I am no longer burdened by the consequences of this world because I believe good will come out of the bad. I've seen good come from bad and have no reason to believe it won't in the future.

If I believe in God, then I have to believe this long experience I have come to know as life is as he, she, or it has planned it. I was given freewill by design. God knew when I was created that I would make these decisions over which I torture myself. And yet I was made the way I was. If I believe God is infallible, then I can stop torturing myself over past decisions, and the inevitability of future mistakes. I suppose it's the desire to have control in this world but if I give God control then I can release the blame I carry and have faith he, she, or it will use my actions for a divine plan. I should embrace the past, not regret it. It's the past, my personal history that has molded me into who I am today.

Chapter Thirty-Four

Smiling, He Wrote . . .

Last night I had a very bizarre dream and, as campy as the idea of the dream may seem, it was one of the happiest experiences I've had in years. It was minutes to show time and the lead skater wasn't there. Even though I had no experience, they asked me to perform in his place. There was loud music; many colorful characters skated around me on the ice. I tried to mimic the idea I had in my mind of a skater's behavior when he's on the ice.

I skated for a few seconds. It was difficult to keep on my feet. I stopped and stood for a moment. I felt the music changing within me and slowly raised my left arm. Then I skated back to the area of the ice in which I had started. I decided to attempt one of the flips I'd seen some of the other skaters perform. I flew into the air and started turning all in the same motion. When I was done with the first rotation I went for a second. I actually felt my body turn at this accelerated speed. The ground, ceiling, and walls moved all around me.

I landed the flip; so I then attempted a second double front flip. I landed that one. Then the dance of light and sound around me was over. A few of the performers and I went into a back room and a man who seemed to be in charge told me he thought I was amazing. I was still full of adrenaline and felt the huge winded smile on my face. Then this man criticized a performer who stood between us holding a guitar. The guitarist said something about it not being that bad. The person in charge gestured to me as if to say, "This guy had no practice and did better than you did." I said something to try to deter the lead man's critiquing but it held little water with him. In those moments I felt what it was like on the other side, the opposite of how I frequently felt when I was growing up. I was the celebrated one. It was almost a parallel to how I've felt most of my life. I radiated self-esteem. I was smiling.

For a few years, I think I forgot how to smile. As a teenager I didn't want to smile because I was slowly becoming embittered toward the world. Eventually I stopped having to force myself not to smile. It became a part of my personality. Years later, I remember trying to smile for pictures and looking and feeling horribly awkward. When I was about twenty, Jo, Nine, and I drove to the beach. By the time we got there the sun had set. We got out of the car. I could smell the ocean. I felt the wind on my face and I smiled. This experience was the inspiration for the line, "Do you remember the electricity of the dawn forgotten beach?" in the poem mentioned in the chapter before entitled "Nine." Now, if I have trouble smiling, I think of the feeling of that warm evening next to the ocean.

I think my dream, whether it was God sent or not, was supposed to symbolize the person I desire to be, or the change that may be coming for me. If this is a symbolism for change for me, it was probably to prepare me. The situation with the guitarist was probably to remind me of what it feels like to be on the other side. If I'm to be celebrated in the future, I hope I don't forget the other side.

I've often felt like I was not made for this world. Many believe this world was intended to be a perfect one but was sent off track by the earth's first inhabitants and the "Original Sin." If it was, then none of us were made for this world.

I have, since writing the chapter entitled "Thirteen", grown new perspective of myself. I have committed acts I now could not imagine committing but felt justified in my actions at the time. I've suspected my father of being disappointed in me. I've since grown to see this disappointment as illogical. I am human. I make mistakes, just as every other person must. I can now laugh at my social awkwardness.

I recall a television show in which a woman was asked a series of questions she would potentially have trouble answering honestly. A lie detector determined whether she was truthful in her answer and could advance to the next question. She failed the question, "Are you a good person?" I believe that, for the first time in my life, I could answer that question with honesty.

This allows me the ability to love others completely. I try to do the best I can in every effort of my life, constantly striving to be better and constantly trying to love every person I meet.

I'm no longer burdened by the seeming lack of consequence in my world. I have the ability to affect my world, even if only in small doses. I often feel like the boy throwing starfish back to the waves but "It made a difference to that one." This slow wearing away of the beached starfish has become my purpose. If I am here for a reason, this is it. I'm here to make the world better in any way I can.

I have finally truly accepted the fact that I'm not in control. I have faith that God will use any misfortune for a purpose. I just have to keep moving in the direction I think God wants me to go. I am not the failure I often believed my father saw me to be. I'm not the child my grandparents often seemed to see me to be. I'm not perfect and should not trouble myself with the lack of perfection I'm bound to incarnate. I can strive to be better, knowing I will fail on occasion. For the first time I can remember, I'm happy with who I am. I am, for the first time in my life, comfortable in my own skin, understanding "my skin" is what I make it. My world is what I make it, so why not make it a happy one?

Chapter Thirty-Five

A Beautiful End

On December 21, 2007 I received a phone call from my mother. Despite the fact that I had a sore throat and my voice hadn't been working as well as I would have liked, I'd intended to go out in the search of employment again but her news would change that. My grandmother was in the hospital in Houston. She had had an aneurism and it was likely just a matter of time. I put my job search on hold and made the trip to be with my family.

My uncle talked me into the family waiting room. As I neared the room, I spotted my grandfather asleep in the room's only recliner. As I moved toward my grandfather, I saw my father in a chair against the wall to my left.

He had on that same leather jacket he'd worn regularly. He was heavier and somewhat discolored in the face. The look on his face was one he'd often worn when dealing with more than he cared to. It seemed defeated, yet enduring. I had noticed I tended to wear this face when experiencing pain as a result of the brain tumor. He stood up and shook my hand. I immediately wrapped my other arm around him and hugged more lovingly than I'd been able to in years.

Two uncles, my grandfather's children, greeted me. They weren't blood but they were family. Then my grandfather stood, with a great smile, to hug me. He asked how I was. I spat out the standard, programmed response, "Good."

He then asked a question that ended with his tears. "Do you wanna go tell your grandma goodbye?"

My father led me to her room in the ICU unit. He said, "Mom, Phil's here." I began to cry. It wasn't a cry spawned out of franticness or hopelessness we often experience as children but a cry from seeing a strong person, whom I loved dearly, so helpless and the sense of finality that came with it.

Dad moved her blanket in an effort to show me something. He went to the other side of the bed and, after examining that side, called me over. He showed me how I could hold her hand as I talked to her. The crying on top of the throat problems made it difficult to speak at all. I mustered a timid whisper, "Grandma, it's Phil. I love you. I'll see you again."

Responding to the brevity in my words, Dad said I could stay with her for a while. He left us alone. I didn't know what to say. I felt the audience of the nurse at work on the other side of the curtain. It was much of the same. I told Grandma I loved her very much. After a few minutes, I returned to the waiting room where family came and left. Grandpa cried as he told his story to other families waiting on their loved ones.

Later, my grandfather spent time next to my grandmother's bed. After my father had spent some time at my grandfather's side, he came back to the waiting area and asked if I wanted to go be with my grandfather for a while. I wasn't sure if he was questioning my desire to or my willingness to. It wasn't that I didn't want to be with them. It was the thought of having to see my grandfather in such a state. Would he want me there? I said, "I can" and my father shook his head.

After some trouble with the ICU doors, I found myself sitting in a chair to the right of my grandfather. The conversation drifted back and forth. We talked about the situation and then we talked about life. He asked how my mother was and we talked about her boyfriend. "Is he a widower?" he asked. In the pursuit of light conversation I mentioned that the word "widower" didn't make sense to me. He explained the difference in a widow and a widower and that if something were to happen to my grandmother he would be a widower. I felt bad for adding the depth of that label to the situation.

I steered the conversation back to rules of English. I stated that I understood and then voiced a somewhat uncertain opinion that the "er" in "widower" should imply action. There was silence. I put my hand on his shoulder and told him, "I know I'm much younger than you but if there is anything I can do . . ."

He said with teary eyes, "I appreciate that, Babe. I'm just devastated." Then he said, "We're still family." Without a second of thought I reassuringly agreed. I asked if he knew what the numbers and lines on the monitor meant. He pointed out the blood pressure and the pulse. There was silence.

A short time later, my aunt, my father and I were asked to come to an office in the ICU area to view films from a CT scan that had been performed earlier. It was a small room with two computer screens, and dark so we could more easily view the screens. The doctor scanned through Grandma's brain, pointing out white areas that represented blood and other figures that represented swelling.

My dad asked if there would be any improvement if the swelling were to go down. The doctor said the swelling would not go down. My dad stayed focused. He asked the number of cases in which the doctor had seen swelling like this decrease. The doctor said there had been none in his experience and that the swelling would likely not go down without an act of God. "What if the swelling *were* to go down?" Dad asked, and then added, "But like you said, 'That's not going to happen.'"

Then the doctor scanned to a different view. The brain in the picture was disfigured. It appeared as if it were in the form of a book, naturally an open book but now folded closed.

Sometime later my father came back into the waiting area and again asked if I wanted to go be with my grandfather. I agreed. This time, my grandfather was sitting in the chair I'd occupied, so I sat to his left. He pointed out something on her face. He said he knew the situation was hopeless but that he was like my father in the way he looked for signs of hope even though there were none. There was silence.

I told him I'd been writing a book. He seemed pleased with the idea and asked, "Is that right?" After a somewhat long stint of silence I felt the desire to pray for her. I looked at my grandfather. His eyes were closed; his head was down. I rose and placed my thumb and middle finger around her forehead, lightly resting near her temples. I thought, "God, let your will be done." After a suspended second, I started to leave. As I passed, my grandfather lovingly gripped my arm.

I said my goodbyes one more time. After the first set of goodbyes, I ended up spending a time by her side, so it just seemed right to reiterate my feelings in an attempt at finality. This time my aunt and uncle were there when I entered.

I told Grandma, "I'll see you again. Okay?" My aunt would later mention seeing a tear on my grandmother's face, an apparent response to my words. We spent a large portion of the night on couches in the hospital lobby. A member of the family had acquired a few blankets. The lobby was huge and the couches were all situated into little conversational areas alongside a couple of chairs, creating alcoves around coffee tables.

In the center of the dimly lit portion of the lobby was a fountain. In the center of the fountain was a statue of a boy riding a dolphin. The sound of the moving water was calming. I awoke once to find a man resting in a chair in the small sitting area where I slept. It was a slightly alienating experience to awake to the sight of a stranger just a few feet away but the feeling of awkwardness was probably unjustified and quickly overcome with tiredness.

I awoke later and was asked by an aunt to move to be near my grandfather. In the tired, disoriented moment I didn't understand her reasoning but obliged anyway. I slept again but awoke later as I did many times during this experience, suddenly and slightly startled. It was an uncle asking if I wanted breakfast. I followed the family into the hospital cafeteria. The cafeteria was very nice. As Dad said, it looked more like a food court than a cafeteria. We ate. Grandpa looked like he was in another world.

Grandma was declared dead at 8:28 a.m. December 22, 2007. She had already flatlined once and, despite her living will which stated "Do not resuscitate", they brought her back because she was signed up to be an organ donor.

Months before, I had mentally written a line that rang true the second I heard this. The line went "Weak ends in a condemn nation when living is just organ preservation." Everyone agreed it was time for grandpa to leave. He told my father he felt like he was abandoning her. My father assured him he wasn't.

Then came the discussion of what was to be done with her body. My grandfather and his two sons were making arrangements. An aunt suggested she would want to be cremated, like her first husband. My father insisted her will expressed the desire to be buried. A friend of my grandmother's said my grandmother would consider it inappropriate to be buried next to my grandfather's first wife.

I interjected the view she had expressed to my grandfather and me many times. After a few glasses of wine, she seemed to take pleasure in telling us she simply wanted to be put in a hole and that we were to play Elvis's "Return to Sender." My view was quickly dismissed, and possibly rightfully so when Dad said, "But that was after a few glasses of wine."

A short time later my uncle ended the phone call with my 14-year old cousin regarding her conversation with my recently deceased grandmother, the conversation mentioned in "My Own Personal God" in which Grandma recognized "the necklace" and said she had no preference regarding what was to be done with her body. My uncle told us my cousin had already connected with Grandma and relayed Grandma's lack of preference when it came to what was to be done with her remains.

Grandpa received a letter from the transplant recipient giving condolences and expressing what a great gift it was. On the 29th Grandma was buried in a cemetery in West Columbia, TX. She didn't want a funeral or a eulogy, so we had a small family gathering. We formed a circle around her coffin and each had a chance to say something in memory of her. Grandpa pointed out that a plot right next to my grandmother's plot had a marker that bore his first name. Then Grandma got her wish. We all stood around her holding hands as Elvis' "Return to Sender" was played through a boom box.

It was sad to lose her but I was content that this was just a part of life. This world has been both kind and unkind. The unkind moments of the future will be inescapable. If there's no changing these inevitable misfortunes then there's no point in fretting over them.

Everything in this world is temporary, even the life I've been given. In the end, the only permanence is the spiritual world. If we feel we were robbed of the years we should have had with our loved ones, we need to remember those years were not ours to begin with. The years we spent with the person were a gift from God.

Throughout the writing of this book, I've learned how my changing perspective forms the world around me and that how I receive the world is completely up to me. Why be angry over a difference in perspective? Why worry about consequence if I have no way of affecting the outcome? I'm content with being here and trying to find happiness in a sometimes seemingly ugly world. If we look hard enough there is beauty in everything. Although we may not be able to change the collective perspective, we as individuals can make small differences in the external world. We cannot force a person to change his or her point of view. We can only change the way we view the world.

Whether this world is a complete fabrication of my mind or everything is exactly as it is perceived, this world is mine. This world is what I make it and the product of how I choose to perceive it. I suppose even the authenticity of this world is up to me. As Albert Einstein said, "Physical concepts are free creations of the human mind, and are not, however it may seem, uniquely determined by the external world."[1] It's been several years now since my experience with cancer and what have I learned? Only that the one absolute is there are none. Of course this is only my interpretation of the evidence.

---

[1] "Physical concepts are," 2010

Bibliography

Adams, C. (2004, March 26). *Is Suicide Against The Law*? The Straight Dope. www.straightdope.com.

Adherents.com (2007). Major Religions of the World Ranked by Number of Adherents. Adherents. www.adherents.com.

Adhiparasakthi Charitable, Medical, Educational and Cultural Trust (2008). *Hinduism - 4000 to 2500 BCE*. The Major World Religions. www.omsakthi.org.

Al Ikhlâs Surah 112. The Unity, Sincerity, Oneness of Allah, Retrieved from http://www.muslimaccess.com/quraan/arabic/112.asp

All definitions were taken from dictionary.reference.com Dictionary.com Unabridged. Retrieved from Dictionary.com website: http://dictionary.reference.com

All scriptures were taken from the English Standard Version featured at www.bible.com except where otherwise noted.

Anderson, Hans Christian (1837). *The Emperor's New Clothes*. deoxy.org/emperors.htm

Arun, Arthur. *The Science of Love*. Your Amazing Brain – The Science of Bristol. www.youramazingbrain.com.

Ash, R. (1997). *The Top 10 of Everything*, DK Publishing, Inc. New York, pg. 160-161. Adherents.com. www.adherents.com.

Assmann, Jan, 'Monotheism and Polytheism' in: Sarah Iles Johnston (ed.), Religions of the Ancient World: A Guide, Harvard University Press (2004), ISBN 0-674-01517-7, pp. 17–31.

Aubuchon, Vaughn, (2009). *The Seven Deadly Sins - Summary Chart*, www.vaughns-1-pagers.com

Barnlund, D. C. *Interpersonal Communication: Survey and Studies*. Boston: Houghton Mifflin, 1968.

Beginning Catholic (2005) *Essential Freedom: Catholic Ten Commandments*. BeginningCatholic.com.

Begley, Sharon. (2008). *The Science of Hypocrisy*, Newsweek. www.newsweek.com

Bellissimo, A. (2009). *The Anger Management Program*. The History Channel/ thesamigroup.com.

BibleHub, (1981, 1998). *Koresh, a Persian King*. Strong's Hebrew Dictionary. BibleHub.com

Bietak, Manfred. 2004. *Review—'A Test of Time' by S.W. Manning*. Bibliotheca Orientalis Vol. 61: 99–222.

Blakeslee, S, & Blakeslee, M. (2007). *The Body Has A Mind Of Its Own*. New York: Random House.

Brainyquotes. *Aristotle Quotes*. (2009). BrainyMedia.com,

Burkert, Walter, Greek Religion: Archaic and Classical, Blackwell (1985), ISBN 0-631-15624-0.

Callender, G. 1999. The Minoans and the Mycenaeans: Aegean Society in the Bronze Age. Oxford University Press. ISBN 0195510283.

Chapanis, A. *Men, Machines, and Models*. American Psychologist, 16:113131, 1961.

Crowell, Benjamin (2011), *Light and Matter*. Especially at Section 4.2, Newton's First Law, Section 4.3, Newton's Second Law, and Section 5.1, Newton's Third Law.

David, Patty and Gelfeld, Vicki, (2014). *Brain Health Research Study*. AARP Research. http://www.aarp.org/content/dam/aarp/research/surveys_statistics/health/2015/2014-Brain-Health-Research-Study-AARP-res-gen.pdf

Davis, Cara. *Finding Focus*. (2009). Atlas of Faiths. Conversant Life. http://www.conversantlife.com.

Deignan, Kathleen (2007). *A Book of Hours: At Prayer with Thomas Merton*. Sorin Books, ISBN 1-933495-05-7.

Deutsch, K. *On Communication Models in the Social Sciences*. Public Opinion Quarterly, 16:356-380, 1952.

DiagnoseMe.com. *High Female Testosterone Level*, (2009), The Analyst. www.diagnose-me.com.

Donne, John. *No Man Is an Island.* Meditation XVII.

Editors of Encyclopedia Britannica (2010). *Limbo.* Encyclopedia Britannica. http://www.britannica.com.

Einstein, Albert. *Before God We Are Equally Wise--And Equally Foolish,* (1879 - 1955). http://www.quotationspage.com/quotes/Albert_Einstein/

Eiseley, Lori (1907 - 1977). *The Starfish Story.* Simply Aware. www.simplyaware.com.

English standard version. (2001). Retrieved from http://bibleresources.bible.com

Evans, R. J. (2005). *The Third Reich in Power 1933–1939.* London: Penguin Books. ISBN 0-7139-9649-8.

Feynman, R. P.; Leighton, R. B.; Sands, M. (2005). *The Feynman Lectures on Physics. Vol. 1* (2nd ed.). Pearson/Addison-Wesley. ISBN 0-8053-9049-9.

Finest Quotes, (1990-2009). *Quotes from the Movie Annie Hall.* http://www.finestquotes.com.

Finest Quotes, (1990-2009). *Quotes from the Movie Men in Black.* http://www.finestquotes.com.

Forest, Jim (2008). *Living with Wisdom: A Life of Thomas Merton* (revised edition). Orbis Books, ISBN 978-1-57075-754-9, illustrated biography.

Forsyth, PY. 1997. *Thera in the Bronze Age.* Peter Lang Publishing. ISBN 0820448893.

Fowles, G. R.; Cassiday, G. L. (1999). *Analytical Mechanics* (6th ed.). Saunders College Publishing. ISBN 0-03-022317-2.

Friedrich, WL. 1999. Fire in the Sea, the Santorini Volcano: Natural History and the Legend of Atlantis. Cambridge University Press. ISBN 0521652901.

Frye, Richard Nelson. *The Heritage of Persia.* Costa Mesa, CA: Mazda, 1993. ISBN 1568590083

Gambotto, Antonella (2004). *The Eclipse: A Memoir of Suicide.* Australia: Broken Ankle Books. ISBN 0-9751075-1-8.

Gartrell, N.K., Loriaux, D.L. & Chase, T.N., (1977). *Plasma Testosterone in Homosexual and Heterosexual Women.* American Psychiatric Association.

Gavin, P., (2012). *The Rise of Adolf Hitler, Hitler Becomes Dictator.* The History Place. www.historyplace.com

Gerbner, G. (1956). *Toward a General Model of Communication.* Audio-Visual Communication Review, 4:171-199.

Gladwell, M (2002). *Tipping Point.* New York, NY: Little, Brown & Company.

Goeschel, Christian (2009). *Suicide in Nazi Germany.* Oxford University Press. ISBN 0-19-953256-7. Sura 19, Mary (Maryam). www.masjidtucson.org.

Graham, Terry (2008). *The Strange Subject - Thomas Merton's Views on Sufism at the Wayback Machine* (archived June 20, 2010). SUFI: a journal of Sufism, Issue 30.

Greer, John Michael; A World Full of Gods: An Inquiry Into Polytheism, ADF Publishing (2005), ISBN 0-9765681-0-1

Haggard, Ted (2009). To King: Haggard to King: I'm Guilty Enough of So Many Things. CNN. CNN.com/

Hakim, S., (2009). *Six Articles of Faith.* IslamReligion.com

Hedberg, Mitch (2009). *Mitch Hedberg Quotes.* Wikiquotes. http://en.wikiquote.org/wiki/Mitch_Hedberg.

Heiden, Konrad (15 September 1933). *Les Débuts Du National-Socialisme.* Revue d'Allemagne (in French) 7 (71).

Hilborn, R.C. (1994). *Chaos and Nonlinear Dynamics.* Oxford University Press.

Hilla, (2007). *Love Words in Hebrew.* IsraelHebrew.com.

Höhne, Heinz (2000) [1969]. The Order of the Death's Head: The Story of Hitler's SS (Der Orden unter dem Totenkopf: Die Geschichte der SS). London: Penguin. ISBN 978-0-14-139012-3.

Holocaust Memorial Center, (2009). *The Holocaust – An Introductory History.* Jewish Virtual Library. www.jewishvirtuallibrary.org/

Huxley, A., (1932). *Brave New World Revisited* (Harper & Brothers, US, 1958; Chatto & Windus, UK, 1959)

Iles Johnston, Sarah; Ancient Religions, Belknap Press (September 15, 2007), ISBN 0-674-02548-2

Jeffcoat, John L. III, (1997-2008). *English Bible History*, Greatsite.com.

Johnson, Raymond, (2009). *Sodomy Laws What Affect Do Sodomy Laws Have On Gay Sex?* About Relationships. gaylife.about.com/

Kaplan, A. (1964). The Conduct of Inquiry: Methodology for Behavioral Science. San Francisco: Chandler.

Kersey Graves (1875). *The World's Sixteen Crucified Saviors.* Adventures Unlimited Press, Chapter 32, Page 279. (1875; Reprinted 2001)

Kershaw, Ian (2008). *Hitler: A Biography.* New York: W. W. Norton & Company. ISBN 0-393-06757-2.

King James Version. Retrieved from http://bibleresources.bible.com

Lackman, R. (1960). *The Model in Theory Construction.* Psychological Review, 67:113-129.

Likins, Peter W. (1973). *Elements of Engineering Mechanics.* McGraw-Hill Book Company. ISBN 0-07-037852-5.

Marion, Jerry; Thornton, Stephen (1995). *Classical Dynamics of Particles and Systems.* Harcourt College Publishers. ISBN 0-03-097302-3.

Marx, Karl, (1843). *Religion Is the Opium of the People.* , A Contribution to the Critique of Hegel's Philosophy of Right.

Marx, Karl. *Karl Marx Quotes.*ThinkExist.com

McDevitt, A., (1997-2007). *Egypt and the Nile*: *Osiris.* Egypttian Myths. http://www.egyptianmyths.net.

Merton, Thomas (1978). *The Seven Storey Mountain.* A Harvest/HBJ Book, ISBN 0-15-680679-7. (see notes for page numbers) Time Traveler, (2005). Retrieved from http://www.pbs.org/wgbh/nova/einstein/hotsciencetwin/

Merton, Thomas (1997). *Learning to Love.* The Journals of Thomas Merton, Volume Six 1966-1967 (1997), ISBN 0-06-065485-6. (see notes for page numbers).

Merton, Thomas, Kathleen Deignan Ed., John Giuliani, Thomas Berry (2003). *When The Trees Say Nothing.* Sorin Books, ISBN 1-893732-60-6.

Moorey, Peter Roger Stuart (1991). *The Biblical Lands.* New York: Peter Bedrick Books. ISBN 0872262472

Mott, Michael (1984). *The Seven Mountains of Thomas Merton.* Harvest Books 1993: ISBN 0-15-680681-9, authorized biography.

National Highway Traffic Safety Administration, (2012). *National Statistics* http://www-fars.nhtsa.dot.gov/Main/index.aspx

Nazi Germany Timeline. Spartacus Educational. http://www.spartacus.schoolnet.co.uk/GERchron.htm

New American Standard Bible, (1995). Retrieved from http://bibleresources.bible.com

New Living Translation, (1996, 2004). Retrieved from http://bibleresources.bible.com

New Testament Words. *Slave.* www.ntwords.com

New World Translation of The Holy Scriptures, (1984). Brooklyn, NY: Watchtower bible and Tract

Newton, Isaac (1726). *Mathematical Principles of Natural Philosophy -English Translation Based On 3rd Latin Edition.* Volume 1, containing Book 1, especially at the section Axioms or Laws of Motion, starting page 19.

Newton, Isaac (1726). Mathematical Principles of Natural Philosophy -English Translation Based On 3rd Latin Edition. Volume 2, containing Books 2 & 3.

NMJ Woodhouse (2003). *Special Relativity.* London/Berlin: Springer. p. 6. ISBN 1-85233-426-6. Nolan, J. & Nolan, C. (Writers). (2000). Memento [Motion Picture].

Olmstead, A. T. (1959). *History of the Persian Empire.* Chicago: University of Chicago Press. ISBN 0226627772

Palou, Christine, and Jean Palou (1967).. *La Perse Antique.* Paris: Presses Universitaires de France.

Paper, Jordan; *The Deities are Many: A Polytheistic Theology*, State University of New York Press (March 3, 2005), ISBN 978-0-7914-6387-1

Paul, A., (1900). Studying Complex and Dynamic Systems to Reveal Patterns of Order (Non-Chaos) Out Of Seemingly Chaotic Behaviors. Explanation of Chaos Theory of Lorenz ('60) and Poincaré.

Penchansky, David, Twilight of the Gods: Polytheism in the Hebrew Bible (2005), ISBN 0-664-22885-2.

Phillips, M. L. *Synesthesia*. Retrieved from http://faculty.washington.edu/chudler/syne.html

Robinson, B.A. (2009, September 17). *Beliefs in the Earth's Age by Old Earth*, Religious Tolerance. www.relilgioustolerance.org.

Robinson, B.A., (2001–2007) Jesus - Pagan link, *Specific similarities between the lives of Jesus and Krishn*a. Religions Tolerance. www.religioustolerance.org

Robinson, B.A., (2001-2007), How American Adults View Themselves, The Shift Away From Christianity And Other Organized Religions. Religious Tolerance. www.religioustolerance.org.

Sayadaw, V. M., (2008). *The Theory of Karma*. Buddha Net. www.buddhanet.net

Seawright, C., (1999-2003), Set (Seth), *God of Storms, Slayer of Apep, Equal to and Rival of Horus*. Tour Egypt. www.touregypt.com.

Sereno, K. K., and Mortensen, C. D. (1970). *Foundations of Communication Theory*. New York: Harper & Row.

Shannon, William H. (1992). *Silent Lamp: The Thomas Merton Story*. The Crossroad Publishing Company, ISBN 0-8245-1281-2, biography.

Shannon, William H., Christine M. Bochen, Patrick F. O'Connell (2002). *The Thomas Merton Encyclopedia*. Orbis Books, ISBN 1-57075-426-8.

Shaw, Jeffrey M. (2014). Illusions of Freedom: Thomas Merton and Jacques Ellul on Technology and the Human Condition. Eugene, OR: Wipf and Stock. ISBN 978-1625640581.

Shirer, William L. (1991) [1960]. *The Rise and Fall of the Third Reich*. London: Arrow Books Ltd. ISBN 978-0749306977.

Society of New York Inc. 10 commandments - god's standards, (2002-2009). Retrieved from http://www.allabouttruth.org/10-commandments.htm

Stackelberg, Roderick (2007). The Routledge Companion to Nazi Germany. New York: Routledge. ISBN 978-0-415-30860-1.

Stein, R. (2004). *Study is First to Confirm That Stress Speeds Aging*. The Washington Post. www.washingtonpost.com

The American Heritage® Dictionary of the English Language, Fourth Edition. Retrieved from Dictionary.com website: http://dictionary.reference.com

The Board of Trustees of the University of Illinois (1995). *General Relativity*. University of Illinois. archive.ncsa.illinois.edu/

The History Place (1996). *The Rise of Adolf Hitler, Hitler Becomes Dictator*. The History Place. www.historyplace.com

The Ovi Team (2009). *Helter Skelter*. Ovi Magazine. www.ovimagazine.org.

Think Exist. (1999 – 2009). *Revenge Is A Confession of Pain*. Latin Proverbs. ThnkExist.com.

Thomson, W (Lord Kelvin), and Tait, P G, (1867). *Treatise On Natural Philosophy, Volume* 1, especially at Section 242, Newton's laws of motion.

Townsley, J., (1998). *Translations of Malakoi and Arsenokoitai through History* (I Cor 6:9), Retrieved from http://www.jeramyt.org/gay/gaytrans.html

Transportation statistics > licensed drivers > total number (most recent) by state, (2003-2009). Retrieved from http://www.statemaster.com/graph/trn_lic_dri_tot_numtransportation-licensed-drivers-total-number

Types of Radiation Used to Treat Cancer, (2009). Retrieved from http://www.cancer.org/docroot/ETO/content/ETO_1_4X_Types_of_r adiation_used_to_treat_cancer.asp

U.S. c-*Store Count Grows to 140,655 Stores* (2006). National Petroleum News, Retrieved from http://www.highbeam.com/doc/1G1-146839618.html

Usually When People Are Sad, t.... (2009). Retrieved from http://quoteworld.org/quotes/12439

Warren, PM. 2006. in E. Czerny, I. Hein, H. Hunger, D. Melman, A. Schwab, *Timelines: Studies in Honour of Manfred Bietak* (Orientalia Lovaniensia Analecta 149). Louvain-la-Neuve, Belgium: Peeters, 2: 305–321. ISBN 904291730X.

Watzlawick, P., Beavin, J., and Jackson, D. (1967). *Pragmatics of Human Communication*. New York: Norton.

Weaver, Brian (2002). *Study Finds that Alcohol Placebo Impairs Memory*. Association for Psychological Science.

Weis, Monica, Paul M. Pearson, Kathleen P. Deignan (2006). *Beyond the Shadow and the Disguise: Three Essays on Thomas Merton*. The

Thomas Merton Society of Great Britain and Ireland, ISBN 0-9551571-1-0.

Willis, B. (1999). E=mc2 explained. Retrieved from http://www.worsleyschool.net/science/files/emc2/emc2.html

Your Sense of Hearing, How You Hear, Retrieved from http://library.thinkquest.org/3750/hear/hear.html

Your Sense of Smell, Retrieved from http://library.thinkquest.org/3750/smell/smell.html

Your Sense of Taste, Retrieved from http://library.thinkquest.org/3750/taste/taste.html

Your Sense of Touch, Retrieved from http://library.thinkquest.org/3750/touch/touch.html

Zeus Publications, (2002). *Information about the Greek God Zeus.* http://www.zeus-publications.com.

Phil Force

Philip C. Force was born July 7, 1984 in Brazoria, TX. Philip was raised in Austin, TX and lived in Boerne, TX for short period of time. The first child of three, Philip has yet to marry or conceive children. He currently holds a BA in Psychology and lives in Austin, TX where he runs his web design company, Blue 3 Designs and writes in his spare time.

Philip had always held a fascination for the human perspective. Psychology would have been a clear choice for his chosen field of work had a learning disability and low self-esteem inspired a lack of effort in his studies. Philip tested for his G.E.D. on September 11th, 2001.

After receiving his diploma, Philip proceeded to live with friends, unable to keep a job for more than a few weeks at most. With a low self-esteem, Philip began to form an enmity toward most of the human race. He eventually found longer-term employment but felt unfulfilled in his work and, after a few months, made the commitment to move to live with his grandparents and attend college courses to study phlebotomy. Philip wouldn't finish his courses that semester, as the growth of a brain tumor would inspire months of treatment and recovery.

Philip acknowledges that his experience with cancer has been the most positive experience of his life. The experience inspired Philip to review his personal history and reevaluate his perspective of the world and himself. Through this experience, Philip found love for himself and every person in his past and present. This change in perspective is documented in Philip's book, Letters From Limbo.

Philip graduated from Ashford University summa cum laude with his BA in Psychology on April 1st, 2013. Philip has not, since completing Letters From Limbo, written any works for which he has sought professional publishing but continues to write fiction and non-fiction to be posted on his blog at http://lettersfromlimbo.com/blog/. Here, one can find works as varying in scope as an article regarding potential benefits of medical marijuana and blurbs written from the perspective of Philip's dog, Avery.

Social Media and Websites

Social Media

Facebook: https://www.facebook.com/pages/Author-Phil-Force

LinkedIn: https://www.linkedin.com/pub/phil-force/26/529/158

Twitter: https://twitter.com/AuthorPhilForce

WordPress Blog: https://authorphilforce.wordpress.com

Websites

Publisher:

dpInk: DonnaInk Publications, L.L.C. http://www.donnaink.com

Mailing List

Discounts, Interviews, Merchandise

In order to become aware of discounts, interviews, signings and promotion campaigns remit email to: lettersfromlimbo@donnaink.com and put "Mailing List" in the subject line. Merchandise will soon be available with special discounts for mailing list members . . . so be certain to send an email confirming your interest!

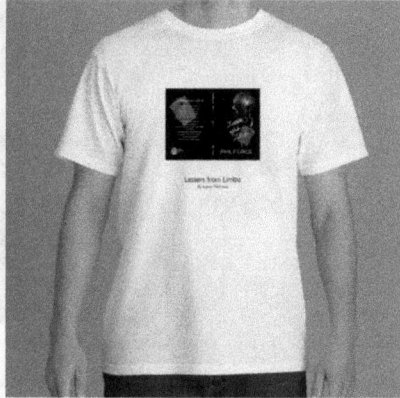

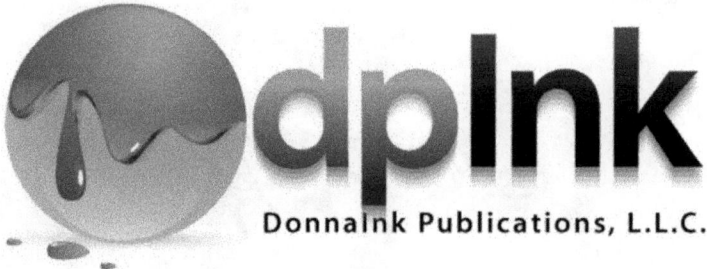

dpInk

Donnaink Publications, L.L.C.

Publisher
www.donnaink.com

For bulk orders, special orders, etc.

Special Markets Division
dpInk: Donnalnk Publications, L.L.C.
129 Daisy Hill Road
Carthage, North Carolina 28327
Email: special_markets@donnaink.com

For Promotions:
Promotions Division
dp**Ink**: Donnalnk Publications, L.L.C.
129 Daisy Hill Road
Carthage, North Carolina 28327
Email: promotions@donnaink.com

ZENCON ART OF
ZEN CONSULTANCY
PR & Marketing

www.ingramcontent.com/pod-product-compliance
Lightning Source LLC
Chambersburg PA
CBHW030934220326
41521CB00040B/2309